Tomart's Encyclopedia & Price Guide to
ACTION FIGURE
COLLECTIBLES

by Bill Sikora & T.N. Tumbusch

A-Team — G.I. Joe

TOMART PUBLICATIONS
Division of Tomart Corporation
Dayton, Ohio

To the Toy Creators...

...who must battle a league of Monday-morning government regulators, consumer advocates, child protectionists, accountants, corporate politics, and the whims of retail chain buyers' wives to get an action figure line to market.

Acknowledgements

This encyclopedia has been a group effort from the beginning. Now in its third version, the list of contributors is ever-growing. Everyone listed here has played a role in making it the best it could be.

Thanks to Bill Jordan and Mike Markowski for their work early on for *G.I. Joe* and *Captain Action*.

We are deeply indebted to many consultants who have improved the accuracy of this book by taking the time to review the manuscript in whole or in part: Anthony Balasco, Raymond Castile, Dr. Jerry Harnish, Ellen Harnish, Jon and Karl Hartman, Mark Huckabone, Suzan Hufferd, G.F. Ridenour, Mike Stannard, Jerry and Joan Wesolowski. Their expertise in the field is an invaluable contribution. Of these, Mark Huckabone, especially, was always there to answer questions, help verify facts, or to provide photographic reference for rare or difficult-to-find figures.

Also contributing to the content were numerous collectors, dealers, and fans who have provided information and/or items for photography, including Rex Abrahams, Mike Blanchard, Steve Crouse, Steve Denny, Brian Doyle, Jim Gilcher, Barry Goodman, Charles Griffith, Chris and Erin Holzinger, Bill Jordan, Jeff Kilian, Israel "Lev" Levarek, Keith Meyer, Steve Miller, Darren & Kathy Murer, Scott Parrish, Karl Price, Deirdre Root, Daniel Rous, Steve Sansweet, David Secrist, Chris Shay, Jim Silva, David Sobliros, Mike VanPlew, Charles Welhelm, Dick Whittick, Andrew Williams, and the many dealers and collectors whose names we unfortunately failed to record. Thanks for all your help with facts and figures.

The cover photography was done with the help of Tom Schwartz and Terry Cavanaugh. Page Imaging was by Type One Graphics, printing by Central Printing and Carpenter Lithographing Company.

The enourmous tasks of photo imaging were completed with the assistance of Nathan Zwilling, Karin Buening, Chuck Jones, Kelly McLees, Chad Stewart, Rebecca Trissel, Denise Tudor, and Susan Tumbusch.

Tomart's Encyclopedia and Price Guide to Action Figure Collectibles is an outgrowth of *Tomart's Price Guide to Action Figure Collectibles*, first published in 1991; revised and updated in 1992.

Revised second printing, 1996

Published by Tomart Publications, Dayton, Ohio 45439-1944.

Library of Congress Catalog Card Number: 90-71163

ISBN: 0-914293-27-3   Manufactured in the United States of America

1 2 3 4 5 6 7 8 9 0   8 7 6 5 4 3 2 1 9 0

FOREWORD

Tomart's Encyclopedia and Price Guide to Action Figure Collectibles is the most complete work on action figures ever assembled. The encyclopedia is comprised of three separate books. It represents the combined research efforts of the staffs of *Tomart's Action Figure Digest*, *Lee's Action Figure News & Toy Review*, plus hundreds of dealers and collectors nation-wide. Nearly 10 years have gone into assembling the photos and information presented. It is a history of what has been produced, complete with collector values of all major action figures from pre-*G.I. Joe* (1964) up to and including lines scheduled for Christmas 1996 release.

An effort has been made to maximize the number of figures shown in full color. It was more difficult to get listings on the same page as the photos...or even close in some cases, but the publisher felt more pictures were better...and the more pictures in color, even better yet! Be sure to review "How to Use This Book" on page 10 before trying to reference any specific figure.

Collecting action figures is still growing fast. It became a serious hobby back in the 1970s, but the growth since 1990 has been geometric. There are several reasons. Some of the greatest popular culture icons from films, TV, and the comics are reproduced in interesting and intriguing ways. They can be found in any flea market or toy show, and usually cost less than older collectible items such as antique toys or robots. What's more, action figures are popular toys which are still being made, and the toy industry doesn't show any signs of stopping. The quality of these miniature sculptures is constantly improving, and they are, in a way, contemporary art...art anyone can own. Furthermore, since 1990 there have been a growing number of publications catering to collectors' interests and education.

Action figures seem to be designed with the collector in mind. They are usually produced as a series, with available figures listed on the back of the package or in a small catalog included inside. The packages encourage young fans and collectors to "collect 'em all!" Toy companies purposely produce smaller quantities of some figures expected not to sell as well as others, or to keep the average cost per figure in line with what the retailer and buying public is willing to pay. They don't purposely withhold them from the market, but what seemed like a wise decision back in March when the figures had to be ordered doesn't always hold true in December when they go on sale. This makes certain figures more desirable, and keeps consumers coming back to the toy stores where they might buy a playset or accessory item when they can't find a particular figure. Demand for the whole set increases when there is one elusive figure.

If all this sounds a bit frivolous, note that many figures are readily sold for more than $1,000 on the secondary collector's market. Even short-packed or error figures you might find currently on sale at a toy store can command as much as a $50 premium from the start. Speculators are around, but are not a major factor due to the abundance of close-out material and constant new product to attract attention and collector interest for lower cost.

A major effort has been made to include every action figure and line, except obvious knock-off figures which are not included. If the manufacturer's name doesn't appear on the package, you won't find the figure in this book. A further distinction is made between action figures and character dolls. Only action figures of fictional characters are included. For example, Farrah Fawcett as Jill in "Charlie's Angels" is included. The Barbie-like Farrah Fawcett fashion doll and outfits are not. Sports figures based on real players are likewise absent. Legends such as Davy Crockett, Long John Silver, other historical and biblical figures are included because they are presented as toys for their play value as period characters rather than personality dolls.

ACTION FIGURES —
THE VALUE IN KNOWING THEIR HISTORY

Action figures were well-established as a top-selling toy category by 1965. They developed as a natural outgrowth of toy soldiers and other miniature figures which had been around since the turn of the century.

The hard plastic Hartland figures of the '50s were an important departure toward the development of the action figure genre. Hartland had produced horse and animal figures in the

'40s. They added riders connected with The Lone Ranger, Roy Rogers, and historical western heroes who were growing in popularity along with a new communications medium called television...a major source for a large majority of action figure lines found at retail.

Hartland figures were not articulated, but came with removable hats, guns, knives, bridles, and other accessories. Riders could be separated from their mounts, but the position left no doubt they belonged on a horse. The first million plastic accessories lost were undoubtedly Hartland hats, Indian feathers, knives and guns.

The Louis Marx Company offered another small, but important line in the late '50s. Throughout the decade they produced detailed single-color figures and playsets. These molded, one-piece figures ranged in size from less than an inch up to around 7" or so. Most averaged around 2½" and

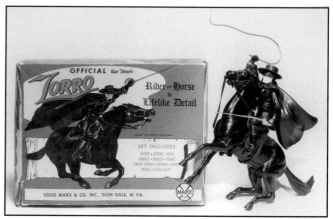

featured comic characters, military, western, knights, doll house, and farm figures. Marx's first move toward producing an action figure-type product were several "playsets" along the lines of Hartland horse and rider sets, but made of solid color, flexible plastic components. The poses on the Zorro, Sleeping Beauty with her Prince, and Johnny Tremain captured amazing speed and excitement in their design.

Mattel introduced the *Barbie* fashion doll in 1959 and signaled some radical changes ahead for boys' toys. The success of the *Barbie* product line became legendary...and a stable product for the Mattel company, going stronger than ever more than 35 years later.

In 1964, Hasbro, then known as Hassenfield Bros., Inc., was the first company to fully develop a male "action figure" equivalent to *Barbie* — G.I. Joe "Action Soldiers." These 12" figures had interchangeable cloth uniforms based on U.S. military issues from World War II. There were vehicles and accessories from the start, but the selection mushroomed with the success of the *G.I. Joe* concept. A nurse, a combat series of foreign soldiers, and a talking version were added in 1967. The *G.I. Joe Adventure Team* was created in 1970, allowing Joe a departure into non-military adventures such as jungle safaris, polar expeditions, and space orbiting. The Arab oil embargo increased plastic prices and the size of *G.I. Joe* was reduced to 8" in 1976. There were no *G.I. Joes* made in the years 1977 to 1981. In 1982, individually named military fig-

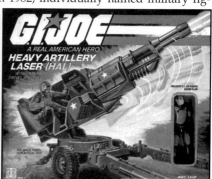

Captain Action, introduced by Ideal Toy Company in 1966, ensured action figures a permanent place in toy manufacturing. *Captain Action* looked like a futuristic airline pilot, but could be converted to leading comic, TV, and super heroes. The conversion was accomplished by changing the costume and full head mask. Even though Ideal gave up the complex licensing arrangement after three years, super heroes have remained an important segment of action figure marketing ever since.

ures were marketed by Hasbro as *G.I. Joe — A Real American Hero*, kicking off a new era of successful figures sold under the *G.I. Joe* name. Figures continued in this size until 1995, when the size was revised to 4½" with the introduction of *Sgt. Savage*. The brand was turned over to Hasbro's Kenner division in 1995. They in turn developed another new approach, marketed under the name *G.I. Joe Extreme*. The 12" figure was re-designed and updated to a modern military look in 1996.

The Marx Company's first major "action figure" line was their *Best of the West* series. Johnny and Jane West, plus the many figures which followed them, were fully-articulated and came with enough accessories to clog many a vacuum cleaner. The line was sold for around 12 years, despite the fact it was not colorful or gimmicky. The original Marx molds have since been acquired by new owners, who are re-making some of the original toys under the new Marx Toy Company name.

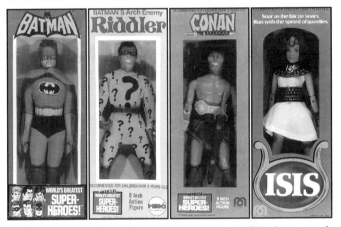

Mego was quick to offer a replacement. In 1972, they issued the first six *World's Greatest Super Heroes*. The series continued through 1982 eventually offering 34 different super heroes and villains. The 8" plastic figures relied largely on lithographed body stockings for costuming with detailed plastic weapons for accessories. There were several vehicles and playsets for added hours of play.

Gilbert attempted to share in Hasbro's action figure success by introducing several figures beginning in 1965. *James Bond 007*, *The Man from U.N.C.L.E.*, and *Honey West* were three of the most popular Gilbert action figure issues.

The popular *Bonanza* TV series was the subject of an interesting 1966 line. The figures, clothes, and all accessories were flexible plastic similar in design to the Marx *Best of the West* series, only smaller.

Mego branched out with figures from films, like *Planet of the Apes* and later *Star Trek: The Motion Picture*; plus the TV series *Star Trek*, *One Million B.C.*, *Dukes of Hazzard*, and *CHiPs*. They also did historic series based on pirates, King Authur, Robin Hood characters, and legendary figures from the American West.

Star Wars was the surprise summer film sensation of 1977. No one anticipated the huge response, so there were no licensed products in the stores. Somehow Kenner Products, then a division of General Mills, Inc., ended up with all rights to toys and games, but there wasn't enough time to get action figures (manufactured in Asia) on the shelves in time for Christmas. To meet the immediate demand, Kenner sold a large cardboard envelope called the "Early Bird Certificate Package" which guaranteed priority delivery of the first four figures by the following February. In March, the first eight figures were available in stores, the next four by summer with nine more on the shelves by Christmas of 1978. It was 1987 before the demand for *Star Wars* figures began to wane. By then 94 figures and over 60 action vehicles and playsets were marketed — many as exclusive products through Sears or Penney's. Additional figures, vehicles, and playsets were produced in conjunction with the animated *Droids* and *Ewoks* TV cartoon series which aired as Saturday morning kids' programs.

Kenner also did figures based on two more films during this period — *Raiders of the Lost Ark* and *Butch Cassidy and the Sundance Kid*. These series seemingly established the 3¾" figure as the standard of the industry.

Mego issued 3¾" sets for *Star Trek: The Motion Picture*, *CHiPs* and *Dukes of Hazzard* along with the larger figures mentioned above...and released the *Love Boat* set in 3¾" only. Mattel did 3¾" sets of *Flash Gordon* and *Clash of the Titans*; while Gabriel did *The Legend of the Lone Ranger* and *Zorro* sets in the same format. There were also a Tri-Star *M*A*S*H* set, Remco's *Universal Monsters* set, and the largest set of action figures ever — *G.I. Joe* — *A Real American Hero* — in the small format.

Mego Corp., the leading action figure company in the '70s, filed for Chapter 11 bankruptcy protection in 1982 and the

day of 8" and 12" action figures with cloth costumes seemed to end with them. The slack in super heroes was quickly taken up by Kenner's *Super Powers Collection* and Mattel's *Marvel Super Heroes Secret Wars* figures.

Just when the pattern of smaller figures seemed set, Mattel introduced muscular 6" *Masters of the Universe* figures. This fantasy line combined sword-and-sorcery with high-tech weaponry in one most successful boy-oriented marketing effort in action figure history. This led to Galoob's *Golden Girl and the Guardians of the Gemstones* and later Mattel's *Princess of Power* for girls. Whereas action figure toys previously resulted from a TV success, deregulation during the Reagan era allowed the development of product-based programs for the the first time. *Masters of the Universe* and *Princess of Power* were the first big successes which resulted — with Mattel collecting royalties instead of paying them — and other companies were swift to follow their example. Both story concepts

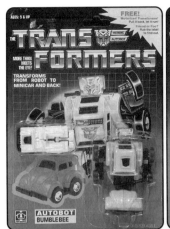

Bravestarr figures could "kill" each other with "laser" blasts to vulnerable spots. *Thundercats* had "fist punching action," *Blackstar* had "laser light" sparking action, and *COPS*, *Robocop*, and others had cap-firing mechanisms to make the play battle more real. Then came digital chip sound effects used in *Sound Team* and small *G.I. Joes*.

The smash successes, such as the fantasy figures and *Transformers*, were imitated many times. Super heroes returned time and again. Then there were the off-the-wall sensations like the *Teenage Mutant Ninja Turtles*, which scored high with collectors from the day the figures hit the market.

were widely copied for other figure lines, and other toy companies saw the value of developing their own toy-oriented TV programming.

Hasbro looked to Japan for help, and came up with another winner, *Transformers*. These robots could be folded like puzzle pieces to become cars, boats, trucks, animals, and enough other objects to keep the line on toy store shelves for more than six years. Other animated programs successful in Japan were imported as a result. *Voltron* and *Robotech* lead the way, but never quite measured up to the success of *Transformers*.

Many other successful action figure lines are covered in this book. Being "just poseable" became passé as interactive figures were introduced. *Captain Power* could shoot objects on the TV screen (which sometimes shot back), *Photon* and

Close behind the tongue-in-cheek *Turtles* sensation came the 1989 *Batman* film...and character popularity unsurpassed in the 1940s or the mid-1960s. The many *Batman* figures produced set a record for the number of different versions of the same character in a series. The 100th version was scheduled for production in 1996. Thus, one character has become a core brand good for many years.

The Marvel Entertainment Group purchased controlling interest in Toy Biz in 1992, and signaled a new trend in the toy business. Previously content with royalties from toy products, property owners seeking a larger share of the pie began to play a new control role in licensed toys...from design to

bottom line. Marketing to the collector with hundreds of dollars to spend became part of more toy company marketing plans. Toy Biz expanded from *Marvel Super Heroes* and *X-Men* offerings to specialized lines for *Spider-Man*, *Fantastic Four*, *Ghost Rider*, and *The Incredible Hulk*; and reorganized *X-Men* into story groups and special packaged sets.

Mighty Morphin Power Rangers was the biggest action figure toy sensation of the first half of the 1990s. It was viewed by many as a greater acceptance of Japanese-style toys, in which very similar products in different colors are the mainstay of the toy business. In time, there may be some vindications of such thinking, but the return of *Star Wars* action figures in 1995 seemed to recapture American kids' interest in what is new, exciting, and different.

Another trend-setter in the mid-90s was Todd McFarlane with *Spawn* and other toy lines. His eye for detail and "what kids like" elevated the art of action figure design and execution several notches.

Tomart's Action Figure Digest has run four reader preference surveys for best figure lines, individual figures, and playsets. Readers have chose Playmates' *Star Trek* as the top line in 1992 and 1993, with *Spawn* grabbing top honors in 1994 and 1995. Both of these lines were excellently sculpted, fully articulated, and finely detailed. In the beginning, posability was the main feature of an action figure. Smaller 3¾" scales made vehicles and playsets with all sorts of play features the main focus of action figure lines. *Masters of the Universe* increased size to accomodate built-in action features in each and every

8

figure. This began a new trend in the action features direction. Size variations have since replaced many accessories to meet retailers price-point goals. Decoration technology offers new opportunities to the toy manufacturer. Products have more detail. They are better replicas of life-size heroes or fanciful characters. They have become art: Art anyone can own. Art appreciated by child and adult alike. Art that is selling an ever-increasing supply of action figures. And since availability breeds collectibility, the future of the action figure hobby seems secure for the foreseeable future.

The common statement found on every action figure package is "Collect Them All!"…and many kids do. Some are so intrigued that they buy one to play with and one to keep mint in the sealed package. The condition of the original box or package has a greater significance in collecting action figures, and is reflected in the way values are reported in this guide.

It is interesting to note the many different companies which have attempted to cash in on the market. At one time or another, most toy companies have offered figures. Hasbro, Mattel, and Playmates have been the most successful. Names like LJN, Mego, and others have arisen, made their mark and disappeared on the strength of action figure lines. Galoob was successful, suffered a long dry spell, and has made a comeback. Well established companies like Colorforms, Ideal, Tonka, Multi-Toys Corp., TYCO, Revell, Matchbox, Horsman, Knickerbocker, Coleco, Buddy L, and others have discovered the pains of unsuccessful action figure offerings. Lines such as *The Last Starfighter*, *Dallas*, small *Alien* and *V* figures were dropped completely when sales prospects did not warrant manufacture. In some cases, just certain figures or playsets were not made…even though they appeared on the back of figure packages.

MARKET REPORT

Action figures were produced by the millions, and are still being made in conjunction with popular movies and television shows. Many are still in the hands of their original owners. The dealer supply is strong for items produced since 1970, so it promises to be an active collecting field for many years to come.

The average action figure can be found for less than $10, but some are easily sold for more than $1000. The most popular collector figures fall in the $12 - $60 range.

Many figures still exist in their original packages. Unlike tin toy or doll afficandos, action figure collectors often refuse to settle for unpackaged items. Mint condition production pieces can be found if one looks hard enough.

Small and easily-lost accessories are also important to the value of any figure. An unopened figure in the original package usually assures completeness. By itself, without accessories, the desirability of all but the rarest figures drops drastically…except, of course, those few figures which did not come boxed or carded.

Figures produced in the last five years or so can frequently be found at close-out prices in large toy chains. Because of character popularity, late additions to the figure line, and short-packed items, certain newly-released figures can become collectible the minute they hit the shelves.

The first kids who owned action figures have grown up to become the first collectors. Although it is a relatively new field, action figures are rapidly becoming one of the fastest-growing collectible markets.

WHAT IS AN ACTION FIGURE?

An action figure is an articulated replica of a fictional character, usually molded in plastic or die-cast metal. This book also lists accessory sets, vehicles, playsets, and other toys which were sold for use with or in conjunction with the fig-ures. "Flexies," "bendies," non-articulated figurines, PVC figures, dolls, and figures representing real personalities are not included unless an interest to action figure collectors has been noted.

Four related factors are of interest to collectors: short-packed or late figures, retailer exclusives, variations, and prototypes.

"Limited Edition" Figures

Toy companies frequently hold back on the production or release of one or more figures in a series. These are shipped only one or two per carton, or advertised but not released immediately. This happens for a variety of reasons, but is seldom done on purpose. There is some benefit to the toy stores and the manufacturers, because people who want a particular character keep coming back only to find the missing item. Characters which are not expected to sell in large quantities often merit lower production runs as well. Even though many limited figures are less popular characters, they can bring higher values to those trying to "collect them all" because of their comparative scarcity.

Production is sometimes limited to a certain amount of 5,000, 10,000, or 100,000. Some of these limited editions are numbered in an attempt to enhance collector appeal. Unless the number is under 1,000, not too many people care…and prices paid for numbers 999 or less usually don't deviate much from others in the numerical series. In reality, every figure made is "limited" to the number produced. Often the number of regular-run figures is less than the number of pieces produced for "limited collector editions." Toy manufacturers have traditionally had a hard time understanding collectors. What often seems to be collectible to them really isn't, and what is highly desirable to collectors is, more often than not, closed out at a loss to the manufacturer.

Retailer Exclusives

When an action figure line acheives best-seller status, the large retailers can afford to buy quantities big enough to demand something special. They want products not available from competitors to get customers to shop at their store or from their catalog. The difference can be anything from a

Sears exclusive *G.I. Joe* Missile Command Headquarters.

packaging or decoration change to a totally unique product. The important thing about retailer exclusives is their tendency to become valuable collectibles. Since they are not universally available, they are often missed because of the short time they are on the shelves. Many retailer exclusives are only available in certain regions of the country or in limited quantities.

Variations

Slight differences in otherwise identical figures are of interest to some collectors. These may be minor changes made by the manufacturer, production mistakes which made it to the retail market, figures produced in different molds, or toys which were changed to comply with government safety standards.

For example, April O'Neil from *Teenage Mutant Ninja Turtles* originally had a plain yellow jumpsuit. A blue stripe was added on later figures. Data figures from *Star Trek: The Next Generation* occasionally came out of the factory with spotted or blue-green faces. Three different variations of the Toy Biz Batman are known to exist, each produced in a different factory. The *Star Wars* Boba Fett was originally planned to included a working rocket launcher, which was discontinued when safety concerns were raised.

Some collectors don't care about variations. Others want every version available, and may be willing to pay higher prices to get them. Variations on limited figures also occur, which makes any version that much harder to find.

A special column on variations appears in each issue of *Tomart's Action Figure Digest*. The department is called "Variation Hunter," and reports even the slightest differences noted by any *AFD* correspondent or special editor.

Two prototypes awarded in contests by *Tomart's Action Figure Digest*.

Prototypes

When a new line of action figures is proposed, a sculptor will hand-make figures, often twice production size, called prototypes. These are very short-run or even one-of-a-kind models which are displayed at toy trade shows, given as samples to prospective toy store buyers, and photographed for the company's catalogs. If the idea doesn't do well at Toy Fair, or if dealer response is poor, the figure may never be pro-

duced. Prototypes are also made for playsets, accessories, and related items. Since a prototype is essentially a "draft" of the product, it will often differ in some respects from the finished version. It is for this reason that many packages indicate the actual figure may be different than the printed image.

Pre-production "vendor-supplied prototypes" (VSPs) and samples do make it into the hands of collectors via contests or connections. These are short-run items of usually less than 100 to satisfy safety, quality control, packaging, and advertising needs. They are less rare than hand-made prototypes, but still highly desirable…especially if production is abandoned.

All prototypes are unique items, and must be evaluated on a case-by-case basis, taking into account the character, the quality of the item, and whether or not the figure was actually produced. The purchase of prototypes is at the buyer's own risk, since an enterprising individual can make their own.

HOW TO USE THIS BOOK

Tomart's Encyclopedia and Price Guide to Action Figure Collectibles was designed to be an authoritative and easy-to-use reference guide. It utilizes an identification and classification system designed to create a standard identification number for each individual figure and associated item.

Try as we have, we have probably missed some figures which will be brought to the publisher's attention and added to future editions. This system contains the framework by which they can be catalogued.

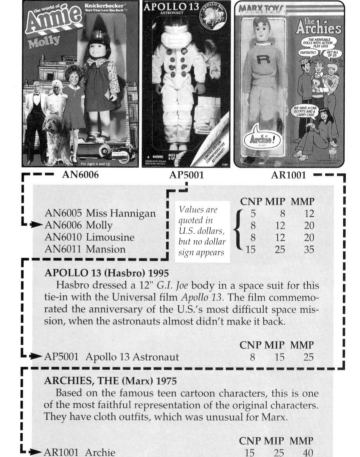

AN6006   AP5001   AR1001

		CNP	MIP	MMP
AN6005	Miss Hannigan	5	8	12
AN6006	Molly	8	12	20
AN6010	Limousine	8	12	20
AN6011	Mansion	15	25	35

Values are quoted in U.S. dollars, but no dollar sign appears

APOLLO 13 (Hasbro) 1995

Hasbro dressed a 12" *G.I. Joe* body in a space suit for this tie-in with the Universal film *Apollo 13*. The film commemorated the anniversary of the U.S.'s most difficult space mission, when the astronauts almost didn't make it back.

		CNP	MIP	MMP
AP5001	Apollo 13 Astronaut	8	15	25

ARCHIES, THE (Marx) 1975

Based on the famous teen cartoon characters, this is one of the most faithful representation of the original characters. They have cloth outfits, which was unusual for Marx.

		CNP	MIP	MMP
AR1001	Archie	15	25	40
AR1002	Jughead	15	25	40

To find a value, note the number under the photo, and match it to the left-hand column in the listings. The first two letters are alphabetical throughout the book. Even though the photos shown above appear on pages 33 and 34, the first two letters are used to find the listings on page 41.

Values throughout all three books are quoted in U.S. dollars, even though no dollar sign ($) appears (i.e. "8" is read as "$8").

The format is based on the name of the figure line found on the package. Code numbers were created based on the first two letters of the series title, with the exception of *Star Wars* (SW). *Masters of the Universe* figures, for example, are found at MA. The later *He-Man* line is found at HE. If the first word in the title is "The," then it is moved to the end of the title and set off by a comma. *The Adventures of Indiana Jones* is alphabetized as *Adventures of Indiana Jones, The*; and the first two letters used for the code are AD.

If, for example, you want to locate a *G.I. Joe* figure, flip through the book until you find classification numbers beginning with GI and read the alphabetical category heading until you reach "*G.I. Joe.*" Classification numbers have been established based on the series name exactly as it appears on the original package, but cross-references have been placed throughout to assist you. Roger Rabbit figures, for example, are listed at the classification *Who Framed Roger Rabbit?*, but you will also find a cross-reference at "Roger Rabbit" which will direct you there.

If the figure is already out of the package and you know the line, it is a simple matter to match the figure to the thousands of photos provided. If you do not know the line, the job becomes much harder because you now have to compare it to each line licensed by the copyright owner molded somewhere on the figure. If there is no copyright in raised or depressed letters somewhere on the figure, it probably isn't worth anything anyway. The historical information describing each line usually mentions who licensed the figure. The best places to look for the copyright notice are on the legs, butt, or bottom of the shoe. Figures with cloth outfits are normally marked on the figure's back underneath the shirt, dress top, or coat.

Each item in the line has been assigned a reference code number consisting of two letters and four numbers. Use of these numbers in secondary market dealer and distributor ads and collector's correspondence is encouraged. Permission to use Tomart's I.D. numbers to buy, sell or trade action figures in lists, letters or ads is hereby granted. All rights for reporting values in newsletters, magazines, books, online, or advisory services are reserved. Written permission must be granted to use Tomart's copyrighted arrangement and identification system. Violators have and will be prosecuted.

The identity code numbers serve to match the correct listing to a nearby photo. Usually, there is a listing for every photo, but not all items listed are depicted. Some items in this three-volume encyclopedia have been previously listed in other publications by Tomart. This book utilizes a code system which is consistent with some, but not all Tomart guides.

THE VALUES IN THIS PRICE GUIDE

Price ranges in this book are divided into three categories: "Complete No Package," "Mint in Package," and "Mint in Mint Package."

Complete No Package (CNP) refers to loose items with all weapons, decals, and other items found in the original bubble pack or box. Figures, accessories, vehicles, playsets, etc. without all the original items are therefore worth less than the value listed for "loose" but complete items.

Mint in Package (MIP) means the unopened figure on a card or in a box which is at least in fine condition with no tears, prominent creases, battered corners, or price sticker damage. The figure will of course be mint, but collectors value the card or box as much, if not more, than the contents. Figures, vehicles, playsets and other accessories may have been opened, decals applied, and assembled — but still complete and undamaged — in a fine or better original box.

The phrase "Mint in Package" can be misleading. This is frequently interpreted by dealers to mean the item *inside* the package is mint, but the package itself could be re-glued, bent, faded, marred, or covered with adhesive tags which are difficult to remove without damage.

Mint in Mint Package (MMP) means the item is in perfect condition, just like it rolled from the manufacturer's assembly line. The highest values for action figures assume the figure is mint, and is complete in a mint package. No price sticker was ever applied, or if so, it was removed without marks or any trace of adhesive. Particular collectors even want the cardboard inserts in the hanger holes to be intact if they are to pay the top price. Boxed items are preferred factory sealed. Mint items were probably original stock, never in circulation, or not used.

| | | | |
| 1 | 2 | 3 | 4 |

Four conditions of an action figure: 1) Loose, no weapons or accessories, worth less than the values quoted in this guide (C-1). 2) Loose with all pieces originally sold in package (C-6 to C-8). 3) Mint in package — frequently quoted by dealers as Mint on Card (MOC) or Mint in Box (MIB) — usually refers to the condition of the figure or accessory. In a hobby where the package can be more valuable than its contents, this is often misleading (package C-6, item C-10). 4) Mint in Mint Package, used to describe and value perfect specimens (package C-10, item C-10).

The values in this guide are based on the experience of the authors and the national panel of dealers and collectors credited in the acknowledgements. The real value any particular item will bring depends on what a buyer is willing to pay. No more. No less. Prices constantly change — up and down.

Another value system which is beginning to gain wide acceptance quotes condition by using the letter "C" and numbers from 1 to 10 to characterize "fair" to "absolute mint" condition. The "MIP" figures quoted in this encyclopedia equate to a C-6; MMP is a solid C-10. Loose action figures are quoted in the C-6 to C-8 range.

Consult *Action Figure Digest's* world wide web page for periodic updates, or check the monthly price guide found in *Action Figure News & Toy Review* for the most accurate swings in the market month to month.

Many factors influence any given transaction. Not the least of these are perceived value, emotional appeal, or competitive drive for ownership. Everything people buy is motivated by a need or a want. There are few who actually need action figure collectibles, but a lot of people buy them out of interest or desire. Dealers usually want the highest returns possible and continually test collectors with higher prices.

Supply and demand have always been important factors in determining value, and are a bit more predictable for those knowledgeable in a given area. These people have a feel for how often an item appears for sale. Since everyone has different experience, however, there are many different ideas on which items are rarer or more valuable.

The availability of the items listed in this book is definitely limited. No one can say precisely how limited. Some of the more recently produced items can still be found in toy and department stores.

The original quantities of vintage items can run anywhere from hundreds up into millions. Generally, items which generated the greatest interest originally were the items produced in the largest quantities. For example, more than 3 million Mego super heroes were made in peak years. Since there were so many produced back then, they still turn up on a regular basis in attics, old toy boxes, closets, and even warehouses.

Action figure production began in the '60s, making it one of the newest collectible fields. All items of character merchandise are collectible, including many produced in the last few years. As such, most aren't old enough to consider the known quantities a valid basis for establishing values.

Parents sometimes purchase low-distribution figures at toy shows for their children because they can't find them in the toy stores. These are often used as toys and reduce the number of collector specimens.

There are rare and even some common items in high demand. The value of these items outperforms the action figure market as a whole — at least until supply catches up with demand. You never know when large quantities of items this new may turn up on closeout 2 or 3 years later.

The notion that the value of collectibles rises automatically with inflation or to the highest price one person was willing to pay has slightly less credibility than the fellow in the alley who offers to sell you a Rolex watch for $50. Values rise and fall at the whim of ready buyers.

The market for an entire action figure collection at retail value is slim and difficult to find. There have been numerous examples in recent years where collections of nostalgia collectibles were sold at auctions or purchased by dealers at a fraction of their estimated value. Except for a very limited number of high demand items, the process of turning a good-sized collection back into cash can be a long and expensive one. Even when a retail buyer can be found, there are sales costs and perhaps a middle man who is working for a percentage.

What it all boils down to is the two ways action figure collectibles are sold: offered at a set price or by auction to the highest bidder.

This book reports market prices based on items sold or traded by dealers and collectors nationwide. It reflects sales on the whole, with the understanding that an auction price is the one all other bidders refused to pay.

Collectors who buy at garage sales, toy store close-outs and flea markets generally purchase for less. Often they have first choice of items offered for sale; sometimes at exceptional bargain prices. But they also incur substantial time and travel expenses.

Mail and other auctions are often preferred by collectors who don't have the time or the ability to visit major shows. Money spent and current resale value also tend to be of less concern to the auction buyer. The winning bidder must outlast the others who need it to "complete" a collection or have some other emotional fix on the item.

It's difficult to say who actually spends more money in pursuit of their collecting interests — the aggressive hunter at lower cost outlets or the auction buyer who pays a premium. This much is sure, there are substantial costs involved beyond the money spent on collectibles by the aggressive buyer not normally considered in the "price", and higher overhead costs which are included in auction sales where the "price" includes everything.

Collecting should be pursued for the interest and satisfaction involved. There are much better investments at most financial institutions. *Fortune, Business Week*, and other business publications have done extensive articles on the pitfalls of speculating in what financial experts term "exotic" investments.

Every attempt has been made to have this price guide reflect the market in its broadest sense. The research effort covers extensive travel each year to attend leading toy, antique, and advertising shows from Boston to Anaheim, California. Mail auctions are monitored and many leading sales lists are received. The up-to-date values in this edition are a compilation of information received through February 1996. All prices shown in this book are U.S. dollar values with the dollar signs removed to permit inclusion of more information. Rarity and other considerations also affect value, and can be measured more precisely.

Rarity

Some items are available for years after they were first offered. Examples of this type include the Mego super heroes, *Micronauts, Star Wars* action figures and other similar items. On the other hand, some figures, like the Ideal *Tarzan* or the Tonka *Smoky the Bear* series were available once or for a brief time.

Rarity doesn't always equate to value. In collecting, the strongest demand is often generated by people wishing to obtain items of special interest. Thus rarity is only a part of value. Character popularity, cross-overs to other collecting fields (such as space adventure, dolls, Disneyana, etc.) and the type of item (figure, vehicle, accessory, playset) may become stronger factors, as other collectors often specialize in areas which cross the action figure line.

Price also has some regional influences. In California and New York, prices are substantially higher. Selling prices are the lowest in the Midwest — especially around Chicago and in Indiana, Ohio, Minnesota and Pennsylvania. Items still become available on a regular basis in these areas, and thereby fulfill demand. Realizing that these regional price situations exist, and that isolated individuals will always let emotions rule in auction bidding, the values represented in this guide are average estimates based on all categories.

Another factor which enhances value is the completeness of the original box or package. Action figure collectors are particularly sensitive in this area. The value of an item is substantially reduced without its original package, and the package must be free of wear, tears, price stickers, damage, or bubble defects if it is to bring the top price. Some figures also included instructions, catalogs, and extra accessories, which must be intact if the item is to realize top value.

Be wary of international merchandise billed as "rare." An interesting aspect in this hobby is the amount of international trading which goes on between collectors in different countries. Such items are usually uncommon in the United States, but many can be easily found in their country of origin. For example, *Star Trek: The Motion Picture* action figures were released in several other countries, but with different serial numbers and languages. The figures themselves were identical. As such, they are considered to be equivalent for the purpose of identification and worth.

Additional Considerations

Condition, like beauty, is in the eye of the beholder. When money becomes involved, the eye seems to take on an added dimension of x-ray vision or rose-colored glasses — depending on whether you are buying or selling.

Rarity, condition, and the amount of material available in the marketplace all have a direct effect on value. The overriding factor, however, is the number of individuals who wish to acquire any given item and have the money to satisfy their desire.

Reread "The Values in this Price Guide" for a full description of condition as it relates to action figure collectibles.

TIPS ON FINDING ACTION FIGURES

Collecting action figures has virtually mushroomed since the late '70s, and there is no want of dealers at toy and character collectible shows who have a large selection of action figures for sale. Finding the special figures may be a bit more difficult, but there are many tools to use.

Publications

Lee's Action Figure News & Toy Review is published monthly, and provides photos, news of new product, articles, and ads. It also features a price guide update each issue. The publishing frequency is monthly. *AFN* also publishes guides on loose figures. Write to *AFN*, 556 Monroe Turnpike, Monroe CT 06468 for subscription information.

Tomart's Action Figure Digest updates prices in this book while providing all-color editorial coverage of new products, hot collecting tips, and feature articles on a wide range of action figure subjects. Reporters from around the world file reports on the London and Tokyo Toy Fairs to support the U.S. staff reporters nation-wide. Columns on variations and action figure finds also appear regularly. To subscribe, write to *Action Figure Digest*, 3300 Encrete Lane, Dayton, OH 45439-1944.

Toy Shop is a classified marketplace for approximately 110 toy classifications. One of them is action figures. Here you will find ads for leading figure dealers and small private classified ads offering specific items for sale. Increasingly, these are auction-type ads with items going to the highest bidder by such and such date. On the whole, expect to pay more if you buy from ads in this publication. To obtain subscription information, contact *Toy Shop*, Circulation Department, 700 E. State St., Iola, WI 54990-0001.

Toy Trader is produced by the publisher of *Antique Trader*. It was designed to compete with *Toy Shop* as a newsprint tabloid. There are articles on all types of toys, a feature that has since been copied by *Toy Shop*. Action figures are available, but only account for 10-20% of the ads presented. Because of the source of its customer base, there are more older toys in this publication than in *Toy Shop*. *Toy Trader* also has an electronic internet trading mall on which they sell ad space. To subscribe, send $15.75 for 12 issues to *Toy Trader*, P.O. Box 1050, Dubuque, IA 52004-9969. If you wish to use a credit card, call 1-800-334-7165. For more information about the Electronic Toy Mall, send e-mail to traderpubs@aol.com.

Ted Hake's mail auction catalog offers many older and rarer action figures along with hundreds of other items of nostalgia. Write Hake's Americana, P.O. Box 1444, York, PA 17405 for subscription details.

Many dealers also publish catalogs for a nominal fee which are available by mail. Most of these are advertised in magazines like *Tomart's Action Figure Digest* and *Lee's Action Figure News & Toy Review*.

Shows

"Toy shows" throughout the U.S. offer ready access to mail-order and other dealers offering action figures. Some of the more prominent ones include the Atlantique City show held each March in Atlantic City, N.J.; the Glendale, CA All-American Collector's Show held each January and August; Antique Toy World shows held May, July, and October at the Kane County Fairgrounds located in St. Charles, IL approximately 40 miles west of Chicago; The Toledo Toy and Character Collectible shows, Lucas County Recreation Center, Maumee, OH; the Toyrific Antique and Collectible Toy Shows in Pasadina, CA; the F/X Shows in Orlando, FL; the New York City Pier shows; and the DeSalle Productions Toy and Doll Show, each spring and fall, Hara Area, Dayton, OH.

Many other local and regional shows can be found listed in *Toy Shop*; *Tomart's Action Figure Digest*, and *Lee's Action Figure News & Toy Review*. And don't forget local antique shows and flea markets.

Toy Stores

It's surprising what you can still find at Kay-Bee, Toy Works, Family Toy Warehouse, Toys "Я" Us, or other toy sales or discount chains. Many desirable items going back to the early '70s were found for the first edition of this book in such stores. Be sure to look on the tops of the shelf units, not only where action figures are sold, but all around the store. The price is often a bargain, too. When traveling, always be on the lookout for out-of-the-way toy stores in small towns. There are times when the assortment received takes years to sell, and reports of valuable finds are quite common. Action figures are new enough that you can expect the unexpected.

Buyout stores are another good source. They are found in most major cities. Such stores are sometimes called dollar or outlet stores, but they all buy stranded warehouse merchandise. Many times you will find toys discontinued 4 or 5 years previously…at sellout prices. Some U.S. discount toy stores have been known to buy even older stock from sources in Canada or other countries.

Finding New Figures

All figures are not issued equally. As soon as speculators learn which ones are packed fewer to an assortment, guess which ones they buy? They also learn when stores restock, and are there right before closing the evening before as the cartons are wheeled into the aisles. Even those who arrive early in the morning on the restock day often find the most desirable figures already sold.

There are two reasons why you can rarely find the toys you want at retail. First of all, the more desirable figures are being produced in lesser quantities than they were prior to 1995. This is because retailers are more afraid of getting stuck with figures that don't sell than they are in promoting the product. They have asked manufacturers to cut the size of assortments from 24 to 16 or fewer figures per case. Thus, they run out of hot products faster. And since the manufacturers base costs on the average price per figure, there are only 2 or 3 short-run figures per 48 count…where there were 4-6 before 1995.

These case-size reductions have contributed to a second problem. Now more than ever, the limited edition or low-packed figures are being removed in the back room or distribution center, and never make it to the retail shelves. The employees who pull them then sell them to flea market or other dealers, who in turn sell them to collectors for two to five times the original retail price…or more. This has given rise to mail-order dealers like Puzzle Zoo, where you can buy the whole set at the suggested retail price (rather than the discounted price offered at Wal-Mart, Target, Toys "Я" Us, and other large retailers) but save the time and gas it can easily take to nail all the figures in the set at a regular retailer.

Removing Price Tags

The condition of the card or box means extra value to the collector. Most commonly, the greatest damage is done by theft-proof price tags. There are a variety of glue solvents on the market which aid in damage-free removal. One of the best, not advertised for this purpose, is Bestine solvent and thinner. Apply liberally with an eye dropper or oilcan applicator, and gently lift off the tag. If there is a sticky residue, apply more Bestine and wipe with a paper towel. Repeat until all residue is removed. The Bestine will dry without a trace. Lighter fluid works in a similar way.

Heating the adhesive with a hair dryer, it is reported, also softens the glue for easier removal.

WHERE TO BUY AND SELL

Many readers select this book because they want to get connected to the action figure network or have figures they wish to sell. Apart from the ideas listed above, special mention of the dealers and collectors who have been particularly helpful to Tomart Publications in publishing this book is due.

Those listed are by no means all the dealers or collectors from whom figures were purchased. They are, however, the ones who were most cooperative, handled figure orders without delay or foul-up, and sent figures in a condition consistent with the way they were advertised. Unfortunately, there were several others who sent shabby material, did not attend to orders promptly, or shorted the order (but made good when it was called to their attention).

This list also contains the names of those dealers and collectors who spent the time to review a fledgling version of the manuscript for this book, made suggestions, and provided estimates of values. Many accepted the challenge, and the people listed here came through. It seems likely they would do the same for anyone wishing to buy or sell. Special areas of interest are included with each name and address.

Action Toys
P.O. Box 102
Holtsville, NY 11742
    Specialists in older rare action figures and toys. Send $1.00 for catalog ($2.00 outside U.S. and Canada)

Amok Time Toys
400 Warwick Road
East Meadow, NY 11554
Phone: (516) 826-4570
    Supplying a wide range of action figure collectibles.

Raymond Castile
208 Gum Tree Dr.
St. Charles, MO 63301
    Collector of monster figures. Also interested in super heroes and figures of the '60s, '70s and '80s.

Cotswold Collectibles
P.O. Box 249
Clinton, WA 98236
    Specializing in G.I. Joe and *Action Man*.

Steve Crouse
3258 Colony Vista Lane
Columbus, OH 43204
Phone (614) 351-7208
    Collector of *Major MATT MASON*

Joe Desris
1202 60th Street
Kenosha, WI 53140
Phone: (414) 657-4737
Fax: (414) 657-4733
    "World's tallest Batman collector." *Batman, Captain Action, G.I. Joe*, Mego and super hero toys.

John DiCicco
57 Bay View Drive (RP)
Shrewsbury, MA 01545
    All types of action figures and collectible toys.

The Earth
4166 Allendale Dr., #3
Cincinnati, OH 45209
    Buyers and sellers of *Star Wars* toys only. No store or showroom.

Figures Inc.
P.O. Box 19482
Johnston, RI 02919
Attn: Anthony Balasco
  Has a catalog of *Star Wars*, super heroes, space, and other collectible figures. Send $2.00 for a copy.

Charles Griffith
705 Mia Avenue
Dayton, OH 45427
Phone: (513) 263-7897
  3¾" *G.I. Joes*, super heroes, one-of-a-kind *G.I. Joe* items.

Ellen & Jerry Harnish
110 Main St.
Bellville, OH 44813
Phone: (419) 886-4782
  G.I. Joe Action Soldiers and Adventure Team, *Captain Action*, Mego and super hero sets. For large quarterly Action, TV, Character Figure and toy catalogue, send $1.00 for postage.

Jon and Karl Hartman
209 W. Rush St.
Kendallville, IN 46755
  Collectors of *Transformers*.

Heroes
23640 W. Highway 120
Grayslake, IL 60030
Attn: Mark Huckabone
Phone: (847) 546-8677
  Mego figures, 3¾" *G.I. Joes*, *Star Wars*, super heroes, and other scarce action figures, vehicles, and playsets

Heroes Unlimited
P.O. Box 453
Oradell, NJ 07649
Phone: (201) 385-1557
  Buyer and seller of all types of action figures.

Suzan Hufferd
6625 Sunbury Dr.
Indianapolis, IN 46241
  Dakin, Sutton, and advertising figures are a specialty. Buy, sell, and trade.

Ted Isaacs
32 Mayfair
Aliso Viejo, CA 92656
  Collector of 3¾" *G.I. Joes*, *Transformers*, and many other action figure lines.

Jeff Kilian
1011 Riverside Ave.
Wichita, KS 67203
Phone: (316) 263-3996
  Collector of 12" *G.I. Joes*.

Lenny Lee
556 Monroe Turnpike
Monroe, CT 06468
  Interested in a wide variety of action figures, especially *G.I. Joe*, super heroes, and unusual items.

Keith Meyer
P.O. Box 4322
North Little Rock, AR 72116
Phone: (501) 758-1444/(501) 791-0000
  Collector/dealer of 1960s action figures, toys and comics. *Major MATT MASON*, *Sea Devils*, *Zeroids*, *Captain Action*, Aurora models, NASA and Sci-Fi-related toys.

Outer Limits
433 Piaset Avenue
Clifton, NJ 07013
  Dealer in a wide variety of space, science fiction, super hero, figures and other toys.

Puzzle Zoo
"The World's Most Unique Toy Store"
1413 Third Street Promenade
Santa Monica, CA 90401
  A retail store devoted to collectors, featuring new, vintage, and imported items. Mail order also availible. Credit card customers call 1-800-627-8523 to order.

G.F. Ridenour
Fun House Toy Co.
P.O. Box 343
Bradford Woods, PA 15015
Phone: (412) 935-1392
  Marx playsets and plastic figures, *Star Wars* & space-related, super heroes, character figures and collectibles.

David Secrist
1128 W. North St.
Springfield, OH 45504
  Wrestling figures only.

Toy Tokyo
Box 337   Box 5607
New York, N.Y. 10021-0009   and   Evanston, IL 60204
Phone: (212) 517-5212   Phone: (312) 381-9941
Fax: (212) 517-5450   Fax: (312) 381-9942
  Toys and collectibles from around the world.

Toys 'N' Stuf
P.O. Box 2037
San Bernardino, CA 92406
Phone: (909) 880-8558
  Older and unusual figures, Mego, super heroes, *Star Wars*, *Major MATT MASON*, store displays, all kinds of TV, movie, and character related toys from around the world.

Tom and T.N.Tumbusch
3300 Encrete Lane
Dayton, OH 45439-1944
  Looking for figures not listed or shown in this series. Toy manufacturer's name must appear on package. Not interested in packaged figures which list "Made in China" as the the only hint to the product's origin. No items available for sale or trade.

Jerry & Joan Wesolowski
22 Allison
Toledo, OH 43605
Phone: (419) 691-1810
  Science Fiction, space, movie, TV, military, character toys, figures, and model kits.

A-TEAM, THE (Galoob) 1984-85

A-Team figures were made in two sizes, each with accessories and playsets. The 6½" figures were sold on blister packs with a cardboard box full of plastic guns, tools, and the like. The Amy A. Allen figure is the rarest of the bunch, since the character left the series before the end of the first season. The 3¾" figures could be found four on a card, or with various playsets and accessories. Figures sold with vehicles had different costumes than those sold on cards.

		CNP	MIP	MMP
6½" figures & accessories A-1001-20				
A-1001	Hannibal	5	10	17
A-1002	B.A. Baracus	5	12	20
A-1003	Face	5	10	17
A-1004	Murdock	5	10	17
A-1005	Amy A. Allen	10	20	30
A-1006	Viper	4	10	15
A-1007	Rattler	4	10	15
A-1008	Cobra	4	10	15
A-1009	Python	4	10	15
A-1010	Off Road Attack Cycle	5	15	30
A-1011	Combat Attack Gyrocopter	5	17	30
A-1020	Command Center	not produced		
3¾" figures and accessories A-1031-50				
A-1031	A-Team figures (4)	10	25	45
A-1032	Bad Guys figures (4)	8	15	25
A-1040	Armored Attack Adventure w/B.A.	12	25	45
A-1041	Interceptor Jet Bomber w/Murdock	15	25	45
A-1042	Tactical Van playset	15	25	50
A-1043	Motorized Patrol Boat w/Hannibal	12	20	35
A-1044	Corvette w/Face	12	25	45
A-1045	Command Chopper	8	15	28
A-1050	Headquarters Camp w/4 figures	15	30	55

AAWF — ALL-AMERICAN WRESTLING FEDERATION (Remco) 1991

A series of Remco knock-offs, designed to capitalize on the success of *WWF*.

	CNP	MIP	MMP
AA8001-02 3-figure cards, ea	1	3	5

ACTION FIGURE! — THE LIFE AND TIMES OF DOONESBURY'S UNCLE DUKE (Andrews and McMeel) 1992

A single action figure of Uncle Duke was issued in conjunction with the publication of the above-titled Doonesbury cartoon collection. The toy is an oddity for collectors.

		CNP	MIP	MMP
AC3001	Book w/figure	10	20	25

ACTION HEROS/ACTION HEROES (Early Light) 1985-86

This is actually two different figure sets, packaged a number of different ways. The first version was a set of unnamed figures sold at Woolworth. The figures are identical to the *Military One* series. The second series was also made for Woolworth, but the same figures were repainted and repackaged the following year for Odd Lots. Woolworth figures had green outfits; Odd Lots figures wore brown.

Version #1 AC4001-08		CNP	MIP	MMP
AC4001	Army	1	2	4
AC4002	Navy	1	2	4
AC4003	Marine	1	2	4
AC4004	Terrorist	1	2	4
AC4005	Pilot	1	2	4
AC4006	Paratrooper	1	2	4
AC4007	Frogman	1	2	4
AC4008	Beret	1	2	4
Version #2 (green) AC4011-15				
AC4011	Medic	1	2	4
AC4012	Flame Thrower	1	2	4
AC4013	Bazooka	1	2	4
AC4014	Rifle (kneeling)	1	2	4
AC4015	Rifle (standing)	1	2	4
Version #3 (brown) AC4021-15				
AC4021	Medic	1	2	4
AC4022	Flame Thrower	1	2	4
AC4023	Bazooka	1	2	4
AC4024	Rifle (kneeling)	1	2	4
AC4025	Rifle (standing)	1	2	4

See also: *Military One*

ACTION JACKSON (Mego) 1974

This was a generic hero-action series, probably designed to compete with *G.I. Joe* and *Big Jim*. The Mustang, Lost Continent and Jungle House playsets were similar to other Mego toys.

		CNP	MIP	MMP
AC5001	Action Jackson, blonde	10	15	35
AC5002	AC5001, black hair	7	15	25
AC5003	AC5001, brown hair	7	15	25
AC5004	AC5001, blonde beard	10	15	30
AC5005	AC5001, black beard	7	15	22
AC5006	AC5001, brown beard	7	15	22
AC5007	Action Jackson, black	20	45	75
AC5011	Strap-On Helicopter	4	10	15
AC5012	Parachute Plunge	4	10	15
AC5013	Parachute Plunge	4	10	15
AC5014	Fire Rescue Pack	4	10	15
Outfits AC5021-38				
AC5021	Rescue Squad	2	5	8
AC5022	Western	2	5	8
AC5023	Scramble Cyclist	2	5	8
AC5024	Jungle Safari	2	5	8
AC5025	Secret Agent	2	5	8
AC5026	Snowmobile Outfit	2	5	8
AC5027	Aussie Marine	2	5	8
AC5028	Air Force	2	5	8
AC5029	Navy	2	5	8
AC5030	Frogman	2	5	8
AC5031	Ski-Patrol	2	5	8
AC5032	Army	2	5	8
AC5033	Fisherman	2	5	8
AC5034	Hockey	2	5	8
AC5035	Baseball	2	5	8
AC5036	Karate	2	5	8
AC5037	Football	2	5	8
AC5038	Surf and Scuba Outfit	2	5	8
Accessories AC5050-62				
AC5050	Campmobile	70	140	200
AC5051	Formula Racer	25	60	125
AC5052	Safari Jeep	25	60	125
AC5053	Adventure Set	35	110	200

AC4008   AC4015   AC4024

AC6001   AC6002   AC6003   AC6004

A-1001

A-1002

A-1003

A-1004

A-1005

A-1006

A-1007

A-1010

A-1011

A-1008

A-1009

A-1020

A-1031

A-1032

A-1040

A-1042

A-1043

A-1044

CNP: Complete, no package, with all weapons and accessories; MIP: Mint in package; MMP: Mint item in Mint package. Values in U.S. dollars. See page 11 for details.

A-1041

A-1050

AA8001   AA8002

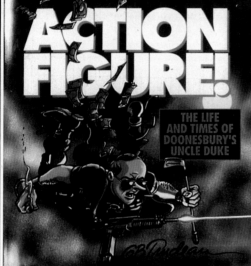

AC3001

AC5005

AC5003   AC5006   AC5007

AC5011

		CNP	MIP	MMP
AC5054	Mustang	10	40	75
AC5055	Snow Mobile	5	15	25
AC5056	Scramble Cycle	8	20	45
AC5057	Rescue Helicopter	18	60	90
AC5058	Dune Buggy	15	50	75
AC5061	Lost Continent playset	20	70	95
AC5062	Jungle House	18	70	95

ACTION PIRATE (Soma) 1991

A set of four cloth-costumed pirates with lever-action arms. Made for Woolworth Co. No names appear on the packages.

		CNP	MIP	MMP
AC6001	Pirate w/patch	1	3	4
AC6002	Pirate w/tattoo	1	3	4
AC6003	Pirate w/scar	1	3	4
AC6004	Pirate w/blue vest	1	3	4

ADDAMS FAMILY, THE (Playmates) 1992-93

The first live-action *Addams Family* film inspired a return of the original animated series, upon which these figures were based.

		CNP	MIP	MMP
AD0501	Gomez	2	5	8
AD0502	Morticia	2	7	12
AD0503	Uncle Fester	2	5	8

18

AC5012   AC5013   AC5014   AC5033

AC5024   AC5027   AC5028   AC5029

AC5030   AC5031   AC5032   AC5034

AC5035   AC5036   AC5037   AC5038

AD0504	Lurch	2	5	8
AD0505	Pugsley	1	8	12
AD0506	Granny	1	5	8
AD0507	Wednesday	not produced		
AD0508	Cousin Itt	not produced		

ADVANCED DUNGEONS & DRAGONS (LJN) 1983-84

LJN Toys introduced a line of *Advanced Dungeons & Dragons* products in 1983, mainly consisting of action figures. Additional non-articulated and wind-up products produced for TSR in conjunction with this line have also inspired interest among action figure collectors, and are listed here as well.

The characters were taken from a Saturday morning TV cartoon series based on the famous TSR role-playing game, which was enjoying a rapid growth period. The detailing in this line is some of the most intricate ever done. All action figures, mounts, monsters and playsets were produced in the same scale.

Good characters appeared on rectangular yellow-gold printed cards; evil characters on dark blue cards. Special figures, more heavily armed, were called "Battle Masters." There were three produced in the first year: Ogre King, Young Male Titan and Northlord the Great. Behir, a serpentine creature with 12 legs and many sharp points, was never made.

19

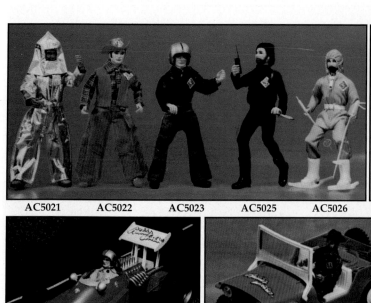

AC5021   AC5022   AC5023   AC5025   AC5026   AC5050

AC5051   AC5052   AC5053

AC5054   AC5055   AC5056

AC5057   AC5061

Battle-Matic Action, Tiamat — the five-headed Dragon, the Snake Cave playset, and "Power Creatures" were the major new announcements for 1984. Melf, Mercion, and Ringlerun were dropped from the "good" assortment in favor of Bowmarc the Crusader, Hawkler the Ranger (originally planned as Falken), and Deeth the female fighter. Grimsword the Knight, Zorgar the Barbarian, and Drex the Warrior were added to the "evil" assortment. All 1984 characters in these two assortments had the increased power of mechanical "Battle-matic Action" (i.e., a button on their back which moved their fighting arm). Card colors for the second year remained the

same, but cards were die-cut with an arch on top curving around to two notches in the side, with rounded corners at the bottom. The Young Male Titan was packaged on a card with a blue background...a mistake in the production department. Three Battle Masters — Pulvereye, Metta Flame, and Mandoom — were added. All six 1984 versions of the Battle Masters included "Shield-Shooters" which fired the heraldic emblem on their shields. All second year figures are rare and prized by collectors. The later Battle Masters are extremely difficult to find.

Bulette, a new monster, was announced for '84, but has never been found. The Power

Creatures wind-ups were extremely limited, and it is unlikly the Snake Cave playset was made.

1983 figures AD1001-11		CNP	MIP	MMP
AD1001	Strongheart	6	18	25
AD1002	Warduke	6	18	25
AD1003	Kelek	6	15	20
AD1004	Mercion	6	15	20
AD1005	Melf	6	25	30
AD1006	Ogre King	8	20	25
AD1007	Ringlerun	8	18	25
AD1008	Zarak	6	20	25
AD1009	Northlord	6	22	30
AD1010	Young Male Titan	6	22	30

| AD0501 | | | | AD0502 | | | | AD0503 | | | | AD0504 | | | |

| AD0505 | | | | AD0506 | | | | AD1001 | | | | AD1002 | | | |

| AD1003 | | | | AD1004 | | | | AD1005 | | | | AD1012 | | | |

AD1011	Skylla	not produced		AD1113	Grimsword	8	45	70	**Mounts AD1131-33**			
AD1012	Peralay	6	25	30	AD1114	Zorgar	10	15	25	AD1131	Nightmare	5	18	25
AD1013	Elkhorn				AD1115	Drex	20	40	60	AD1132	Destrier	5	18	25
1984 figures AD1101-27				AD1116	Kelek	10	25	40	AD1133	Bronze Dragon	5	20	30
AD1101	Strongheart	8	25	30	AD1121	Ogre King	20	45	60	**Mount and Action Figure Gift Sets AD1135-37**			
AD1102	Elkhorn	8	25	30	AD1122	Northlord	20	45	60	AD1135	Nightmare w/AD1111	15	25	35
AD1103	Bowmarc	25	45	60	AD1123	Young Male Titan	20	45	60	AD1136	Destrier w/AD1101	15	25	35
AD1104	Valkeer	8	35	50	AD1124	Pulvereye	30	50	75	AD1137	Bronze Dragon			
AD1105	Bowmarc (evil card)				AD1125	Metta Flame	30	50	75		w/AD1101	15	25	35
AD1106	Deeth	20	45	60	AD1126	Mandoom	30	50	75	**Articulated Monsters AD1141-46**			
AD1111	Warduke	8	25	30	AD1127	Hawkler	35	55	80	AD1141	Hook Horror	5	15	20
AD1112	Zarak	8	25	30						AD1142	Behir	not produced		

CNP: Complete, no package, with all weapons and accessories; MIP: Mint in package; MMP: Mint item in Mint package. Values in U.S. dollars. See page 11 for details.

AD1006

AD1007

AD1008

AD1009

AD1010

AD1013

AD1170

AD1101

AD1103

AD1105

AD1106

AD1123   AD1126   AD1125

AD1122   AD1121   AD1124

AD1136

AD1111   AD1112   AD1113   AD1114

AD1115   AD1123   AD1127   AD1163

AD1131   AD1132   AD1133

AD1141   AD1143   AD1182

AD1151   AD1161   AD1162   AD1201

AD1203   AD1205   AD1215   AD1217

AD1221   AD1225   AD1231   AD1233

AD3001   AD3002   AD3003   AD3004

AD1143	Dragonne	5	15	20	AD1152	5-Headed Hydra	4	10	15	**Power Creatures (wind-ups) AD1161-63**			
AD1144	Bulette	not produced			AD1153	Chimera	4	10	15	AD1161	Terrasque	25	50	75
Rubber Monsters AD1151-55					AD1154	Carrion Crawler	3	7	10	AD1162	Pernicon	25	50	75
AD1151	Roper	4	10	15	AD1155	Neo-Otyugh	3	7	10	AD1163	Cave Fisher	25	50	75

AD3005	AD3006	AD3007	AD3008

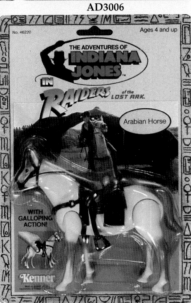

AD3009	AD3020	AD3021

AD3022	AD3023	AD3024

AD1170	Tiamat the Five-Headed Dragon	30	75	100
AD1181	Snake Cave playset	not produced		
AD1182	Fortress of Fangs	35	55	75
Solid Figures AD1201-37				
AD1201	Skeletons of Sith	4	10	15
AD1203	Troglodyte/Goblin	3	7	10
AD1205	Bullywugs of the Bog	3	7	10
AD1207	Orcs of the Broken Bone	3	7	10
AD1209	Grell	4	10	15
AD1211	Minotaur	3	7	10
AD1213	Bugbear/Goblin	3	7	10
AD1215	Terrible Troll/Goblin	3	7	10
AD1217	Shambling Mound	4	10	15
AD1219	Spectre/Lich	3	7	10
AD1221	Odious Ogre	4	10	15
AD1223	Umber Hulk	3	7	10
AD1225	Fire Elemental	3	7	10
AD1227	Elves of the Woodland	3	7	10
AD1229	Sarke Mercenaries	3	7	10
AD1231	Dwarves of the Mountain King	3	7	10
AD1233	Heroic Men-At-Arms	4	10	15
AD1235	Steadfast Men-At-Arms	4	10	15
AD1237	Stalwart Men-At-Arms	4	10	15

ADVENTURES OF INDIANA JONES, THE (Kenner) 1982-83

Raiders of the Lost Ark was a surprise success film which few anticipated. If Kenner had not already had a relationship with Lucasfilm Limited producing the highly-successful *Star Wars* toy line, there might not have been any *Adventures of Indiana Jones* figures at all.

Catalogs and cards relate a two-year marketing span for the line. The figures were under-produced in the first year, and a big demand resulted. In the second year Kenner packed only two or three figures of Indiana Jones per

CNP: Complete, no package, with all weapons and accessories; MIP: Mint in package; MMP: Mint item in Mint package. Values in U.S. dollars. See page 11 for details.

AL1001	AL1002	AL1004	AL1005
AL1007	AL1009	AL1021	AL1023
AL1025	AL1027	AL1029	AL1031
AL1033	AL1035	AL1037	AL1039

case, and only one Marion Ravenwood. Interest in the line died when shoppers couldn't find the featured characters. The packing of Toth and the Cairo Swordsman was so unbalanced that the figures could still be found on closeout shelves ten years after their initial release.

Collector interest in *Adventures of Indiana Jones* figures is unique. The lead character's popularity has continued to grow with each successive film and video release. It is a short but valuable set consisting of nine action figures (plus two more which were not available on cards), two accessories, and three playsets. Interest is further fueled by the existence of a 12" Indy figure (see IN1801) and the normally plain-boxed figure of Belloq in a ceremonial robe, which is available carded in extremely limited supply.

The carded Belloq figure was never sold in stores, but a few samples were produced. These, along with some extra cards, are known to exist.

Several of the *Adventures of Indiana Jones* figures had spring-action arms. The first four comprised the original release of the series, with Belloq in ceremonial robe available as a mail-in premium. The Arabian Horse was a re-

| AL1051 | AL1053 | AL1055 | AL1057 |

| AL1059 | AL1061 | AL1063 | AL1065 |

| AL1067 | AL1069 | AL1071 | AL1073 |

| AL1015 | AL1041 | AL1043 |

make of the 1979 *Butch and Sundance* horses, and was sold on a card. Special figures of Indiana Jones, the Monkey Man, and Marion Ravenwood were included in various playsets.

	CNP	MIP	MMP
AD3001 Indiana Jones	25	70	95
AD3002 Toht	3	10	12
AD3003 Marion Ravenwood	40	200	260
AD3004 Cairo Swordsman	5	10	14
AD3005 Sallah	6	18	35

AD3006 Indiana Jones in German uniform	10	30	48
AD3007 German Mechanic	6	15	19
AD3008 Belloq	10	22	35
AD3009 Belloq in ceremonial robe (mail-in)	10	15	20
AD3010 AD3009 on card	10	400	600
AD3011 Indiana Jones in desert disguise (from AD3022)	10	-	-

AD3012 Monkey Man (from AD3023)	10	-	-
AD3013 Marion Ravenwood PVC (from AD3023)	10	-	-
AD3020 Arabian Horse	20	60	80
AD3021 Well of the Souls	25	50	65
AD3022 Map Room	18	25	40
AD3023 Streets of Cairo	15	30	45
AD3024 Desert Convoy Truck	10	30	45

See also: *Indiana Jones; Indiana Jones and the Temple of Doom*

AL1081

AL1107

AL1111

AL1113

AL5110

AL1121   AL1123   AL1125

AL5150

AL5152

AL5154

AL5156

ALADDIN (Mattel) 1992-95

Mattel figures based on Disney's animated feature *Aladdin* were originally sold on character-specific blister cards. The first versions of Aladdin and Jafar only included accessories. Smaller figures of Abu and Iago, created for the Aladdin & Jafar Action Figure Playset, were later added to the individually-carded figures.

In 1995, the card art was changed to tie-in with the television series. The new card was generic, and not all figures appeared on the card backs. Some of the old figures were freshened with minor paint changes, and new characters were added.

4½" movie figures		CNP	MIP	MMP
AL1001	Aladdin	2	5	7
AL1002	Aladdin & Abu	3	6	8
AL1004	Jafar	2	5	7
AL1005	Jafar & Iago	3	6	8
AL1007	Genie	2	5	7
AL1009	Jasmine & Rajah	3	6	8
AL1011	Aladdin & Jafar set	6	10	15
AL1013	Jasmine, Rajah, & Genie set	6	10	15
AL1015	Cave of Wonders	8	13	18
AL1021	Baseball Player Genie	4	9	12
AL1023	Frenchman Genie	4	9	12
AL1025	Top Hat 'n Tails Genie	4	9	12
AL1027	Prince Ali	2	5	7
AL1028	Princess Jasmine	2	5	7

AL1029	Parade Leader Genie	4	8	12
Figures with "Battle Action" AL1031-37				
AL1031	Aladdin	4	9	12
AL1033	Jafar	4	9	12
AL1035	Evil Genie Jafar	4	9	12
AL1037	Palace Guard Rasoul	4	9	12
AL1039	Sultan	4	9	12
AL1041	Prince Ali & Parade Leader Genie set	8	15	20
AL1043	Princess Jasmine, Sultan set	8	15	20
AL1045	Final Battle Playset	6	13	18
4½" television figures AL1051-AL1081				
AL1051	AL1002, repainted	2	5	7
AL1053	Aladdin in purple	2	5	7
AL1055	Prince Ali	2	5	7

AL5158 AL5160 AL5162 AL5164

AL5166 AL5170 AL51 AL5176

AL5176 AL5178 AL5179 AL5180

AL1057	AL1005 on TV card	2	6	8	AL1067	Sultan	3	7	9	AL1081	Anchors Away
AL1059	Genie	2	6	8	AL1069	Captain Murk	3	7	9		Sailing Ship	6	15	20
AL1061	Parade Leader Genie	4	8	13	AL1071	Abis Mal	3	7	9	AL1101	Giant Genie	12	24	34
AL1063	Jasmine w/birdcage	2	6	8	AL1073	Mekanicles	3	7	9	AL1105	Tourist Genie	15	25	35
AL1065	Jasmine w/Iago	2	6	8	AL1075	Fashoum	3	7	9	AL1107	Genie of the Lamp (15")	10	20	30

CNP: Complete, no package, with all weapons and accessories; MIP: Mint in package; MMP: Mint item in Mint package. Values in U.S. dollars. See page 11 for details.

AL5185   AL5186   AL5187   AL5191

AL5192   AL5193   AL5194   AL5195

AL5183
(assembled sections)

AL1110	Aladdin (street clothes)	8	15	25
AL1111	Aladdin (wedding)	8	15	25
AL1113	Jasmine	8	15	25
AL1114	Jasmine (wedding)	8	15	25
AL1115	Jasmine & Rajah			
	Friendship set	10	20	35
AL1117	Magic Carpet Giftset	10	20	35
AL1119	Fashion Genie (plush)	8	15	25
Water Jewel Magic figures AL1121-23				
AL1121	Aladdin	8	15	25
AL1123	Jasmine	8	15	25
AL1125	Arabian Lights Jasmine	8	15	25

See also: *Bubble Princess; Musical Princess; Perfume Princess*

ALIEN (Kenner) 1979

The Kenner Alien figure is one of the most highly-sought pieces among collectors of action figures, space adventure and horror items. Most *Alien* merchandise was taken off the shelves because the creature was considered too frightening. Kenner had also prepared a 4½" figure line, which was killed when the large figure was withdrawn.

The figure — which has retracting inner teeth, spines on its back, and a plastic dome covering its head — is rarely found intact. At least one manufacturer has made reproductions of the plastic dome. Mint condition figures in the original box are occasionally seen, but always with a high price tag. The complete figure includes a poster.

When *Aliens* returned to popularity in the early '90s, a limited edition reissue of this classic figure was considered, but the idea was shelved at the time.

AL5251

AL5253

AL5254

AL5252

AL5260

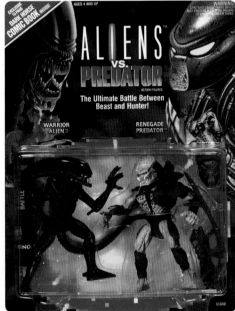

AL5601

AI6002

AM1000

	CNP	MIP	MMP
AL5110 Kenner Alien figure	150	350	460

See also: *Maxx FX*

ALIENS (Kenner) 1992-95

The popularity of the *Aliens* films demanded the return of merchandise. The initial line was fantastic, featuring five marines based on characters from the films, and four aliens loosely based on H.R. Geiger's classic creature. Each of the original figures included a mini-comic.

The monster figures were well received, but Kenner packed too many marines into the assortments. The monsters sold quickly, but humans were left hanging on the shelves,

dampening retailer enthusiasm for the line. Kenner further hampered the line by failing to introduce many new figures in the second year.

Lack of retailer interest caused Kenner to cancel American shipment of the Hudson, O'Mally, and Vasquez figures. American collectors imported large quantities of these three figures from Australia, Singapore, the U.K., and other foreign markets, and the figures continue to bring high values.

U.K. retailers were more receptive to the line, and took steps to keep it going. At Christmas time in 1994, U.K. Toys "Я" Us and Woolworth stores released a six-piece pop-up Space Base. Individual sections were taped to

the backs of random figures.

The *Aliens vs. Predator* 2-pack (see AL5601) gave sales a boost in 1993, and the Hive playset included an exquisite Alien Queen.

Kenner had production difficulties with several 1994 aliens. Poor retail performance resulted, causing the cancellation of the proposed 1995 *Hive War* line.

First series		CNP	MIP	MMP
AL5150	Lt. Ripley	5	10	15
AL5152	Bishop	5	10	15
AL5154	Sgt. Apone	5	10	15
AL5156	Hicks	5	10	15
AL5158	Drake	5	10	15

AM1001

AM1005

AM3039

AM3091

AM3101

AM3102

AM3105

AM4001

AM4002

AM4003

AM4004

AM4005

AM4007

AM4006

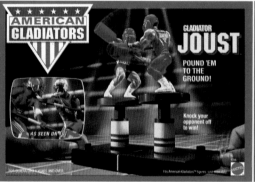

AM4021

AM4022

AM4023

AM4024

AM4025

SITTING BULL — AM7001

DAVEY CROCKETT — AM7002

WYATT EARP — AM7003

WILD BILL HICKOK — AM7004

COCHISE — AM7005

BUFFALO BILL CODY — AM7006

AM7015

AM7020

AM7030

AN3503   AN3501   AN3502

AN4007

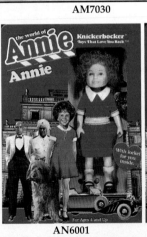

AN6001

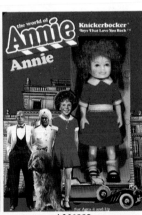

AN6002

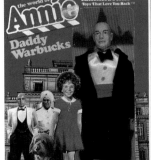

AN6003

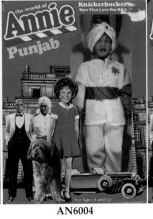

AN6004

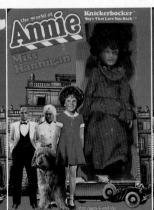

AN6005

AN6006

AP5001

AN6010　　　　　　　　　　　AR1001　　　　　AR1002

AR1003　　　　AR1004　　　　　BA1001　　　　　BA1002　　　　　BA1005

BA2012　　　　BA2013　　　　BA2033　　　　BA2035　　　　BA2036

BA2501　　　　BA2505　BA2507　　BA2501　　BA2503　　BA2509　　BA2511　　　　BA2511

AL5160 Scorpion Alien	5	10	15	AL5183 Space Base sections,			
AL5162 Gorilla Alien	5	10	15	six different, ea. (UK)	20	25	30
AL5164 Bull Alien	5	10	15	**Third series marines (foreign release only)**			
AL5166 Alien Queen	5	10	15	AL5185 Hudson	15	25	40
Second series				AL5186 O'Malley	15	25	40
AL5170 Flying Queen Alien	8	15	20	AL5187 Vasquez	25	45	70
AL5172 ATAX Disguise	8	15	20	**Fourth series**			
Third series				AL5191 Wild Boar Alien	8	10	15
AL5175 Queen Face Hugger	8	12	16	AL5192 Night Cougar Alien			
AL5176 Rhino Alien	5	10	15	(repaint of AL5177)	8	10	15
AL5177 Panther Alien	5	10	15	AL5193 Alien Arachnid	8	10	15
AL5178 Snake Alien	8	12	16	AL5194 King Alien	10	15	20
AL5179 Killer Crab Alien	5	10	15	AL5195 Swarm Alien			
AL5180 Mantis Alien	8	12	16	(electronic)	10	14	20

Accessories and Playsets

AL5251 Power Loader	8	14	18
AL5252 E.V.A.C. Fighter	10	15	20
AL5253 Stinger XT-37	8	14	18
AL5254 Electronic Hovertread	8	14	18
AL5260 Hive Playset	20	35	50

ALIENS VS. PREDATOR (Kenner) 1993

Kenner's second *Alien* line began in 1992. The 1993 series was sold to the trade as *Aliens vs. Predator,* but this theme only appeared on one two-pack. *Aliens* continued as an independent line, and the *Predator* line was added as a new series.

34

BA5005

BA5006

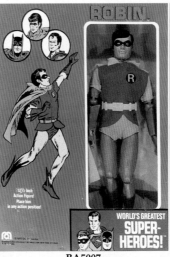

BA5007

BA5008

BA5011

BA5012

BA5013

BA5016

BA5017

BA5020

BA5021

BA5022

BA5023

BA5024

		CNP	MIP	MMP
AL5601	Warrior Alien/ Renegade Predator	7	15	25

ALL-STAR WRESTLERS (Remco) 1985

A series of figures based on the American Wrestling Association (AWA).

		CNP	MIP	MMP
AL6001	Legion of Doom Road Warriors	8	12	20
AL6002	High Flyers	8	12	20
AL6003	Fabulous Freebirds	8	12	20
AL6004	Gagne's Raiders	8	12	20
AL6005	Long Riders	8	12	20

		CNP	MIP	MMP
AL6011	Rick Martel vs. Baron Von Raschke	12	22	28
AL6012	Ric Flair vs. Larry Zbyszko	12	22	28
AL6025	All Star Wrestling Ring	4	10	15

	BA5025	BA5030	BA5040
BA5201	BA5202	BA5203	BA5204	BA5205
BA5206	BA5211	BA5212	BA5213	BA5214

AMAZING SPIDER-MAN, THE (Mego) 1978-81

Mego made a 12½" figure of the Amazing Spider-Man in 1978. It was originally designed with magnetic hands and feet, but this version was never produced. The following year, a similar figure was sold with a fly-away action attachment. The Web-Spinning version of the figure had a hollow right arm which a child filled with a special solution to produce "webs."

This section includes only those figures which were sold under the name *The Amazing Spider-Man*. Figures sold under the name *Spider-Man* and figures which were made as part of a larger series appear elsewhere in the appropriate sections.

		CNP	MIP	MMP
AM1000	Spider-Man, boxed	25	50	60
AM1001	Spider-Man, carded	25	40	50
AM1002	w/fly-away action	25	45	75
AM1005	Web-Spinning Spider-Man	45	125	150

See also: *Captain Action, Comic Action Heroes; Die-Cast Super Heroes; Marvel Super Heroes; Marvel Super Heroes Secret Wars; Maximum Carnage; Official World's Greatest Super Heroes; Pocket Super Heroes; Spider-Man*

AMERICAN DEFENSE (Agglo) 1985, (Remco) 1986

The name *American Defense* is a trademark owned by K-mart. The figures first appeared as a K-mart exclusive series in 1985. Enemy characters were called "The Demon Enemy." The figures were sold 2 on a card. The same figures, individually packaged, were later sold in other chains (such as Meijer's) under the name *National Defense* (see listing NA7001).

Remco took over the line in 1986. The figures were originally sold 2 on a card, but eventually switched to individual packaging. Later production runs were re-issues of earlier characters, with new colors, vests, firing backpacks, and a colored liquid to shoot. Remco also produced the same figures as *U.S. Forces— Defenders of Peace* (see US1001). Colors and names were changed for the latter series.

Infrared BATMAN

BA5215

Catwoman

BA5216

Scarecrow

BA5217

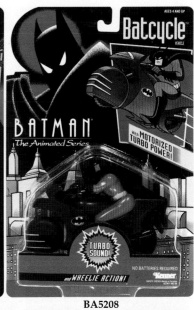

Batcycle

BA5208

Hoverbat

BA5221

B.A.T.V.

BA5222

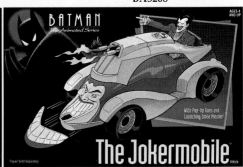

The Jokermobile

BA5223

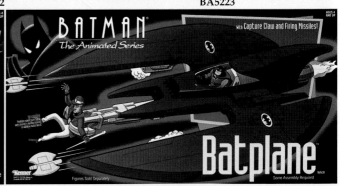

Batmobile

BA5224

Batplane

BA5225

Bat-Signal Jet

BA5226

Robin Dragster

BA5227

Batcave Command Center

BA5229

Agglo AM3001-08	CNP	MIP	MMP
AM3001 Bazooka Marine/UDT	1	5	9
AM3002 Machine Gunner/ Army Infantry	1	5	9
AM3003 Marine/Ranger	1	5	9
AM3004 Pilot/Special Forces	1	5	9
AM3005 Commando/Green Beret	1	5	9
AM3006 Enemy Leader/Enemy Undersea Officer	1	5	9
AM3007 Enemy Weapons Officer/ Assault Team Officer	1	5	9
AM3008 Enemy Spy Leader/ Enemy Flight Officer	1	5	9
Remco AM3011-3104			
AM3011 Defender/Flame	1	5	9
AM3012 Karate King/Ramrod	1	5	9
AM3013 Black Belt/Mac Tough	1	5	9
AM3014 Bush Fighter/Sky Fighter	1	5	9
AM3021 Defender	1	5	9
AM3022 Mac Tough	1	5	9
AM3023 Karate King	1	5	9
AM3024 Black Belt	1	5	9
AM3025 Ramrod	1	5	9
AM3026 Sky Fighter	1	5	9
AM3027 Bush Fighter	1	5	9
AM3028 Flame	1	5	9
AM3039 Forest Green	1	5	9
AM3040 Control	1	5	9
AM3051 Underground	1	4	6
AM3052 Paraforce (brown)	1	4	6
AM3053 Paraforce (green)	1	4	6
AM3054 Dr. Care	1	4	6
AM3055 Frogman	1	4	6

CNP: Complete, no package, with all weapons and accessories; MIP: Mint in package; MMP: Mint item in Mint package. Values in U.S. dollars. See page 11 for details.

BA5231

BA5232

BA5233

BA5234

BA5237

BA5235

BA5236

BA5252

BA5253

BA5241

BA5242

BA5243

BA5244

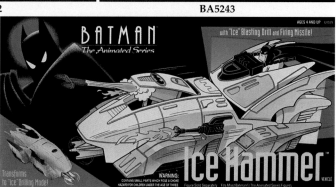

BA5261

AM3056	Sheriff Goldstar	1	4	6	AM3071	Tiger Claw	1	2	3	AM3103	Jet Streak vehicle	3	8	10
AM3057	Inspector Vision	1	4	6	AM3072	Swamp Man	1	2	3	AM3104	Rough Trax vehicle	3	8	10
AM3061	Heavy Metal	1	3	5	AM3073	Slugger	1	2	3	AM3105	Road Raider	3	8	10
AM3062	Claw	1	3	5	AM3091-6	Liquid Fighters, ea	1	2	3	AM3106	Sky Raider	3	8	10
AM3063	Top Flight	1	3	5	AM3098	Liquid Fighter refills	.50	1	2				

AM3064 General Iron Boot 2 4 6   AM3101 Sky Scanner vehicle 3 8 10   **See also:** *National Defense; U.S. Forces—*
AM3065 Yeti 2 4 6   AM3102 Attack Trike vehicle 3 8 10   *Defenders of Peace; U.S. Military*

BA5251	BA5254	BA5255	BA5258

BA5271	BA5272	BA5273	BA5274	BA5275

BA5276	BA5277	BA5278	BA5281	BA5282

AMERICAN GLADIATORS (Mattel) 1991-92

A "macho" set of figures based on the stars of the popular TV sport-challenge show. The blue challenger was only available in the competition two-pack.

		CNP	MIP	MMP
AM4001	Gladiator Gemini	2	7	10
AM4002	Gladiator Turbo	2	7	10
AM4003	Gladiator Nitro	2	7	10
AM4004	Gladiator Laser	2	7	10
AM4005	Red Challenger	2	7	10
AM4006	Competition 2-Pack w/ Laser/Blue Challenger	4	10	12

AM4007	Gladiator Zap (1992)	3	8	12
AM4021	Gladiator Joust	5	7	10
AM4022	Gladiator Atlasphere	5	7	10
AM4023	Gladiator Assault	5	7	10
AM4024	Gladiator Wall	5	7	10
AM4025	Gladiator Eliminator	5	7	10

AMERICAN HEROES — See *Great Heroes of Time*

AMERICAN WEST SERIES, THE (Mego) 1973-75

A lesser-known Mego series, released as part of the *Official World's Greatest Super Heroes* line. Figures were originally sold in boxes, but later a few were produced on bubble-pack cards. Some carded figures were specially labeled for S.S. Kresge, (which later became K-mart). The boxed figures are more common, and bring lower values. Kresge cards are sometimes preferred by Mego collectors. The Shadow stallion was a remote-controlled horse that wagged its tail while it walked, similar to the *Planet of the Apes* action stallion.

Boxed Figures AM7001-06	CNP	MIP	MMP
AM7001 Sitting Bull	30	35	45
AM7002 Davy Crockett	45	95	150

CNP: Complete, no package, with all weapons and accessories; MIP: Mint in package; MMP: Mint item in Mint package. Values in U.S. dollars. See page 11 for details.

BA5283   BA5284   BA5285   BA5286   BA5287

BA5265   BA5295   BA5296

BA5501   BA5502   BA5503   BA5504   BA5505

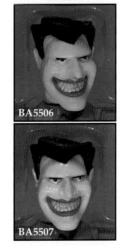

BA5506   BA5508   *Adv. of Batman and Robin* replaced *Animated Series* in 1996

BA5507

AM7003	Wyatt Earp	30	35	75
AM7004	Wild Bill Hickok	30	35	75
AM7005	Cochise	40	55	85
AM7006	Buffalo Bill Cody	30	35	75

Carded Figures AM7011-16

AM7011	Sitting Bull	30	60	95
AM7012	Davy Crockett	45	85	150
AM7013	Wyatt Earp	30	60	95
AM7014	Wild Bill Hickok	30	60	95
AM7015	Cochise	40	90	110
AM7016	Buffalo Bill Cody	30	60	95
AM7020	Shadow (horse)	75	95	150
AM7030	Dodge City playset	100	175	225

ANIMANIACS (Warner Bros. Studio Stores) 1995

Large vinyl figures of Yakko, Wakko, and Dot were sold exclusively at the Warner Bros. Studio Stores.

		CNP	MIP	MMP
AN3501	Yakko	8	-	-
AN3502	Wakko	8	-	-
AN3503	Dot	8	-	-

ANIMAX (Schaper) 1986

Humanoid animal warriors with animal-shaped vehicles. Each was sold with a mini-comic.

		CNP	MIP	MMP
AN4001	Max Action	1	4	6
AN4002	Rhinox	1	4	6
AN4003	Tarmac	1	4	6
AN4004	Tiger Trakker	1	4	6
AN4005	X-Tingtor	1	4	6
AN4006	Torrendus	1	4	6
AN4007	Grease Kicker	1	4	6
AN4008	Gross Out	1	4	6
AN4011	Max Action w/Jungle Max	2	5	8
AN4012	Rhinox w/Off Road Rhino	2	5	8
AN4013	Tarmac w/Power Horse	2	5	8
AN4014	Tiger Trakker w/Turbo Tiger	2	5	8
AN4015	X-Tingtor w/Obliterator	2	5	8
AN4016	Torrendus w/Bullveriser	2	5	8
AN4017	Grease Kicker w/Dreadful Dragster	2	5	8
AN4018	Gross Out w/Road Hog	2	5	8

ANNIE (Knickerbocker) 1982

The *Little Orphan Annie* comic strip dates back to August 5, 1924. This series, however, was produced as part of the build-up for the live-action movie musical. The Annie doll was originally sold with a child-sized plastic locket which was eliminated in later production. Each figure was 6" - 7" tall, and was sold in a cardboard window box.

		CNP	MIP	MMP
AN6001	Annie w/locket	5	9	15
AN6002	Annie w/o locket	4	7	10
AN6003	Daddy Warbucks	5	8	12
AN6004	Punjab	5	8	12
AN6005	Miss Hannigan	5	8	12
AN6006	Molly	8	12	20
AN6010	Limousine	8	12	25
AN6011	Mansion	15	25	40

APOLLO 13 (Hasbro) 1995

Hasbro dressed a 12" *G.I. Joe* body in a space suit for this tie-in with the Universal film *Apollo 13*. The film commemorated the anniversary of the U.S.'s most difficult space mission, when the astronauts almost didn't make it back.

		CNP	MIP	MMP
AP5001	Apollo 13 Astronaut	8	15	25

ARCHIES, THE (Marx) 1975

Based on the famous teen cartoon characters, this is one of the most faithful representations of the original characters. They have cloth outfits, which was unusual for Marx.

		CNP	MIP	MMP
AR1001	Archie	15	25	40
AR1002	Jughead	15	25	40
AR1003	Betty	15	30	45
AR1004	Veronica	15	25	40
AR1022	Jalopy	25	40	70

ASTERIX — See *Play Asterix*

BABAR (Bikin) 1989

Babar, King of the Elephants, is a children's storybook character who first appeared in 1931. The Bikin figures are vinyl-flocked, and were shipped on bubble-pack cards. There are seven in all, but smaller figures were sold two on a card. King Babar and Queen Celeste originally cost $2 more than the others.

		CNP	MIP	MMP
BA1001	King Babar	3	5	8
BA1002	Queen Celeste	3	5	8
BA1003	Arthur	2	4	6
BA1004	Flora & Pom	2	4	6
BA1005	Zephir & Alexander	2	4	6

BAD GUYS, THE (Remco) 1982-84

These were villains designed as adversaries for other Remco military lines, but could also be used with small *G.I. Joe* and other military figures. Some of their accessories were identical to *Sgt. Rock* items, but produced in different colors.

The Bad Guys BA1011-14		CNP	MIP	MMP
BA2011	Snake	1	5	8
BA2012	Hawk	1	5	8
BA2013	Shark	1	5	8
BA2014	Scorpion	1	5	8
BA2015	Wolf	1	5	8
BA2016	Vulture	1	5	8
BA2017	Grizzly	1	5	8
BA2018	Hammer Head	1	5	8
BA2019	Buzzer	1	5	8
BA2031	Guerrilla Enemy Camp Set (similar to SG5023)	2	6	10
BA2032	Assault Raft Invasion Set (similar to SG5024)	2	6	10
BA2033	Hidden Ambush Gunner's Nest (similar to SG5025)	2	6	10
BA2034	Battle Action Amphibious Destroyer (similar to SG5031)	2	6	10
BA2035	Power Anti-Aircraft Weapon (sim. to SG5032)	2	6	10
BA2036	Rocket Attack Mobile Unit (similar to SG5033)	2	6	10
BA2041	Big Bad Chopper	2	6	10

See also: *A-Team; Sarge Team; Sgt. Rock*

BANANA SPLITS — See *Dakin and Dakin-Style Figures*

BANANAS IN PAJAMAS (Tomy) 1996

Figures aimed at preschoolers, based on the Sachs Family Entertainment television show.

		CNP	MIP	MMP
BA2501	B1	1	3	5
BA2503	B2	1	3	5
BA2505	Morgan	1	3	5
BA2507	Amy	1	3	5
BA2509	Rat in a Hat	1	3	5
BA2511	Lulu	1	3	5

BARNEY (Child Dimension) 1993

The purple dinosaur whom pre-schoolers loved and adults came to hate mushroomed to a brief stint as a merchandise superstar...and faded just as fast. The figures were also short-lived. Figures were intended for preschoolers, and had only limited articulation.

		CNP	MIP	MMP
BA3001	Barney	2	5	8
BA3002	Baseball Barney	2	5	8
BA3003	Top Hat Barney	2	5	8
BA3004	Baby Bop	2	5	8
BA3005	Ballerina Baby Bop	2	5	8
BA3006	Beddy Bye Baby Bop	2	5	8

BATGIRL — See *Comic Heroines*

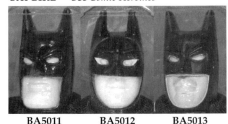

BA5011   BA5012   BA5013

BATMAN (Mego) 1979, (Toy Biz) 1989, (Takara) 1989

Figures in this section were based on the comics and the 1989 film. Mego made 12½" figures which featured magnetic hands and feet. Fly-Away action was a string attachment which was later included with the figures.

The Toy Biz figures were released in conjunction with the 1989 *Batman* film. They were sold in packages similar to the *DC Comics Super Heroes* line, but with the *Batman* logo. Variations in the Batman figure have been found, and some collectors want all three.

The 1989 *Batman* film also inspired a 12" Batman figure made in Japan by Takara. Though never sold in the U.S., many of these figures have been imported by collectors.

Special Edition *Batman* figures sold exclusively at the Warner Bros. Studio Stores in 1995-96 are listed in the *Legends of Batman* section (see LE2301-13). Other Batman figures which were produced as part of a series are listed elsewhere in the appropriate sections.

Mego		CNP	MIP	MMP
BA5005	Batman, 12½"	40	75	120
BA5006	Magnetic Batman	75	165	275
BA5007	Robin, 12½"	120	225	300
BA5008	Magnetic Robin	75	145	225
BA5009	Robin, 9½	75	225	300

Toy Biz				
BA5011	Batman, square jaw	5	10	14
BA5012	Batman, round jaw	5	10	14
BA5013	Batman, painted face	5	10	14
BA5015	Joker, curled hair	6	12	25
BA5016	Joker	5	10	15
BA5017	Bob the Joker's Goon	7	15	30
BA5020	Batmobile w/shroud	15	35	55
BA5021	Batmobile, no shroud	10	22	40
BA5022	Batcycle	5	10	15
BA5023	Joker Cycle	5	10	15
BA5024	Joker Van	10	32	45
BA5025	Batwing	10	25	35
BA5031	Batcave	15	30	50

Takara				
BA5040	12" Batman	50	125	175

See also: *Batman — The Animated Series; Batman — Mask of the Phantasm; Batman Forever; Batman Returns; Captain Action; Comic Action Heroes; Dark Knight Collection; DC Comics Super Heroes; Die Cast Super Heroes; Legends of Batman; Official World's Greatest Super Heroes; Pocket Super Heroes; Super Powers Collection*

CNP: Complete, no package, with all weapons and accessories; MIP: Mint in package; MMP: Mint item in Mint package. Values in U.S. dollars. See page 11 for details.

BA5401	BA5402	BA5403	BA5404	BA5405

BATMAN — THE ANIMATED SERIES
(Kenner) 1992-95, (McDonald's) 1993

The new *Batman* films (starting in 1989) sparked a new animated TV show. Most of the line was dominated by the same Batman figure, repainted in a variety of deco combinations and packaged with different accessories. Old vehicle molds from other Kenner lines were used periodically, and several mechanisms were re-used throughout the series.

Rapid Attack Batman (a repainted Combat Belt Batman) and Tornado Batman were originally part of the *Batman — Mask of the Phantasm* line, but were later sold on *Animated Series* packages. Battle Helmet Batman, a repaint of Infrared Batman, was available only as a mail-in premium from Warner Home Video. Collector demand is higher for the comparatively scarce villains, many of which were originally packaged only 1 or 2 per case.

Batman — Mask of the Phantasm figures produced in conjunction with this line appear in the next section.

Batman — The Animated Series was also featured in a national McDonald's Happy Meal promotion, which ran from October 29 - November 25, 1993. Four of the eight premiums were 3" action figures. A non-jointed figure of Batman, very similar to the action figure, was offered as a premium for children under 3.

In 1996, this line was re-named *The Adventures of Batman and Robin*.

First Kenner Series (1992)		CNP	MIP	MMP
BA5201	Combat Belt Batman	15	30	50
BA5202	Turbo Jet Batman	5	12	20
BA5203	Robin	6	12	28
BA5204	Riddler	15	30	50
BA5205	Two-Face	8	15	25
BA5206	Penguin	20	45	85
BA5208	Batcycle	6	12	20
Second Kenner Series (1993)				
BA5211	Bruce Wayne	5	12	18
BA5212	The Joker	6	12	20
BA5213	Man-Bat	7	15	20
BA5214	Sky Dive Batman	5	10	15
BA5215	Infrared Batman	5	10	15
BA5216	Catwoman	10	25	40
BA5217	Scarecrow	8	16	25
BA5221	Hoverbat	5	10	15
BA5222	B.A.T.V.	5	10	15
BA5223	Jokermobile	7	18	25
BA5224	Batmobile	10	20	40
BA5225	Batplane	8	20	35
BA5226	Bat-Signal Jet	5	10	15
BA5227	Robin Dragster	100	275	375
BA5228	Batskiboat	8	18	25
BA5229	Batcave Com. Center	10	25	50
Third Kenner Series (1993-94)				
BA5231	Lightning Strike Batman	5	10	15

BA5232	Knight Star Batman	5	10	15
BA5233	Mr. Freeze	7	15	18
BA5234	Clay Face	7	15	20
BA5235	High Wire Batman	5	10	15
BA5236	Mech-Wing Batman	5	10	15
BA5237	Ninja Robin	5	15	18
BA5241	Aero Bat	4	7	14
BA5242	Hydro Bat	4	7	14
BA5243	Electronic Crime Stalker	5	10	20
BA5244	Bruce Wayne Street Jet	12	17	26
Fourth Kenner Series (1994)				
BA5251	Anti-Freeze Batman	5	10	15
BA5252	Power Vision Batman	5	10	15
BA5253	Ground Assault Batman	5	10	15
BA5254	Dick Grayson	5	10	15
BA5255	Poison Ivy	7	18	25
BA5258	Ninja Power Pack Batman & Robin	3	6	14
BA5261	Ice Hammer	5	10	20
BA5265	12" Ultimate Batman	10	20	40
Fifth Kenner Series (1994-95)				
BA5271	Rapid Attack Batman	3	6	12
BA5272	Tornado Batman	3	6	12
BA5273	Bola Trap Robin	3	6	9
BA5274	Killer Croc	5	15	27
BA5275	Bane	5	10	20
BA5276	Radar Scope Batman	3	6	9
BA5277	Cyber Gear Batman	3	6	9
BA5278	Glider Robin	8	15	30
Sixth Kenner Series: "Crime Squad" (1995)				
BA5281	Air Assault Batman	3	6	9
BA5282	Land Strike Batman	3	6	9
BA5283	Torpedo Batman	3	6	9
BA5284	Ski Blast Robin	3	6	9
BA5285	Piranha Blade Batman	3	6	9
BA5286	Sea Claw Batman	3	6	9
BA5287	Stealthwing Batman	3	6	9
BA5288	Battle Helmet Batman (WHV mail-in)	5	10	16
BA5295	Crime Squad Batcycle	8	10	15
BA5296	Triple Attack Jet	5	10	16
McDonald's Happy Meal Premiums (1993)				
BA5401	Batman w/cape	1	3	5
BA5402	Catwoman w/leopard	1	3	5
BA5403	Batgirl	1	3	5
BA5404	Riddler	1	3	5
BA5405	Non-jointed Batman (under 3 premium)	2	3	8

See also: *Adventures of Batman and Robin, The*

BATMAN — MASK OF THE PHANTASM
(Kenner) 1994

Animated-style Batman figures from the December, 1993 animated feature *Batman — Mask of the Phantasm* were sold in 1994. This was a spinoff line of *Batman — The Animated Series*, and the two lines cross-promoted each other on package backs.

Joker figures were originally shipped with blue faces. A running change was made, and subsequent figures had white faces. Rapid Attack Batman and Tornado Batman were later repackaged and sold as part of the *Batman — The Animated Series* line.

Traditionally shy of female figures, Kenner packaged Phantasm one per case. This figure dominates collector interest in the line.

		CNP	MIP	MMP
BA5501	Rapid Attack Batman	4	11	15
BA5502	Tornado Batman	4	11	15
BA5503	Retro Batman	4	11	15
BA5504	Total Armor Batman	4	11	15
BA5505	Decoy Batman	4	11	15
BA5506	Jet Pack Joker, blue face	8	15	30
BA5507	BA5506, white face	8	12	25
BA5508	Phantasm	8	20	35

BATMAN FOREVER (Kenner) 1995-96

The third live-action *Batman* film produced in the '90s was a box-office smash, renewing collector interest in old and new *Batman* figures. As usual, the line featured an overabundance of Batman figures, with harder-to-find villains. Transforming Dick Grayson featured a quick-change mask feature, made possible by color-changing paint. The mask on original figures appeared when cold water was applied, but it wasn't visible in the package. Later versions of the figure featured a mask which *disappeared*, and was thus visible on the packaged figure.

First Series (1995)		CNP	MIP	MMP
BA5511	Blast Cape Batman	3	6	9
BA5512	Fireguard Batman	3	6	9
BA5513	Manta Ray Batman	3	6	9
BA5514	Night Hunter Batman	3	6	9
BA5515	Sonar Sensor Batman	3	6	9

BA5550

BA5511			**BA5512**			**BA5513**			
BA5516			**BA5518**			**BA5519**			
BA5522			**BA5523**			**BA5517**			**BA5524**

BA5511 Blast Cape Batman with Assault Blades and Launching Attack Cape!

BA5512 Fireguard Batman with Spinning Attack Cape Action!

BA5513 Manta Ray Batman with Firing Sea Sled and Pop-Out Breathing Gear!

BA5514 Night Hunter Batman with Claw Glider Wing and Night Vision Goggles!

BA5515 Sonar Sensor Batman with Flying Disc Blaster

BA5516 Transforming Bruce Wayne with Quick-Change Bat Suit and Battle Blades!

BA5518 Hydro Claw Robin with Aqua Attack Launcher and Diving Gear!

BA5519 Street Biker Robin with Launching Grappling Hooks

BA5520 Transforming Dick Grayson with Crime Fighting Suit and Sudden-Reveal Mask!

BA5554 Skyboard Robin with Missile-Blasting Pursuit Vehicle

BA5522 Two-Face with Turbo-Charge Cannon and Good/Evil Coin!

BA5523 The Riddler with Trapping Brain-Drain Helmet!

BA5517 Deluxe Attack Wing Batman with Power-Flex Attack Cape

BA5524 Deluxe Martial Arts Robin with Ninja Kicking Action and Battle Weapons

BA5516	Transforming				BA5524	Martial Arts Robin	3	6	9
	Bruce Wayne	3	6	9	BA5531	Robin Cycle	5	10	20
BA5517	Attack Wing Batman	3	6	9	BA5532	Batmobile	7	18	25
BA5518	Hydro Claw Robin	3	6	9	BA5533	Batwing	6	15	22
BA5519	Street Biker Robin	3	6	9	BA5534	Batboat	6	15	22
BA5520	Transforming Dick				BA5537	Ultimate Batman	10	15	25
	Grayson with				BA5540	Wayne Manor Batcave	10	20	40
	"appearing" mask	3	6	9	BA5541	Batcave	35	75	90
BA5521	BA5520 with				BA5550	Guardians of Gotham	5	10	13
	"disappearing" mask	3	6	9	**Second Series (1995-96)**				
BA5522	The Riddler	5	8	10	BA5551	Batarang Batman	3	6	9
BA5523	Two-Face	4	7	10	BA5552	Ice Blade Batman	3	6	9

BA5553	Power Beacon Batman	3	6	9
BA5554	Skyboard Robin	4	7	10
BA5555	Photon Armor Batman	3	6	9
BA5556	Wing Blast Batman	3	6	9
BA5557	Sonar Sensor Bruce Wayne	3	6	9

BATMAN RETURNS (Kenner) 1992-94

This series was an extension of Kenner's *Dark Knight Collection*, re-named to coincide with the release of the 1992 film *Batman Returns*. The Powerwing and Thunderwhip Batman figures were briefly available as part of

BA5531

BA5532

BA5537

BA5533

BA5534

BA5540

BA5541

BA5551

BA5552

BA5553

BA5651

BA5653

the *Dark Knight Collection* in 1991. They were repainted and repackaged for this series, with accessories molded in different colors.

The Bruce Wayne Custom Coupe includes a special edition (that is, repainted) Bruce Wayne figure.

		CNP	MIP	MMP
BA5651	Arctic Batman	5	12	18
BA5653	Air Attack Batman	5	12	18
BA5655	Deep Dive Batman	5	12	18
BA5657	Powerwing Batman	5	12	18
BA5659	Thunderwhip Batman	6	14	25
BA5661	Laser Batman	5	12	18
BA5663	Robin	5	12	18
BA5667	The Penguin	10	25	45
BA5669	Penguin Commandos	8	15	30
BA5671	Catwoman	6	12	20
BA5680	Laser Blade Cycle	5	12	18

BA5655   BA5657   BA5659   BA5661   BA5663

BA5667   BA5671   BA5686

BA5680   BA5682   BA5688

BA5690   BA5692

BA5711 **BA5713** **BA5715** **BA5717**

BA5731 **BA5751** **BA5753** **BA5755**

BA5696 **BA5700**

BA5682	Sky Blade vehicle	10	15	25		BA5711	Crime Attack Batman	8	20	35		BA5735	Rocket Blast Batman	15	30	50
BA5684	Robin Jet Foil Cycle	8	15	25		BA5713	Sky Winch Batman	8	20	35		BA5740	15" Batman	10	20	45
BA5686	Sky Drop Airship	10	25	40		BA5715	Shadow Wing Batman	8	20	35		BA5745	Batmobile	15	35	55
BA5688	Umbrella Jet	5	10	18		BA5717	Bruce Wayne	4	12	18		**Series II Figures and Accessories (1994)**				
BA5690	Batmissile Batmobile	15	25	35		**Toys "Я" Us Exclusive Figures BA5721-23**						BA5751	Hydro Charge Batman	4	8	12
BA5692	Bruce Wayne Custom Coupe	10	15	30		BA5721	Bola Strike Batman	10	25	35		BA5753	Jungle Tracker Batman	4	8	12
BA5694	Turbojet Batwing	12	25	45		BA5722	Claw Climber Batman	10	25	35		BA5755	Night Climber Batman	4	8	12
BA5696	Batskiboat	10	20	35		BA5723	Polar Blast Batman	10	25	35		BA5757	Toxic Guard Batman	not produced		
BA5700	Batcave Command Center Playset	15	30	55		**1993 Figures and Accessories**						BA5761	Camo Attack Batmobile	10	20	45
						BA5731	Aero Strike Batman	10	12	18					
						BA5733	Firebolt Batman	15	30	50					

BA5694

BA5733

BA5735

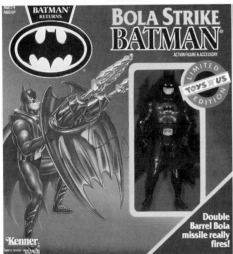

BA5721

BA5722

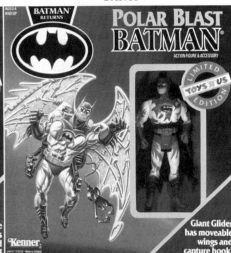

BA5723

BA5745

BA5761

BATTLE BEASTS (Hasbro) 1987

Each of these figures was a 2" animal in body armor. They came packaged two on a card or in boxed sets of ten. A heat-sensitive liquid crystal sticker on each figure revealed their elemental strength: fire, wood, or water. All three stickers could appear on the same figure, and the card encouraged kids to play a modified "rock-paper-scissors" game. The names of the 62 figures were listed on a premium poster, but did not appear on the packages.

Warriors/Series I	CNP	MIP	MMP
BA6001-28 Assorted Beasts, 14 packages, ea	2	5	10
Series II			
BA6031-54 Assorted Beasts, 12 packages, ea	2	5	10
Series III			
BA6061-84 Assorted Beasts 12 packages, ea	2	5	10

Battle Chariots BA6101-03			
BA6101 Big Horn	5	10	15
BA6102 Deer Stalker	5	10	15
BA6103 Tearin' Tiger	5	10	15
Transport Stations BA6105-07			
BA6105 Shocking Shark	5	10	15
BA6106 Wood Beetle	5	10	15
BA6107 Blazing Eagle	5	10	15

BATTLE BRAWLERS (Kenner) 1986

These two figures were designed to fight each other. They featured spring-loaded body parts which attacked or showed battle damage.

	CNP	MIP	MMP
BA6501 Crackarm	7	15	20
BA6502 Hammertail	7	15	20

BATTLE TROLLS (Hasbro) 1992

Trolls seem to be revived as a toy sensation about every 25 years. Hasbro released several assortments of these ugly dudes as a Troll spoof before the category faded once again.

Assortment I BA7201-08	CNP	MIP	MMP
BA7201 Cap 'n Troll	1	3	5
BA7202 Count Trollula	1	3	5
BA7203 Nunchuk Troll	1	3	5
BA7204 Sgt. Troll	1	3	5
BA7205 T.D. Troll	1	3	5
BA7206 Troll-Clops	1	3	5
BA7207 Tollaf	1	3	5
BA7208 Trollminator	1	3	5
Assortment II BA7211-18			
BA7211 Franken Troll	1	3	5
BA7212 General Troll	1	3	5
BA7213 Officer PaTroll	1	3	5
BA7214 Punk Troll	1	3	5
BA7215 Roadhog Troll	1	3	5
BA7216 Sir Trollahad	1	3	5
BA7217 Super Troll	1	3	5
BA7218 Trollbot	1	3	5

CNP: Complete, no package, with all weapons and accessories; MIP: Mint in package; MMP: Mint item in Mint package. Values in U.S. dollars. See page 11 for details.

BA5740

BA6001

BA6101

BA6501

BA6502

BA7201-08

BA7202

BA7211-18

BA7221-28

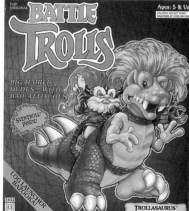

BA7231

BA7232

BA8100

BA8102

BA8104

BA8105

BA8106

BA8107

BA8108

BA8109

BA8110

BA8120

BA8130

BA8131

Assortment III BA7221-28

BA7221	Ace Troll	1	3	5
BA7222	Jacques CousTroll	1	3	5
BA7223	K.O. Troll	1	3	5
BA7224	Quick Draw McTroll	1	3	5
BA7225	Slapshot Troll	1	3	5
BA7226	Thrasher Troll	1	3	5
BA7227	Troll-timate Wrastler	1	3	5
BA7228	Wolfman Troll	1	3	5
BA7231	Trollasaurus	1	3	5
BA7232	Capture Net	1	3	5

BATTLESTAR GALACTICA (Mattel) 1978

Six small *Battlestar Galactica* figures were fairly common, the rest were comparatively rare. Daggits were molded in tan or brown versions, but there is little or no difference in value. The most difficult figures are the gold Cylon Commander, Baltaar, Boray, and Lucifer. Figures were sold individually on cards or in boxed sets. Cylon Commander and Lucifer were also available as mail-in premiums. Two larger figures, a Colonial Warrior and Cylon Centurian, were also produced. The gun molded into the right hand of each figure included a clear plastic piece about an inch long, which is frequently broken or missing. The body mold for the large figures closely resembled the *Major MATT MASON* Captain Lazer doll.

Trendmasters acquired the *Battlestar Galactica* license in 1996, and began plans for a new line.

| BA8501 | BA8502 | BA8503 | BA8504 | BA8505 | BA8506 |

| BA8511 | BA8512 | BA8513 | BA8523 |

| BA8524 | BA8531 | BE0201 | BE0203 | BE0205 | BE0207 |

		CNP	MIP	MMP
BA8100	Adama	8	20	35
BA8102	Starbuck	8	25	45
BA8103	Daggit (tan or brown)	8	20	35
BA8104	Cylon Centurian	10	35	50
BA8105	Cylon Commander	25	75	125
BA8106	Imperious Leader	5	10	15
BA8107	Ovion	8	20	35
BA8108	Baltaar	25	75	125
BA8109	Boray	15	50	85
BA8110	Lucifer	20	65	120
BA8120	Boxed set of 6: Ovion, Imperious Leader, Cylon Centurian, Daggit (br.), Adama, Starbuck	-	85	150
BA8121	Boxed set of 4: Imperious Leader, Cylon Centurian, Daggit (brown), Ovion	-	70	120
BA8122	Boxed set of 3: Baltaar, Cylon Commander, Lucifer	-	75	125
12" figures				
BA8130	Cylon Centurian	30	75	120
BA8131	Colonial Warrior	15	40	50

BATTLETECH (TYCO), 1995

FASA's popular wargame was adapted for a TV animated series. "Battlemechs" produced by TYCO were released in conjunction with the show. A two-inch figure was included with each 'mech, but there were only a few different molds repainted throughout the line. The packaging art for Banshee was changed to better display the toy's action features. In 1996, most of the line was redecorated. The toys were clunky and bland when compared with the superior craftsmanship and detail of the *Exosquad* line, which was in its third year at the time.

		CNP	MIP	MMP
Powersuit/Elemental Assortment				
BA8501	Infiltrator	3	6	10
BA8502	Sloth	3	6	10
BA8503	Toad	3	6	10
Repainted "Tiger Camo" Powersuits (1996)				
BA8504	Infiltrator	4	8	12
BA8505	Sloth	4	8	12
BA8506	Toad	4	8	12
Light 'Mech Assortment				
BA8511	Hunchback	3	6	10
BA8512	Bushwacker	3	6	10
BA8513	Banshee	3	6	10
BA8514	Banshee (repackaged)	3	6	10
Repainted "Tiger Camo" Light 'Mechs (1996)				
BA8515	Hunchback	4	8	12
BA8516	Bushwacker	4	8	12

		CNP	MIP	MMP
Medium 'Mech Assortment				
BA8523	Axman	4	8	12
BA8524	Thor	4	8	12
Repainted Medium 'Mechs (1996)				
BA8525	Axman	4	8	12
BA8526	Thor	4	8	12
Heavy 'Mechs				
BA8531	Mauler	10	15	20
BA8532	Mauler repaint	10	15	20

B.C. BIKERS (Street Kids) 1992, (Ace Novelty) 1993

This unusual line featured "chrome age" humanoid dinosaurs on motorcycles. The figures were repainted and repackaged when Ace Novelty picked up the line in 1993.

Street Kids		CNP	MIP	MMP
BC2001	Crank	3	6	9
BC2003	Revv	3	6	9
BC2005	Scales	3	6	9
BC2007	Tarr	3	6	9
Ace Novelty (repainted)				
BC2011	Crank	3	6	9
BC2013	Revv	3	6	9
BC2015	Scales	3	6	9
BC2017	Tarr	3	6	9

BEAST WARS — See *Transformers*

| BC2001 | BC2003 | BC2005 | BC2007 | BC2017 |

| BE0211 | BE0212 | BE0213 | BE0215 | BE0218 | BE0219 |

BEAUTY AND THE BEAST (Burger King) 1991, (Mattel) 1991-94

Four action figures inspired by the Disney film were given away as Burger King Kid's Club premiums.

Beauty and the Beast characters were also part of a series of 12" characters treated like dolls, with additional versions and fashions typical of a *Barbie*-type product.

Burger King Premiums		CNP	MIP	MMP
BE0201	Beast	1	3	4
BE0203	Belle	1	4	6
BE0205	Chip	1	5	8
BE0207	Cogsworth	1	2	3
Mattel				
BE0211	Belle in house dress	8	16	22
BE0212	Beast/Prince	10	20	25
BE0213	Belle in yellow gown	10	20	25
BE0215	Belle "Be Our Guest" Gift Set	12	25	35
BE0217	Belle in Winter Dress	9	18	22
BE0218	Musical Wedding Belle	10	20	25
BE0219	Wedding Prince	8	15	20
BE0221	Library Fashion	3	7	10
BE0222	Dinner Fashion	3	7	10

See also: *Bubble Princess; Musical Princess; Perfume Princess*

BEDKNOBS & BROOMSTICKS (Horsman) 1971-72

One of the more unusual items in the action figure field is Horsman's Self-Propelled Action Bed, marketed in conjunction with the Disney film *Bedknobs and Broomsticks*. A female figure is included which resembles Angela Lansbury.

		CNP	MIP	MMP
BE0501	Action Bed w/figure	35	95	125

BEETLEJUICE (Kenner) 1990

The first series of figures was based on the film *Beetlejuice*. Later figures were unrelated to the film, but were transforming figures similar in style to the *Real Ghostbusters* line.

BE0501

		CNP	MIP	MMP
BE1001	Adam Maitlan the Headless Ghost	2	8	10
BE1002	Harry the Haunted Hunter	2	8	10
BE1003	Otho the Obnoxious	2	8	10
BE1004	Shish Kebab Beetlejuice	2	8	10
BE1005	Showtime Beetlejuice	2	8	10
BE1006	Spinhead Beetlejuice	2	8	10
Second series/Neighborhood Nasties BE1011-16				
BE1011	Exploding Beetlejuice	3	10	10
BE1012	Hungry Hogg	3	10	15
BE1013	Old Buzzard	3	10	15
BE1014	Shipwreck Beetlejuice	3	8	10
BE1015	Street Rat	3	10	15
BE1016	Teacher Creature	3	10	15
BE1021	Creepy Cruiser	5	8	12
BE1023	Phantom Flyer	3	8	12
BE1025	Vanishing Vault	5	15	20
BE1050	Talking Beetlejuice	10	20	25

BEST OF THE WEST (Marx) 1965-76, 1993

This series is one of the most common early action figure groups. Many pieces of molded soft plastic clothing and personal accessories were included with each figure. Having a single item missing detracts from the highest value. Packaging for the line was modified every few years, but these variations do not currently affect the value. This may change as collectors become more aware of the differences. The following designations are used in the photo identification numbers to indicate package variations:

A — The original packaging style, printed in 1965-66. Each package shows a drawing of the enclosed toy. Packages vary widely, using different typefaces for character names. As many as three different packaging variations are known to exist for the Johnny West figure alone within this category.

B — These boxes incorporated photos of the toys, against an artwork background. They were produced from 1967-69.

C — "Mod" boxes, produced from 1970-73, featured photos of the toys against brightly-colored backgrounds.

D — The year 1974 was the first time that the line had a family packaging look. All packages feature the "Best of the West" logo.

E — In 1975-76, the name of the series was changed to "Johnny West Adventure." Boxes again featured illustrations of the figures rather than photographs. The name of the toy appeared in a blue color bar across the box. Until this time, most accessories had been molded in consistent colors. Beginning with style E packaging, different color plastics were used. "Quick-draw action" figures were introduced in 1975. Items in this packaging style are less common than the other four, but thus far no difference in value has been identified.

The Marx company name and many of the original molds were later sold. "Reproduction" items began appearing in the early 1990's. The most widely known of these is the "Johnny West," which is a Captain Maddox head on a blue Johnny West body. Special thanks to G. F. Ridenour for his assistance with this section.

		CNP	MIP	MMP
BE6001	Johnny West	25	40	75
BE6002	Jane West	25	40	75
BE6003	Jaimie West	18	35	50
BE6004	Jay West	18	35	50
BE6005	Janice West	18	35	50

CNP: Complete, no package, with all weapons and accessories; MIP: Mint in package; MMP: Mint item in Mint package. Values in U.S. dollars. See page 11 for details.

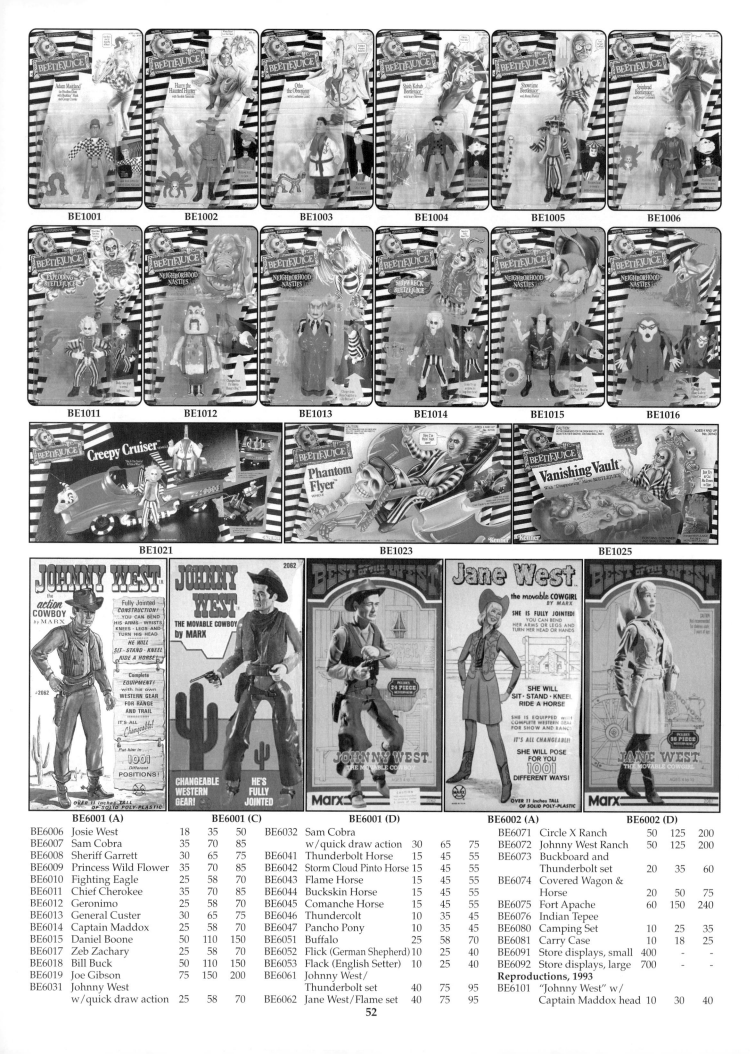

BE1001 **BE1002** **BE1003** **BE1004** **BE1005** **BE1006**

BE1011 **BE1012** **BE1013** **BE1014** **BE1015** **BE1016**

BE1021 **BE1023** **BE1025**

BE6001 (A) **BE6001 (C)** **BE6001 (D)** **BE6002 (A)** **BE6002 (D)**

BE6006	Josie West	18	35	50	BE6032	Sam Cobra				
BE6007	Sam Cobra	35	70	85		w/quick draw action	30	65	75	
BE6008	Sheriff Garrett	30	65	75	BE6041	Thunderbolt Horse	15	45	55	
BE6009	Princess Wild Flower	35	70	85	BE6042	Storm Cloud Pinto Horse	15	45	55	
BE6010	Fighting Eagle	25	58	70	BE6043	Flame Horse	15	45	55	
BE6011	Chief Cherokee	35	70	85	BE6044	Buckskin Horse	15	45	55	
BE6012	Geronimo	25	58	70	BE6045	Comanche Horse	15	45	55	
BE6013	General Custer	30	65	75	BE6046	Thundercolt	10	35	45	
BE6014	Captain Maddox	25	58	70	BE6047	Pancho Pony	10	35	45	
BE6015	Daniel Boone	50	110	150	BE6051	Buffalo	25	58	70	
BE6017	Zeb Zachary	25	58	70	BE6052	Flick (German Shepherd)	10	25	40	
BE6018	Bill Buck	50	110	150	BE6053	Flack (English Setter)	10	25	40	
BE6019	Joe Gibson	75	150	200	BE6061	Johnny West/				
BE6031	Johnny West					Thunderbolt set	40	75	95	
	w/quick draw action	25	58	70	BE6062	Jane West/Flame set	40	75	95	

BE6071	Circle X Ranch	50	125	200
BE6072	Johnny West Ranch	50	125	200
BE6073	Buckboard and			
	Thunderbolt set	20	35	60
BE6074	Covered Wagon &			
	Horse	20	50	75
BE6075	Fort Apache	60	150	240
BE6076	Indian Tepee			
BE6080	Camping Set	10	25	35
BE6081	Carry Case	10	18	25
BE6091	Store displays, small	400	-	-
BE6092	Store displays, large	700	-	-
Reproductions, 1993				
BE6101	"Johnny West" w/			
	Captain Maddox head	10	30	40

BE6003 (D)

BE6006 (C)

BE6006 (D)

BE6006 (E)

BE6007 (A)

BE6007 (D)

BE6011 (A)

BE6012 (B)

BE6012 (D)

BE6013 (B)

BE6014 (B)

BE6014 (D)

BE6015 (A)

BE6017 (B)

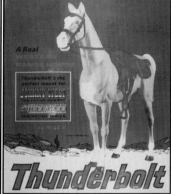

BE6041 (A)

BE6041 (D)

BE6043 (B)

BE6044 (D)

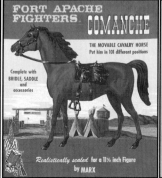

BE6045 (A)

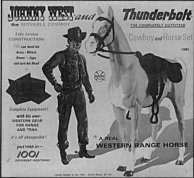

BE6061 (A)

53

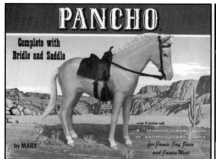

BE6047 (B)

BE6047 (D)

BE6051 (B)

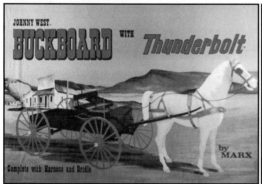

BE6073 (A)

BE6073 (E)

BE6074 (D)

BE6076 (A)

BE6080 (C)

BI0301

BI0402

BI0401

BI0403

BI0404

BI0503

BI-TRONS (Gordy International) 1984

Another *Transformers* knock-off.

		CNP	MIP	MMP
BI0301	BAT-L	1	3	5
BI0302	TRUXX	1	3	5

BIBLE CHARACTERS (Praise Unlimited) 1984-85

Even religious groups have shown an interest in action figures, this time as an educational tool. Each figure in this series was a major character in an Old Testament story. A child-size suit of armor was sold in conjunction with the series.

		CNP	MIP	MMP
BI0401	David the Shepherd Boy	3	8	12
BI0402	Goliath the Philistine Giant	3	8	12
BI0403	Judah the Christian Soldier	3	8	12

BI0404	Judah's Chariot w/horse	4	12	14
BI0410	Noah's Ark	10	20	25

See also: *Great Heroes of Time*

BIBLE GREATS (Rainfall Toys) 1987

Another Old Testament-oriented series. The Mego-style figures were sold on cards or in boxed sets. Each package included an illustrated booklet.

		CNP	MIP	MMP
BI0501	Noah w/dove	3	8	12
BI0502	Daniel w/gold necklace	3	8	12
BI0503	Joseph w/coat of many colors	3	8	12
BI0504	Moses w/tablets	3	8	12
BI0505	Samson w/real hair and jawbone	3	8	12
BI0506	Ruth w/basket	3	8	12

BI0507	Deborah w/walking stick	3	8	12
BI0508	Esther w/gold crown	3	8	12
BI0509	Gideon w/horn & sword	3	8	12
BI0510	Joshua w/sword & spear	3	8	12
BI0511	David and Goliath, card	7	12	18
BI0521	David and Goliath, box	7	12	18
BI0522	Goliath, in box	5	10	14
BI0525	Jonah & the Whale	5	10	14

See also: *Great Heroes of Time*

BIG BOY — See *Dakin and Dakin-Style Figures*

BIG JIM (Mattel) 1973-76

Big Jim was Mattel's non-military answer to *G.I. Joe*. The character stressed sports, action and adventure rather than guns and combat. Figures had action features such as swinging arms and flexing biceps.

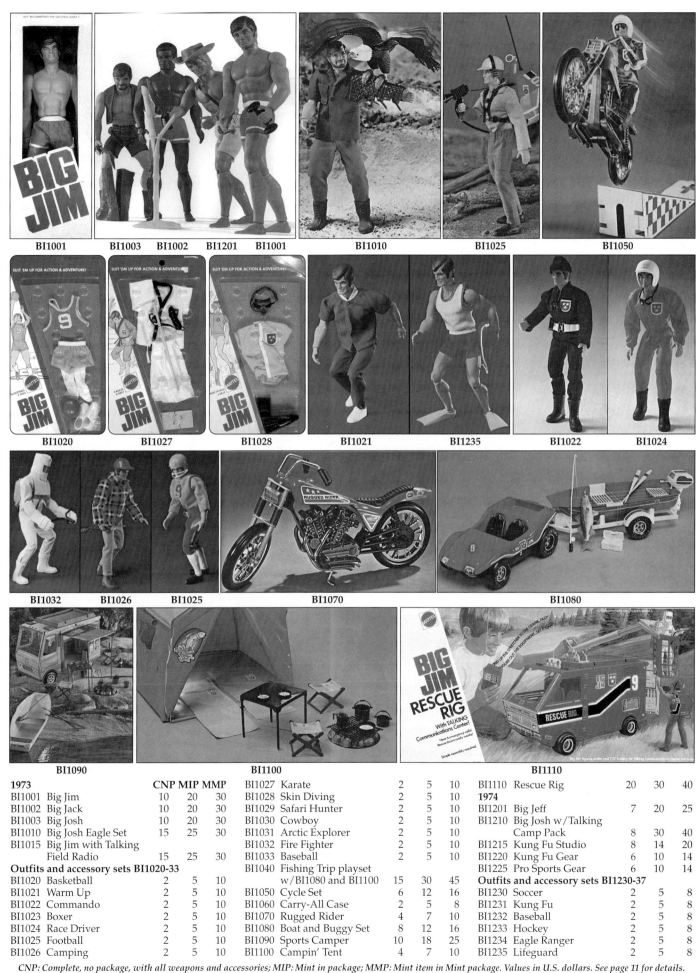

| BI1001 | BI1003 | BI1002 | BI1201 | BI1001 | | BI1010 | | BI1025 | | BI1050 |

| BI1020 | BI1027 | BI1028 | BI1021 | BI1235 | BI1022 | BI1024 |

| BI1032 | BI1026 | BI1025 | BI1070 | BI1080 |

| BI1090 | BI1100 | BI1110 |

1973		CNP	MIP	MMP
BI1001	Big Jim	10	20	30
BI1002	Big Jack	10	20	30
BI1003	Big Josh	10	20	30
BI1010	Big Josh Eagle Set	15	25	30
BI1015	Big Jim with Talking Field Radio	15	25	30
Outfits and accessory sets BI1020-33				
BI1020	Basketball	2	5	10
BI1021	Warm Up	2	5	10
BI1022	Commando	2	5	10
BI1023	Boxer	2	5	10
BI1024	Race Driver	2	5	10
BI1025	Football	2	5	10
BI1026	Camping	2	5	10

BI1027	Karate	2	5	10
BI1028	Skin Diving	2	5	10
BI1029	Safari Hunter	2	5	10
BI1030	Cowboy	2	5	10
BI1031	Arctic Explorer	2	5	10
BI1032	Fire Fighter	2	5	10
BI1033	Baseball	2	5	10
BI1040	Fishing Trip playset w/BI1080 and BI1100	15	30	45
BI1050	Cycle Set	6	12	16
BI1060	Carry-All Case	2	5	8
BI1070	Rugged Rider	4	7	10
BI1080	Boat and Buggy Set	8	12	16
BI1090	Sports Camper	10	18	25
BI1100	Campin' Tent	4	7	10

BI1110	Rescue Rig	20	30	40
1974				
BI1201	Big Jeff	7	20	25
BI1210	Big Josh w/Talking Camp Pack	8	30	40
BI1215	Kung Fu Studio	8	14	20
BI1220	Kung Fu Gear	6	10	14
BI1225	Pro Sports Gear	6	10	14
Outfits and accessory sets BI1230-37				
BI1230	Soccer	2	5	8
BI1231	Kung Fu	2	5	8
BI1232	Baseball	2	5	8
BI1233	Hockey	2	5	8
BI1234	Eagle Ranger	2	5	8
BI1235	Lifeguard	2	5	8

CNP: Complete, no package, with all weapons and accessories; MIP: Mint in package; MMP: Mint item in Mint package. Values in U.S. dollars. See page 11 for details.

BI1210   BI1215   BI1220   BI1225

BI1230   BI1232   BI1233   BI1234   BI1236   BI1031   BI1030   BI1237

BI1240   BI1250   BI1260   BI1270

BI1300   BI1301   BI1302   BI1303   BI1304

BI1320 BI1321 BI1322 BI1323 BI1324 BI1325 BI1326   BI1310

BI1236	Pilot	2	5	8	**1975**	
BI1237	Jungle Set	4	8	12	BI1300	U.S. Olympic Ski Run	5	8	15
BI1240	Jungle Truck	4	10	15	BI1301	Gold Medal Boxer Big Jim	7	20	25
BI1250	Jungle Adventure	5	8	15	BI1302	Gold Medal Big Jim U.S.			
BI1260	Devil River Trip	5	8	15		Olympic Boxing Match			
BI1270	Sky Commander Jet	5	8	15		(includes BI1301)	7	30	40
					BI1303	The Incredible Dr. Steel	8	45	75

BI1304	Big Jim with Talking			
	Back Pack	7	25	35
BI1310	Baja Beast vehicle	7	12	16
U.S. Olympic Uniforms BI1320-35				
BI1320	U.S. Olympic Soccer	2	5	10
BI1321	Woodsman	2	5	10
BI1322	U.S. Olympic Judo-Karate	2	5	10

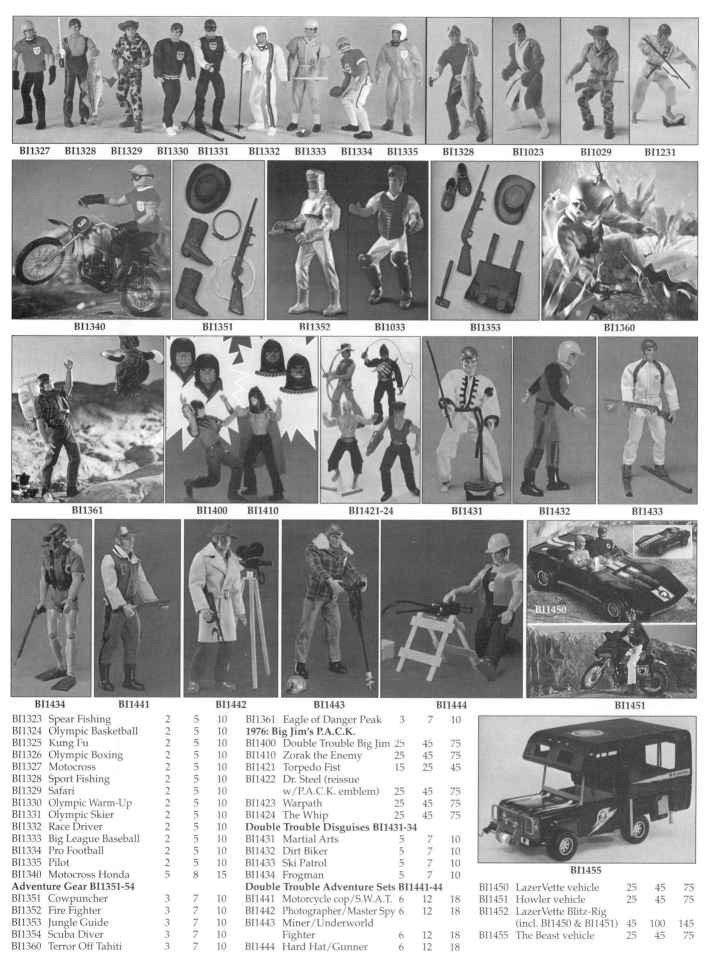

| BI1327 | BI1328 | BI1329 | BI1330 | BI1331 | BI1332 | BI1333 | BI1334 | BI1335 | BI1328 | BI1023 | BI1029 | BI1231 |

| BI1340 | BI1351 | BI1352 | BI1033 | BI1353 | BI1360 |

| BI1361 | BI1400 | BI1410 | BI1421-24 | BI1431 | BI1432 | BI1433 |

BI1450

| BI1434 | BI1441 | BI1442 | BI1443 | BI1444 | BI1451 |

BI1323	Spear Fishing	2	5	10
BI1324	Olympic Basketball	2	5	10
BI1325	Kung Fu	2	5	10
BI1326	Olympic Boxing	2	5	10
BI1327	Motocross	2	5	10
BI1328	Sport Fishing	2	5	10
BI1329	Safari	2	5	10
BI1330	Olympic Warm-Up	2	5	10
BI1331	Olympic Skier	2	5	10
BI1332	Race Driver	2	5	10
BI1333	Big League Baseball	2	5	10
BI1334	Pro Football	2	5	10
BI1335	Pilot	2	5	10
BI1340	Motocross Honda	5	8	15

Adventure Gear BI1351-54

BI1351	Cowpuncher	3	7	10
BI1352	Fire Fighter	3	7	10
BI1353	Jungle Guide	3	7	10
BI1354	Scuba Diver	3	7	10
BI1360	Terror Off Tahiti	3	7	10

| BI1361 | Eagle of Danger Peak | 3 | 7 | 10 |

1976: Big Jim's P.A.C.K.

BI1400	Double Trouble Big Jim	25	45	75
BI1410	Zorak the Enemy	25	45	75
BI1421	Torpedo Fist	15	25	45
BI1422	Dr. Steel (reissue w/P.A.C.K. emblem)	25	45	75
BI1423	Warpath	25	45	75
BI1424	The Whip	25	45	75

Double Trouble Disguises BI1431-34

BI1431	Martial Arts	5	7	10
BI1432	Dirt Biker	5	7	10
BI1433	Ski Patrol	5	7	10
BI1434	Frogman	5	7	10

Double Trouble Adventure Sets BI1441-44

BI1441	Motorcycle cop/S.W.A.T.	6	12	18
BI1442	Photographer/Master Spy	6	12	18
BI1443	Miner/Underworld Fighter	6	12	18
BI1444	Hard Hat/Gunner	6	12	18

BI1455

BI1450	LazerVette vehicle	25	45	75
BI1451	Howler vehicle	25	45	75
BI1452	LazerVette Blitz-Rig (incl. BI1450 & BI1451)	45	100	145
BI1455	The Beast vehicle	25	45	75

CNP: Complete, no package, with all weapons and accessories; MIP: Mint in package; MMP: Mint item in Mint package. Values in U.S. dollars. See page 11 for details.

BI1601 BI1603 BI1605 BI1607 BI1609

BI1611 BI1613 BI1615 BI1617 BI1651

BI1621

BI1625

BI1627

BI1629

BIKER MICE FROM MARS (Galoob) 1994

Biker Mice From Mars was a syndicated TV series produced by New World Animation. The show premiered in 1993, and figures by Galoob followed in 1994. The line only lasted a year in the U.S., but enjoyed better success in the U.K., where it continued into 1996.

		CNP	MIP	MMP
BI1601	Throttle	2	5	8
BI1603	Vinnie	2	5	8
BI1605	Modo	2	5	8
BI1607	Lawrence Limburger	2	5	8
BI1609	Dr. Karbunkle	2	5	8
BI1611	Greasepit	2	5	8
BI1613	Charley	5	10	12
BI1615	Lectromag	4	8	10
BI1617	Evil Eye Weevil	4	8	10
BI1621	Throttle's Martian Monster Bike	4	8	12
BI1623	Vinnie's Radical Rocket Sled	4	8	12
BI1625	Modo's Mondo Chopper	4	8	12
BI1627	Greasepit's Grunge Cycle	4	8	12
BI1629	Radical Rider Set (Vinnie w/BI1623)	4	8	12
BI1631	Super Sidecar	4	8	12
BI1633	Throttle's Blazin' Cycle	4	8	12
BI1641	Dr. Karbunkle's Transporter & Secret Lab	10	18	24
BI1643	Scoreboard Hideout	8	16	22
Mega Mice (12"+)				
BI1651	Throttle	6	10	12
BI1652	Vinnie	6	10	12
BI1653	Modo	6	10	12
Sports Bro's				
BI1661	Home-Run Throttle	3	6	9
BI1662	Slam-Dunk Vinnie	3	6	9
BI1663	Touchdown Modo	3	6	9
Freedom Fighters BI1671-84				
BI1671	Tail-Whippin' Throttle	3	6	9
BI1672	Rad Rebel Vinnie	3	6	9
BI1673	Commando Modo	3	6	9
BI1674	Rimfire	3	6	9
BI1681	Throttle's Spike Bike	4	8	12
BI1682	Vinnie's Rebel Rocket	4	8	12
BI1683	Mondo's Commando Cruiser	4	8	12
BI1684	Sky Commander	3	6	9
BI1691	Napoleon Brie	3	6	9
Biker Knights BI1695-97				
BI1695	Totalizer Throttle	4	8	10
BI1696	Armatron Modo	4	8	10
BI1697	Invincible Vinnie	4	8	10
BI1701	Throttle's Tromper ATV	4	8	10
BI1702	Vinnie's Rattler ATV	4	8	10
BI1703	Modo's Duneripper ATV	4	8	10
BI1711	Four-By	4	8	10

BILL & TED'S EXCELLENT ADVENTURE (Kenner) 1991

Bill & Ted's excellent figures were supposed to be totally cool with their radical transforming features and bodacious built-in speakers. The figures could be hooked up to a child's cassette player to rock 'n roll most triumphantly with the help of a tape and speaker attachment (sold separately). Their release was also most excellently timed to coincide with their second film, *Bill and Ted's Bogus Journey*. Unfortunately, the concept didn't produce anything close to excellent sales, and was written off as a major bummer. A Napoleon figure was planned, but never produced.

BI1631

BI1633

BI1641

BI1643

BI1661

BI1662

BI1663

BI1671

BI1672

BI1673

BI1674

BI1691

BI1696

BI1711

BI2001

BI2002

	CNP	MIP	MMP
BI2001 Bill	5	8	12
BI2002 Ted	5	8	12
BI2003 Rufus	6	10	15
BI2004 Genghis Khan	5	10	15
BI2005 Billy the Kid	5	10	15
BI2007 The Grim Reaper	6	12	25
BI2008 Abe Lincoln	5	10	15
BI2009 Napoleon	not produced		
BI2010 Jam Session Two-Pack	6	12	20
BI2015 Wild Stallyns Speaker & Tape			
BI2020 Phone Booth	2	4	5
	6	10	15

BIONIC MAN — See *Six Million Dollar Man, The*

59

BI2003 BI2004 BI2005 BI2007 BI2008

BI2010 BI2015 BI2020 BI3004

BI3001 BI3002 BI3003 BI3005 BI3006 BI3007

BI3011 BI3012 BI3013 BI3014 BI3015 BI3016

BIONIC SIX (LJN) 1986

This series of die-cast metal and plastic figures was based on a Saturday morning animated adventure series. F.L.U.F.F.I. the ape-like robot figure was hard to get early on, but was available in abundance as sales of the line slackened.

		CNP	MIP	MMP
BI3001	Bunji	3	8	10
BI3002	Helen	3	8	10
BI3003	Jack	3	8	10
BI3004	F.L.U.F.F.I.	4	10	15
BI3005	J.D.	3	8	10
BI3006	Eric	3	8	10
BI3007	Meg	3	8	10
BI3011	Mechanic	4	10	15
BI3012	Glove	3	8	10
BI3013	Madame-O	3	8	10
BI3014	Dr. Scarab	4	10	15
BI3015	Chopper	3	8	10
BI3016	Klunk	4	10	15
BI3021	M.U.L.E.S. Van	8	20	30
BI3022	Bionic Dirt Bike	4	10	15
BI3023	Bionic Quad Runner	4	10	15
BI3024	Laser Aero Chair	4	10	15
BI3025	Flying Laser Throne	4	10	15
BI3031	Secret Headquarters	10	25	40

BIONIC WOMAN, THE (Kenner) 1976-78

The *Bionic Woman* was a spinoff of *The Six Million Dollar Man*. The figure included small plastic arm and leg modules. Bionic ears were simulated by a pinging noise when the head was turned. Doll-style outfits were sold for the figure, including a two-piece evening outfit which only came with the Dome House. A smaller figure of the Bionic Woman came with the cycle sets.

The original figure came dressed in a NASA-style white shirt with stripes. The second version wore a blue jump suit, and the packaging logos were updated to reflect the

BI3021

BI3022

BI3023

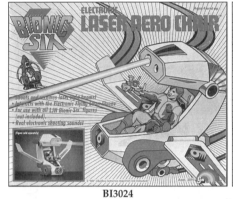

BI3024

BI3025

BI3031

BI5001

BI5003

BI5005

BI5011

BI5012

BI5013

BI5014

BI5021

BI5031

BI5035

BI5056

change. Special thanks to Mike VanPlew for his assistance in updating this section.

	CNP	MIP	MMP
BI5001 Jaime Sommers	15	40	70
BI5003 BI5001 w/Mission Purse	20	65	125
BI5005 Fembot	20	95	175
Designer Collection Fashions (white shirt label) BI5011-14			
BI5011 Gold Evening Gown	5	15	25
BI5012 White Pant Suit	5	15	25

BI5013 Denim Pant Suit	5	15	25
BI5014 Tennis and Swimming Coordinates	10	15	25
BI5021 Bionic Beauty Salon	10	25	45
BI5031 Dome House w/evening gown (similar to SI7041)	25	40	75
BI5035 Carriage House	35	85	150
Designer Collection Fashions (blue jumpsuit label) BI5051-57			
BI5051 Country Comfort	4	12	20
BI5052 Gold Dust	4	12	20

BI5053 Peach Dream	4	12	20
BI5054 Casual Day	4	12	20
BI5055 Blue Mist	4	12	20
BI5056 Floral Delight	4	12	20
BI5057 Silk 'N' Satin	4	12	20
Designer Budget Fashions BI5061-68			
BI5061 Lime Lite	3	8	15
BI5062 Red Dazzle	3	8	15
BI5063 Lunch Date	3	8	15
BI5064 Lilac Butterfly	3	8	15
BI5065 Siesta	3	8	15

CNP: Complete, no package, with all weapons and accessories; MIP: Mint in package; MMP: Mint item in Mint package. Values in U.S. dollars. See page 11 for details.

BI5051-57, BI5061-68   BI5062   BI5071

BI5081   BI5085   BL5150

BL5130   BL5131   BL5132   BL5133   BL5134

BI5066	Classy Culottes	3	8	15
BI5067	Elegant Lady	3	8	15
BI5068	Party Pants	3	8	15

Accessories BI5071-81

BI5071	Bubblin' Bath 'n Shower	30	75	135
BI5081	Sports Car	25	75	175
BI5083	Bionic Classroom (Sears)	35	100	175
BI5085	Travel Communicase	5	12	20
BI5087	Bionic Cycle	20	50	100
BI5089	Tower and Cycle set	35	75	125

See also: *Six Million Dollar Man, The*

BLACK HOLE, THE (Mego) 1980

Ten small figures from The Black Hole were sold individually on cards. Three others (BL5138-40) were only available outside the United States. The robots are generally harder to find. Six 12" figures were also produced.

3¾" action figures BL5130-40   CNP MIP MMP

BL5130	Captain Holland	5	15	25
BL5131	Kate McCrae	5	12	20
BL5132	Dr. Durant	8	20	45
BL5133	Pizer	8	20	45
BL5134	V.I.N.Cent.	25	40	75
BL5135	Harry Booth	5	12	18
BL5136	Dr. Reinhardt	5	12	18
BL5137	Maximillian	20	40	75

BL5138	Old B.O.B.	60	125	250
BL5139	S.T.A.R.	60	150	295
BL5140	Humanoid	100	200	400
BL5141	Sentry Robot	25	50	80

12" figures BL5150-55

BL5150	Captain Holland	20	35	50
BL5151	Kate McCrae	20	45	75
BL5152	Dr. Durant	20	40	85
BL5153	Pizer	20	35	50
BL5154	Harry Booth	20	40	75
BL5155	Hans Reinhardt	20	35	50

BLACKSTAR (Galoob) 1983-85

Original *Blackstar* figures are more difficult to find. Figures released from 1984 on had "Laser Light" built into the figure, which was a spark mechanism similar to that on a cigarette lighter. Each figure came packaged on a card with a PVC figure of a Trobbit or Demon. Mara was a low-production figure for the first series, replaced by Klone in 1984.

Original Figures BL6001-08   CNP MIP MMP

BL6001	Blackstar and Trobbit	6	12	18
BL6002	Mara and Trobbit	6	12	18
BL6003	Overlord w/Demon	6	12	18
BL6004	Neptul w/Demon	6	12	18
BL6005	Palace Guard w/Demon	6	12	18

BL6006	Kadray w/Demon	6	12	18
BL6007	Tongo w/Demon	6	12	18
BL6008	Gargo w/Demon	6	12	18

Later Figures w/"Laser Light" BL6011-25

BL6011	Blackstar and Trobbit	4	10	15
BL6012	Klone and Trobbit	4	10	15
BL6013	Overlord w/Demon	4	10	15
BL6014	Neptul w/Demon	4	10	15
BL6015	Palace Guard w/Demon	4	10	15
BL6016	Kadray w/Demon	4	10	15
BL6017	Tongo w/Demon	4	10	15
BL6018	Gargo w/Demon	4	10	15
BL6021	Vizir w/Demon	4	10	15
BL6022	White Knight w/Demon	4	10	15
BL6023	Devil Knight w/Demon	4	10	15
BL6024	Lava Loc Monster w/Demon	4	10	15
BL6025	Meuton the Wasp Man w/Demon	4	10	15
BL6031-36	Individual Trobbits, 6 different, on card	2	4	8
BL6037-39	Individual Demons, 3 different, on card	2	4	8
BL6050	Gift set w/BL6001, BL6003, and BL6008	24	45	65
BL6051	Trobbit Gift set	10	16	30
BL6060	Warlock, green wings	8	12	16
BL6061	BL6060, yellow wings	5	10	14

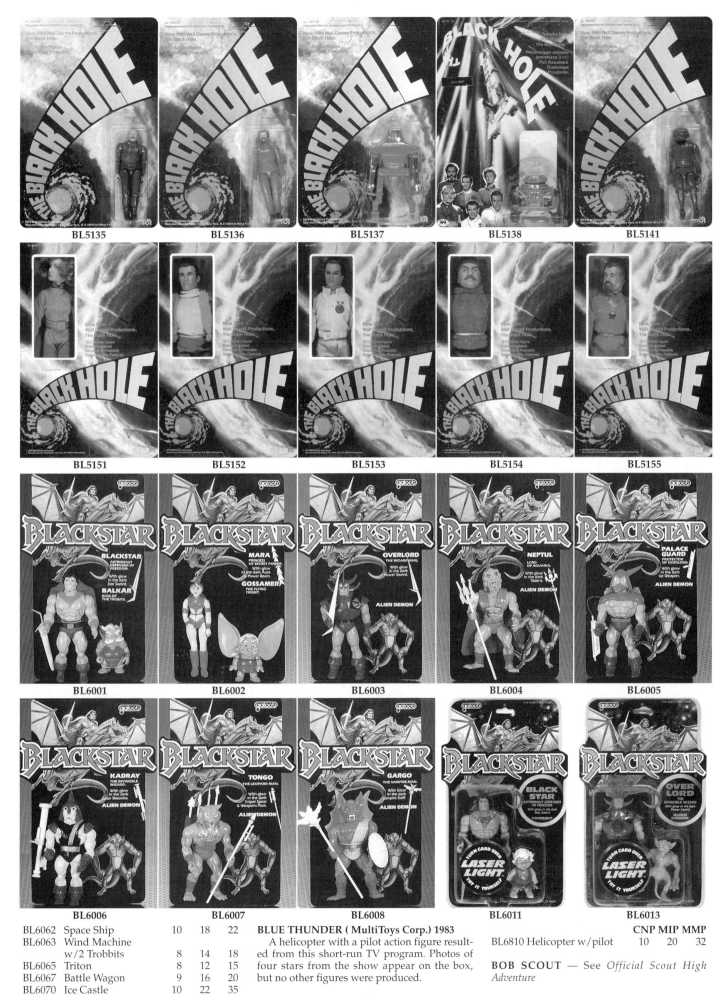

| BL5135 | BL5136 | BL5137 | BL5138 | BL5141 |

| BL5151 | BL5152 | BL5153 | BL5154 | BL5155 |

| BL6001 | BL6002 | BL6003 | BL6004 | BL6005 |

| BL6006 | BL6007 | BL6008 | BL6011 | BL6013 |

BL6062	Space Ship	10	18	22
BL6063	Wind Machine			
	w/2 Trobbits	8	14	18
BL6065	Triton	8	12	15
BL6067	Battle Wagon	9	16	20
BL6070	Ice Castle	10	22	35

BLUE THUNDER (MultiToys Corp.) 1983

A helicopter with a pilot action figure resulted from this short-run TV program. Photos of four stars from the show appear on the box, but no other figures were produced.

CNP MIP MMP

| BL6810 Helicopter w/pilot | 10 | 20 | 32 |

BOB SCOUT — See *Official Scout High Adventure*

63

BL6014

BL6015

BL6016

BL6017

BL6018

BL6021

BL6022

BL6024

BL6061

BL6012

BL6023

BL6025

BL6031

BL6051

BL6062

BL6063

BL6065

BONANZA (American Character) 1966

The *Bonanza* "action men" were among the earliest action figures ever made, and were more articulated than most. Each came in a cardboard box with numerous accessories.

Bonanza fans will note that the Outlaw figure looks suspiciously like Parnell Roberts, who left the show shortly before the release of the figures. His figure was converted by adding a painted mustache and a change of clothes.

Horses had "action hoofs" with ball bearings. Figures and horses were sold separately or together in "stable" packages. More than 70 plastic accessories were included with the 4 in 1 wagon.

64

BL6067

BL6810

BL6070

BO2002

BO2003

BO2002   BO2023   BO2021

BO2023

BO2041

BO4002

BO4013

BO4022

BO4031

BO4041

BO4043

BO4046

Action Men BO2001-04	CNP	MIP	MMP
BO2001 Ben	40	75	100
BO2002 Little Joe	40	75	100
BO2003 Hoss	40	75	100
BO2004 Outlaw	45	85	115

Range Horses BO2011-14

	CNP	MIP	MMP
BO2011 Ben's Palomino	25	65	100
BO2012 Little Joe's Pinto	25	65	100
BO2013 Hoss's Stallion	25	65	100
BO2014 Outlaw's Mustang	30	75	115

Action Men and Horses BO2021-23			
BO2021 Ben and Palomino	65	175	220
BO2022 Little Joe and Pinto	65	175	220
BO2023 Hoss and Stallion	65	175	220
BO2041 4 in 1 Wagon	35	70	85

BONE AGE (Kenner) 1988

This was a series of caveman figures, some of which came with skeletal dinosaurs. The dinosaur bones were inter-changeable, and could be reassembled into warlike vehicles such as tanks and bombers.

Ice Clan BO4001-05	CNP	MIP	MMP
BO4001 Nord	2	4	5
BO4002 Skog (also sold as Mok)	2	4	5
BO4003 Tund the Thunderous	2	4	5
BO4004 Brog (came w/BO4046)	1	-	-
BO4005 Zur (came w/BO4048)	1	-	-

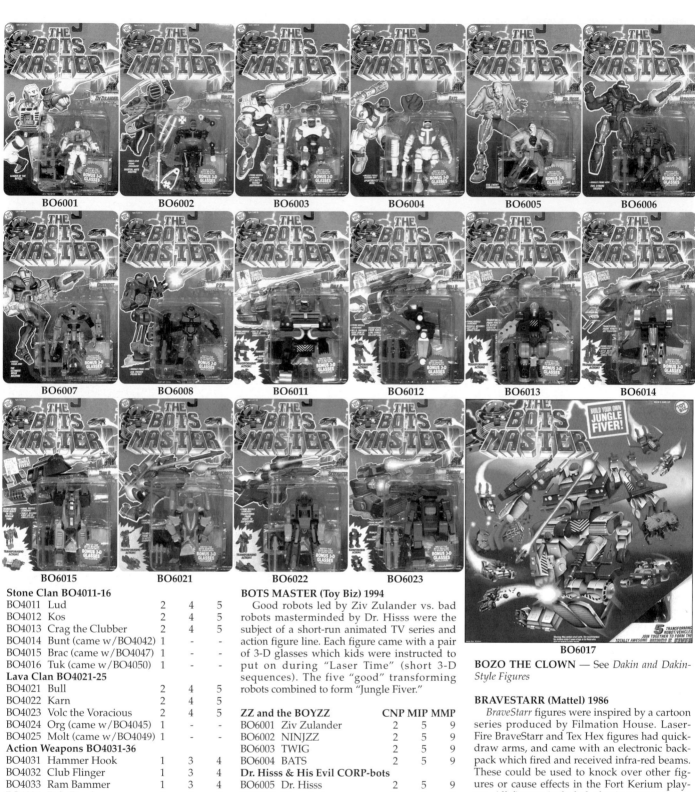

BO6001	BO6002	BO6003	BO6004	BO6005	BO6006
BO6007	BO6008	BO6011	BO6012	BO6013	BO6014
BO6015	BO6021	BO6022	BO6023		

BO6017

Stone Clan BO4011-16

BO4011	Lud	2	4	5
BO4012	Kos	2	4	5
BO4013	Crag the Clubber	2	4	5
BO4014	Bunt (came w/BO4042)	1	-	-
BO4015	Brac (came w/BO4047)	1	-	-
BO4016	Tuk (came w/BO4050)	1	-	-

Lava Clan BO4021-25

BO4021	Bull	2	4	5
BO4022	Karn	2	4	5
BO4023	Volc the Voracious	2	4	5
BO4024	Org (came w/BO4045)	1	-	-
BO4025	Molt (came w/BO4049)	1	-	-

Action Weapons BO4031-36

BO4031	Hammer Hook	1	3	4
BO4032	Club Flinger	1	3	4
BO4033	Ram Bammer	1	3	4
BO4034	Bola Bomber	1	3	4
BO4035	Spear Slinger	1	3	4
BO4036	Tangle Trap	1	3	4

Dinosaurs BO4041-50

BO4041	Brontus w/Volc	10	22	30
BO4042	Codus w/Bunt	5	10	16
BO4043	T-Rex w/Crag	8	20	28
BO4044	Tritops w/Tund	8	18	25
BO4045	Stegus w/Org	8	18	25
BO4046	Ptero w/Brog	6	16	22
BO4047	Deitron w/Brac	6	16	22
BO4048	Dynacus w/Zur	5	10	16
BO4049	Plesior w/Molt	5	10	16
BO4050	Anklor w/Tuk	8	18	25

BONE BRIGADE — See *Ghost Battallion/Bone Brigade*

BOTS MASTER (Toy Biz) 1994

Good robots led by Ziv Zulander vs. bad robots masterminded by Dr. Hisss were the subject of a short-run animated TV series and action figure line. Each figure came with a pair of 3-D glasses which kids were instructed to put on during "Laser Time" (short 3-D sequences). The five "good" transforming robots combined to form "Jungle Fiver."

ZZ and the BOYZZ		CNP	MIP	MMP
BO6001	Ziv Zulander	2	5	9
BO6002	NINJZZ	2	5	9
BO6003	TWIG	2	5	9
BO6004	BATS	2	5	9
Dr. Hisss & His Evil CORP-bots				
BO6005	Dr. Hisss	2	5	9
BO6006	Humabot	2	5	9
BO6007	Greenbot	2	5	9
BO6008	P.P.B	2	5	9
Transforming Robots (Jungle Fiver)				
BO6011	Half B.	2	5	9
BO6012	Heli B.	2	5	9
BO6013	Hover B.	2	5	9
BO6014	Jet B.	2	5	9
BO6015	Tank B.	2	5	9
BO6017	Box set w/BO6011-15	10	15	24
Army Bots (evil transforming robots)				
BO6021	Chopperbot	2	5	9
BO6022	Skyfighter	2	5	9
BO6023	Tankbot	2	5	9

BOY SCOUTS — See *Official Scout High Adventure*

BOZO THE CLOWN — See *Dakin and Dakin-Style Figures*

BRAVESTARR (Mattel) 1986

BraveStarr figures were inspired by a cartoon series produced by Filmation House. Laser-Fire BraveStarr and Tex Hex figures had quick-draw arms, and came with an electronic back-pack which fired and received infra-red beams. These could be used to knock over other figures or cause effects in the Fort Kerium play-set. All figures included plastic accessories, a nugget of kerium ("source of all power in the galaxy!"), a comic and a poster.

		CNP	MIP	MMP
BR1001	Laser-Fire BraveStarr	5	15	25
BR1002	Laser-Fire Tex Hex	5	15	25
BR1003	Marshal BraveStarr	5	15	25
BR1004	Thirty/Thirty	8	19	30
BR1005	Tex Hex	8	19	30
BR1006	Skull Walker	8	19	30
BR1007	Sand Storm	5	15	25
BR1008	Handle Bar	5	15	25
BR1009	Thunder Stick	5	15	25
BR1010	Deputy Fuzz	8	19	30
BR1011	Outlaw Scuzz	8	19	30
BR1020	Neutra-Laser	8	18	30

BR1001	BR1002	BR1004	BR1006	BR1007

BR1008	BR1011	BR1030	BR2003

BR8005	BR8021	BR8101

BR1021	Laser-Fire Backpack	8	19	30
BR1030	Fort Kerium	15	40	60

BRAVO COMPANY/BRAVO MISSION/U.S. COMMANDO SQUAD (Small World Toys) 1987

A G.I. Joe knock-off molded in die-cast metal. No names were given to the figures. This series has been sold under a variety of names with similar packages.

		CNP	MIP	MMP
BR2001	Green uniform, helmet	1	3	5
BR2002	Green uniform, cap	1	3	5
BR2003	Green, cap, beard	1	3	5

BR2004	Green, beret, beard	1	3	5
BR2005	Brown uniform, ski cap	1	3	5
BR2006	Black uniform, ski mask	1	3	5

BRONZE BOMBERS (Olmec) 1989, 1996

The original Bronze Bombers line was similar to 3¾" *G.I. Joe — A Real American Hero* figures. K-mart's name appears on some packages, but it was not an exclusive line.

The line was revived in 1996, using actual *G.I. Joe* molds salvaged from Hasbro's abandonment of the line. African tribal shields were added. Figures were packaged 4 per card with a special comic book.

1989		CNP	MIP	MMP
BR8001	Map Man Jackson	1	3	5
BR8002	Shaka Johnson	1	3	5
BR8003	Arrow Hawk	1	3	5
BR8004	Marc "Kaboom" Walters	1	3	5
BR8005	Wayne "Golden" Alexander	1	3	5
BR8006	A.J. Moon	1	3	5
BR8007	Agent Telepathy	1	3	5
BR8008	The Baron	1	3	5
BR8009	Charles "Chilly Pop" Battle	1	3	5
BR8010	Cool Breeze	1	3	5
BR8011	Hi Tech	1	3	5

CNP: Complete, no package, with all weapons and accessories; MIP: Mint in package; MMP: Mint item in Mint package. Values in U.S. dollars. See page 11 for details.

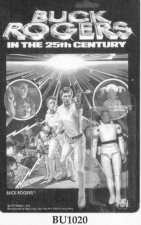

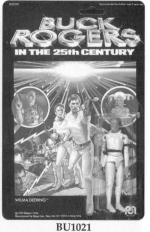

| BU0501 | BU0505 | BU0509 | BU1020 | BU1021 |

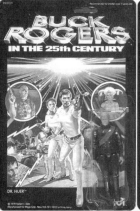

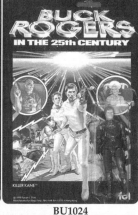

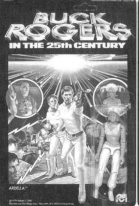

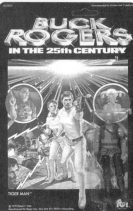

| BU1022 | BU1023 | BU1024 | BU1025 | BU1026 |

| BU1027 | BU1028 | BU1031 | BU1032 |

		CNP	MIP	MMP
BR8012	Sure Fire	1	3	5
BR8021	Battle Copter	2	5	7
BR8022	Motorcycle	1	4	6
BR8023	Hovercraft	2	5	7

1996

| BR8101 | 4-packs w/comic, ea | 4 | 6 | 8 |

BRUCE LEE — See *Legend Bruce Lee, The*

BUBBLE PRINCESS (Mattel) 1995-96

A collection of Disney princess characters, following the success of Musical Princess and Perfume Princess. Bubble solution could be stored in an enclosed base or the figure itself.

		CNP	MIP	MMP
BU0501	Belle	2	4	7
BU0503	Cinderella	2	4	7
BU0505	Jasmine	2	4	7
BU0507	Sleeping Beauty	2	4	7
BU0509	Snow White	2	4	7

See also: *Musical Princess; Perfume Princess*

BUCK ROGERS (Mego) 1979

This series was produced in conjunction with the 1979 film and TV series update of the 1930's character. Ardella is a new or mis-spelling of a female character originally called Ardala. Buck gained new robot friends in keeping with the droids more deftly presented in the *Star Wars* films.

		CNP	MIP	MMP
3¾" figures and accessories BU1020-35				
BU1020	Buck Rogers	10	40	65
BU1021	Wilma Deering	7	40	50
BU1022	Doctor Huer	5	12	25
BU1023	Twiki	8	32	50
BU1024	Killer Kane	5	12	20
BU1025	Ardella	5	12	25
BU1026	Tiger Man	8	18	35
BU1027	Draconian Guard	6	15	25
BU1028	Draco	5	12	20
BU1030	Land Rover	8	18	25
BU1031	Star Fighter	10	25	60
BU1032	Draconian Marauder	10	25	45
BU1033	Star Fighter Command Center	15	60	95
BU1035	Laserscope Fighter	15	35	45
BU1037	Starsearcher	20	60	125
12½" figures BU1040-46				
BU1040	Buck Rogers	20	40	75
BU1041	Walking Twiki	25	55	125
BU1042	Doctor Huer	25	50	85
BU1043	Killer Kane	25	45	85
BU1044	Draco	25	45	85
BU1045	Tiger Man	40	80	140
BU1046	Draconian Guard	40	80	140

See also: *Captain Action*

BUCKY O'HARE (Hasbro) 1991

Inspired by Continuitys TV/comic books, Bucky O'Hare was the hero of S.P.A.C.E. (Sentient Protoplasm Against Colonial Encroachment). Color variations exist, but do not significantly affect values.

		CNP	MIP	MMP
BU2001	#1 Bucky O'Hare	1	5	9
BU2003	#2 Dead-Eye Duck	1	5	9
BU2005	#3 Willy DuWitt	1	5	9
BU2007	#4 Toadborg	1	5	9
BU2009	#5 A.F.C. Blinky	1	5	9
BU2011	#6 Toad Air Marshall	1	5	9
BU2013	#7 Bruiser the Berserker Baboon	1	5	9
BU2015	#8 Al Negator	1	5	9
BU2017	#9 Commander Dogstar	1	5	9
BU2019	#10 Storm Toad Trooper	1	5	9
Vehicles				
BU2050	Righteous Indignation	not produced		
BU2051	Toad Croaker	6	10	20
BU2052	Toad Double Bubble	6	10	20

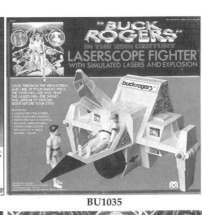

BU1033

BU1035

BU1041

BU1037

BU1040

BU1043

BU2503

BU2001

BU2003

BU2005

BU2007

BU2009

BU2011

BU2013

BU2015

BU2017

BU2019

BU2051

69

BU2052

BU4001

BU4001   BU4002   BU4003   BU4004

BU4201

BU4202

BU4203

BU4204

BU4551

BU4552

BU4553

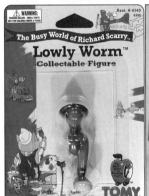

BU5011

BU5001   BU5003   BU5005   BU5007   BU5009   BU5011 BU5021   BU5023   BU5025

BU5031   BU5032

BUDDY CHARLIE (Marx)

Four figures were produced exclusively for Montgomery Ward by Marx. The figures were compatible with 12" *G.I. Joe* figures, and had cloth accessories rather than the usual rubber clothing associated with Marx figures. Service insignia appeared on the figure's dog tags.

BU2501	Soldier	40	100	220
BU2502	Sailor	40	100	220
BU2503	Airman	40	100	220
BU2504	Marine	40	100	220

BUG BOTS (Buddy L) 1984

Insect-like robot figures. Each figure had motorized action when pushed along the floor.

		CNP	MIP	MMP
BU4001	Bee Bot	1	2	3
BU4002	Cosmic Crawler	1	2	3
BU4003	Galactic Creeper	1	2	3
BU4004	Dragon Drone	1	2	3

BUGMEN OF INSECTA (Multi-Toys) 1983

The action figure equivalent of B movies, these low-quality toys were humanoid insects with plastic weapons. Each came with a drone, either a spider, roach, or fly.

		CNP	MIP	MMP
BU4201	Spiderman	1	2	4
BU4202	Stag Beetle	1	2	4
BU4203	Killer Bee	1	2	4
BU4204	Grasshopperman	1	2	4
BU4205	Tiger Beetle	1	2	4
BU4206	Black Widow	1	2	4

BUMP IN THE NIGHT (Street Players) 1994-95

Figures based on the claymation series.

		CNP	MIP	MMP
BU4551	Mr. Bumpy	1	3	4
BU4552	Molly Coddle	1	3	4
BU4553	Squishington	1	3	4

BUSY WORLD OF RICHARD SCARRY (Tomy) 1995-96

Busytown figures were produced in conjunction with the Nickelodeon animated series. The first wave of figures was available only through independent toy stores in 1995, shipping to major retail chains in early 1996. Pull-back-and-go vehicles were sold with figures.

1995		CNP	MIP	MMP
BU5001	Hilda Hippo	1	3	5
BU5003	Bananas Gorilla	1	3	5
BU5005	Mr. Frumble	1	3	5
BU5007	Sgt. Murphy	1	3	5
BU5009	Huckle Cat	1	3	5
BU5011	Lowly Worm	1	3	5
BU5015	BU5003 w/Banana Car	2	6	8
BU5017	BU5007 w/motorcycle	2	6	8
BU5019	BU5011 w/Apple Car	2	6	8
1996				
BU5021	Rudolf von Flugel	1	3	5
BU5023	Sally Cat	1	3	5
BU5025	Fix-it Fox	1	3	5
BU5031	BU5001 w/Roller Skate	2	6	8
BU5032	BU5005 w/Pickle Car	2	6	8

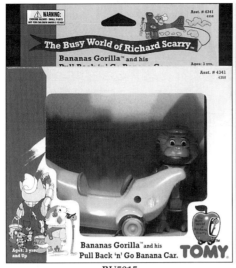

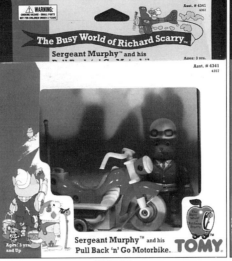

BU5015   BU5017   BU5019

BU6001   BU6002   BU6003   BU6004   BU6005

BU6010   BU6011   BU6020

BUTCH AND SUNDANCE: THE EARLY DAYS (Kenner) 1979

The 1979 movie Butch Cassidy and the Sundance Kid inspired this series of figures. Each had a button-controlled arm for "fast-draw action." Similar controls made the horse figures "gallop." Two additional figures came with the Mint Wagon.

	CNP	MIP	MMP
BU6001 Butch Cassidy	5	15	28
BU6002 The Sundance Kid	5	15	28
BU6003 Marshall LeFors	8	20	30
BU6004 Sheriff Bledsoe	8	20	30
BU6005 O.C. Hanks	8	20	30
BU6010 Bluff	10	25	45
BU6011 Spurs	10	25	45
BU6020 Mint Wagon	15	40	80
BU6021 Saloon playset	20	65	85

BUTTERFLY WOMAN (Olmec) 1986

The female counterpart to Sun-Man. Each figure was packaged with a mini-comic.

BU7001   BU7003

	CNP	MIP	MMP
BU7001 Butterfly Woman	2	5	7
BU7003 Amandla	2	5	7
BU7005 Felina	2	5	7

CADILLACS AND DINOSAURS (TYCO) 1993

This storyline is set in the 26th century — the Xenozoic Era — where dinosaurs have returned, and are armed with futuristic weaponry (strangely similar to TYCO's earlier Dino-Riders — some old molds were revived). Add in a hero with a modified 1953 Cadillac convertible and a forgetable cast of bad guys, and you've got Cadillacs and Dinosaurs. Various Cadillac and other automotive trademarks were used under license from General Motors.

	CNP	MIP	MMP
CA1001 Jack "Cadillac" Tenrec	3	6	10
CA1002 Hammer Terhune	3	6	10
CA1003 Hannah Dundee	3	6	15
CA1004 Vice Terhune	3	6	10
CA1005 Mustapha Cairo	3	6	10
CA1006 Jungle Fighting Jack	3	6	10
CA1011 Zeke	3	6	12
CA1012 Hermes	3	6	12
CA1021 Glider	5	8	12

CNP: Complete, no package, with all weapons and accessories; MIP: Mint in package; MMP: Mint item in Mint package. Values in U.S. dollars. See page 11 for details.

CA1001

CA1002

CA1003

CA1004

CA1005

CA1006

CA1011

CA1012

CA1021

CA1022

CA1023

CA1031

CA1032

| CA1022 | Tribike | 5 | 8 | 12 | CA1031 | Triceratops | 8 | 12 | 15 | CA1041 | Jack's Garage | not produced |
| CA1023 | Cadillac | 10 | 15 | 20 | CA1032 | Kentrosaurus | 8 | 12 | 15 | **See also:** *Dino-Riders* | |

CAPTAIN ACTION (Ideal) 1966-68

Today we think in terms of collecting a whole set of action figures. Back in 1966 "action figures" were a new concept patterned after the success of the *Barbie* doll. *G.I. Joe* was a smash in 1964 with a parade of different uniforms and barrage of carded accessories.

It was natural for the Ideal Toy Company to stick close to this proven success formula when they conceived *Captain Action*, a unique character who could turn into just about any hero popular with boys. The transformation was accomplished by changing uniforms and adding a rubber mask created true to the likeness of the character being impersonated. The first year, *Captain Action* could become Superman, Batman, Aquaman, Steve Canyon, The Lone Ranger, Flash Gordon, Captain America, or The Phantom. Licensing so many different character properties for a single line was a feat — even back then — and would probably be impossible today.

Super hero characters have turned out to be some of the most successful and steady-selling action figures. This first offering was really a collection of comic book heroes. In 1965, when the toys were being developed, no one at Ideal could have predicted the tremendous boost the line would receive from the Adam West *Batman* TV show, which began airing shortly thereafter. *Batman* took the nation by storm and triggered a "pop" revival of virtually every cartoon character. These characters remained popular until the mid-'70s.

The second year, Flash Gordon and Sgt. Fury were dropped in favor of Spider-Man, The Green Hornet, Tonto and Buck Rogers. "Video-Matic" flasher rings were added to the costume and accessory boxes. Action Boy was introduced along with costume ensembles for Robin, Aqualad and Superboy. Six accessory packs were added to give *Captain Action* addi-

tional powers when he just wanted to be himself, plus a turbo rocket-firing Silver Streak Amphibian car.

Dr. Evil was the major addition the third year. The standard figure came in a blue smock-type suit with sandals, disguise mask, medallion, and laser gun. He was available boxed or in a gift set which included an extra lab coat, Oriental disguise, and 5 inter-galaxial deadly weapons: a reducer, hypnotic eye, ionized hypo, laser ray gun and thought control helmet. This gift set is commonly referred to as "Dr. Evil's laboratory", even though no such name appears on the box.

There was a playset/carrying case depicting several *Captain Action* and super hero characters on the exterior, but nonetheless called Dr. Evil's Sanctuary.

Ideal marketed four *Comic Heroines* at the same time as Captain Action, but no connection was promoted. (See CO1501-04)

Captain Action was discontinued by 1970. The Ideal Toy Company was eventually purchased by CBS as a diversification move. It was reorganized with other CBS properties and lost its identity, even though CBS later sold all its toy company properties. Ideal continues to operate out of England, selling toys throughout Europe. Mego came along in 1972 and dominated the super hero figure category for the next 12 years.

		CNP	MIP	MMP
CA3001	Captain Action, 1966 (Lone Ranger in red shirt)	150	250	450
CA3003	CA3001 re-issue box (Lone Ranger in blue shirt, Christmas 1966)	150	250	450
CA3004	CA3001 in 1967 box w/Parachute	200	350	750
CA3005	CO3001 in 1967 photo box (Christmas 1967)	150	490	850

Dr. Evil the Sinister Invader of Earth 1967

CA3011	Dr. Evil, 1967	175	250	425
CA3012	Dr. Evil Gift Set	375	1250	2000
CA3013	Dr. Evil Sanctuary (carry case)	800	1200	2300

Superhero Costumes for Captain Action

CA3020	Superman (1966)	95	325	600
CA3021	1967 re-issue w/ring	110	375	800
CA3022	Batman (1966)	100	325	600
CA3023	1967 re-issue w/ring	110	375	800
CA3024	Aquaman (1966)	95	300	500
CA3025	1967 re-issue w/ring	110	350	600
CA3026	Capt. America (1966)	125	325	650
CA3027	1967 re-issue w/ring	140	350	850
CA3028	Phantom (1966)	95	300	575
CA3029	1967 re-issue w/ring (w/pistols or 45s)	110	325	875
CA3030	Lone Ranger, (1966) red shirt	100	350	1000
CA3031	1967 re-issue w/blue shirt and ring	150	450	800
CA3032	Steve Canyon (1966)	95	225	350
CA3033	1967 re-issue w/ring	110	250	875
CA3034	Flash Gordon (1966)	125	350	600
CA3035	1967 re-issue w/ring	140	375	475
CA3036	Sgt. Fury (1966)	100	360	600
CA3037	Spider-Man (1967)	250	2500	4500
CA3038	Tonto (1967)	200	550	1500
CA3039	Buck Rogers (1967)	200	600	1400
CA3040	Green Hornet (1967)	400	3000	4400

Action Boy

CA3043	Action Boy (1967)	225	500	1000
CA3044	1967-68 re-issue w/ space suit	250	550	1200

Superhero Costumes for Action Boy

CA3045	Aqualad (1967)	200	450	800
CA3046	Superboy (1967)	200	525	875
CA3047	Robin (1967)	200	450	850

Captain Action Accessories

CA3051	Directional Communicator	75	225	325
CA3052	Power Pack	75	225	325

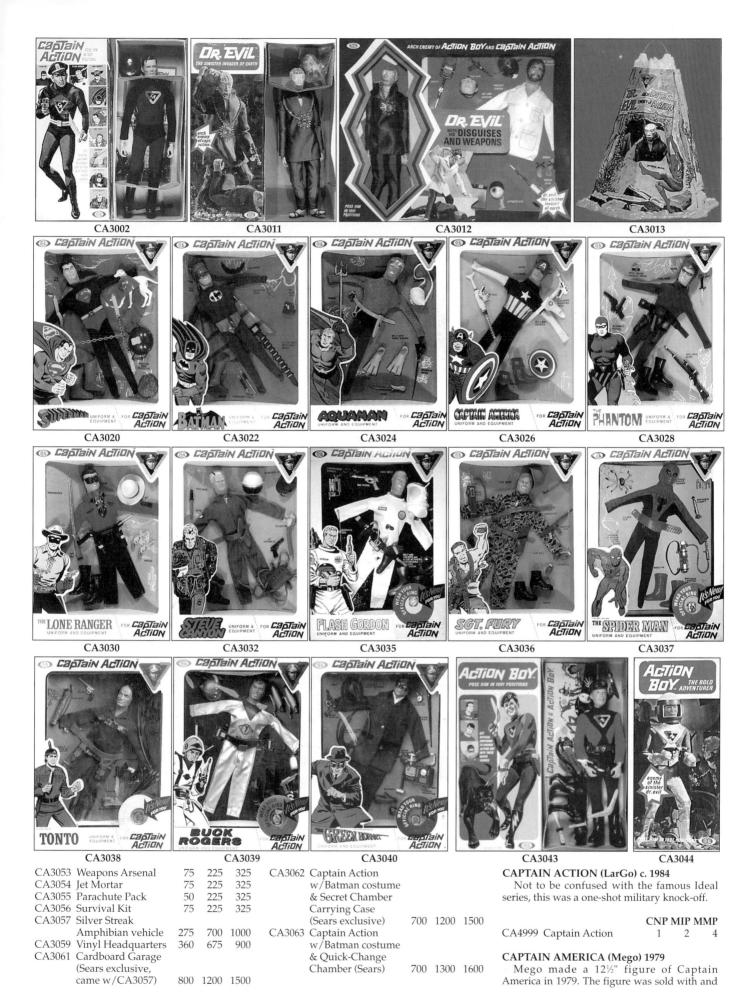

CA3002   CA3011   CA3012   CA3013

CA3020   CA3022   CA3024   CA3026   CA3028

CA3030   CA3032   CA3035   CA3036   CA3037

CA3038   CA3039   CA3040   CA3043   CA3044

CA3053	Weapons Arsenal	75	225	325
CA3054	Jet Mortar	75	225	325
CA3055	Parachute Pack	50	225	325
CA3056	Survival Kit	75	225	325
CA3057	Silver Streak			
	Amphibian vehicle	275	700	1000
CA3059	Vinyl Headquarters	360	675	900
CA3061	Cardboard Garage			
	(Sears exclusive,			
	came w/CA3057)	800	1200	1500

CA3062	Captain Action			
	w/Batman costume			
	& Secret Chamber			
	Carrying Case			
	(Sears exclusive)	700	1200	1500
CA3063	Captain Action			
	w/Batman costume			
	& Quick-Change			
	Chamber (Sears)	700	1300	1600

CAPTAIN ACTION (LarGo) c. 1984

Not to be confused with the famous Ideal series, this was a one-shot military knock-off.

| | CNP | MIP | MMP |
| CA4999 Captain Action | 1 | 2 | 4 |

CAPTAIN AMERICA (Mego) 1979

Mego made a 12½" figure of Captain America in 1979. The figure was sold with and

| | | CA3045 | | CA3046 | | CA3047 |

CA3052   CA3056   CA3057

CA4999   CA6001   CA6501   CA6502   CA6503   CA6511

CA6512   CA6513   CA6521   CA6522   CA6523   CA6524

without a fly-away action attachment. Captain America figures which were made as part of a series appear elsewhere in the appropriate sections.

CNP MIP MMP

CA6001 Captain America
w/fly-away action   65   100   150

See also: *Captain Action; Comic Action Heroes; Iron Man; Marvel Super Heroes; Marvel Super Heroes Secret Wars; Official World's Greatest Super Heroes; Pocket Super Heroes*

CAPTAIN PLANET (Tiger Toys) 1991-95

Captain Planet figures were created by Tiger for the Turner Broadcasting System. They were politically correct, safe, educational, ethnically balanced, packaged on recycled cards, and everything parents could want in a toy. Someone remembered that toys are for kids late in the first year of the series, and produced a few figures which squirt water or make "sludge."

Like many educational figures, the series died at retail, but a trickle of product made from recycled molds continued to ship to K-mart after the first two years. The New Adventures of Captain Planet consisted only of repaints made from earlier molds.

CNP MIP MMP

CA6501 Captain Planet   1   2   5

		CNP	MIP	MMP
CA6502	Planeteer Wheeler	1	2	5
CA6503	Ma-Ti and Kwame	2	4	8
CA6511	Verminous Skumm	1	2	5
CA6512	Dr. Blight	1	2	5
CA6513	Duke Nukem	1	2	5
CA6520	Captain Planet w/ Color Change	2	4	8
CA6521	Linka Planeteer	3	6	8
CA6522	Gi Planeteer	2	3	5
CA6523	Sly Sludge	2	3	5
CA6524	Hoggish Greedly	2	3	5
CA6540	Eco-Cycle	1	3	8
CA6542	Eco-Sub	3	4	8
CA6544	Geo-Cruiser	3	4	8
CA6546	Skumm-O-Copter	2	10	20
CA6548	Toxic Cannon	2	4	6

CNP: Complete, no package, with all weapons and accessories; MIP: Mint in package; MMP: Mint item in Mint package. Values in U.S. dollars. See page 11 for details.

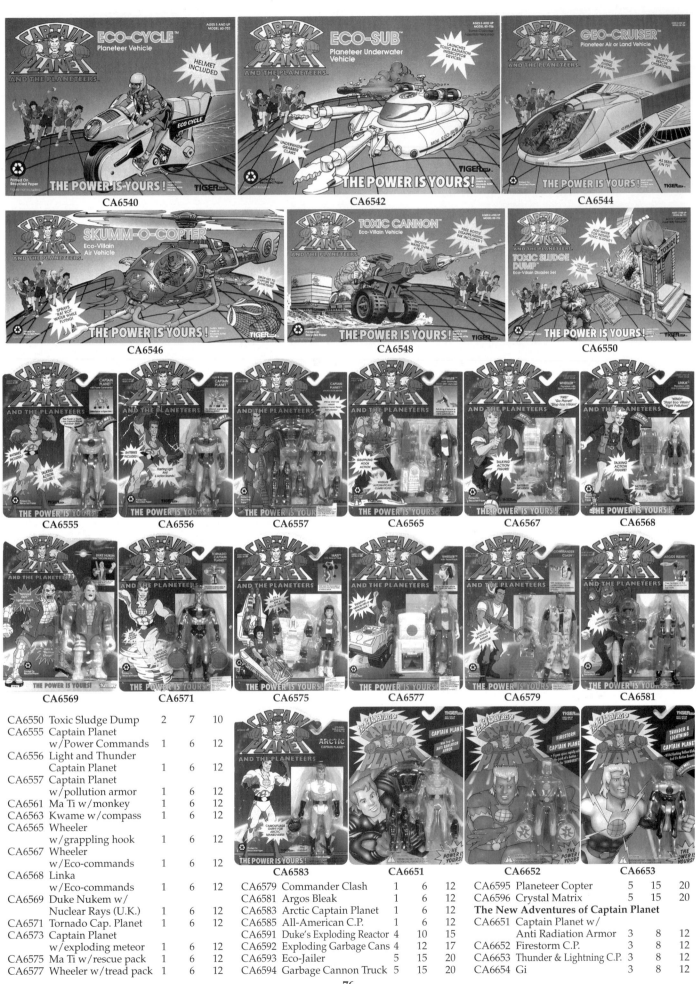

CA6540   CA6542   CA6544

CA6546   CA6548   CA6550

CA6555   CA6556   CA6557   CA6565   CA6567   CA6568

CA6569   CA6571   CA6575   CA6577   CA6579   CA6581

CA6583   CA6651   CA6652   CA6653

CA6550	Toxic Sludge Dump	2	7	10
CA6555	Captain Planet w/Power Commands	1	6	12
CA6556	Light and Thunder Captain Planet	1	6	12
CA6557	Captain Planet w/pollution armor	1	6	12
CA6561	Ma Ti w/monkey	1	6	12
CA6563	Kwame w/compass	1	6	12
CA6565	Wheeler w/grappling hook	1	6	12
CA6567	Wheeler w/Eco-commands	1	6	12
CA6568	Linka w/Eco-commands	1	6	12
CA6569	Duke Nukem w/Nuclear Rays (U.K.)	1	6	12
CA6571	Tornado Cap. Planet	1	6	12
CA6573	Captain Planet w/exploding meteor	1	6	12
CA6575	Ma Ti w/rescue pack	1	6	12
CA6577	Wheeler w/tread pack	1	6	12
CA6579	Commander Clash	1	6	12
CA6581	Argos Bleak	1	6	12
CA6583	Arctic Captain Planet	1	6	12
CA6585	All-American C.P.	1	6	12
CA6591	Duke's Exploding Reactor	4	10	15
CA6592	Exploding Garbage Cans	4	12	17
CA6593	Eco-Jailer	5	15	20
CA6594	Garbage Cannon Truck	5	15	20
CA6595	Planeteer Copter	5	15	20
CA6596	Crystal Matrix	5	15	20

The New Adventures of Captain Planet

CA6651	Captain Planet w/Anti Radiation Armor	3	8	12
CA6652	Firestorm C.P.	3	8	12
CA6653	Thunder & Lightning C.P.	3	8	12
CA6654	Gi	3	8	12

| CA6591 | CA6593 | CA6595 |

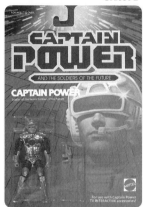 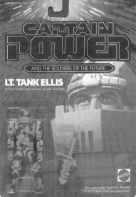  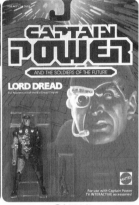 

| CA7001 | CA7002 | CA7003 | CA7004 | CA7011 |

| CA7012 | CA7013 | CA7014 | CA7015 | CA7016 |

| CA7032 | CA7033 | CA7034 |

CA6655	Kwame	3	8	12
CA6656	Linka	3	8	12
CA6657	Ma Ti	3	8	12
CA6658	Wheeler	3	8	12

CAPTAIN POWER (Mattel) 1987

Captain Power toys were designed to interact with a television set. Encoded signals were broadcast with the TV show, which determined hits or "destroyed" the toy. Videotapes were sold so kids could play when the show wasn't on the air. Four of the figures (CA7013-18) comprised a second series, saw lower distribution, and are more difficult to find.

		CNP	MIP	MMP
CA7001	Captain Power	2	6	10
CA7002	Lt. Tank Ellis	3	8	14
CA7003	Major Hawk Masterson	4	9	16
CA7004	Lord Dread	2	6	10

CA7011	Soaron Sky Sentry	3	8	14
CA7012	Blastarr Ground Guardian	3	6	12
CA7013	Sgt. Scout Baker	4	8	15
CA7014	Cpl. Pilot Chase	8	12	17
CA7015	Col. Stingray Johnson	8	15	20
CA7016	Tritor	10	20	35
CA7017	Dread Commander	25	75	150
CA7018	Dread Trooper	25	75	150
CA7031	Magnacycle	5	12	15

CNP: Complete, no package, with all weapons and accessories; MIP: Mint in package; MMP: Mint item in Mint package. Values in U.S. dollars. See page 11 for details.

PHANTOM STRIKER

CA7035

DREAD STALKER

CA7036

INTERLOCKER

CA7041

TRANS-FIELD COMMUNICATION STATION

CA7044

TRANS-FIELD BASE STATION

CA7045

POWER BASE

CA7051

CA8001	CA8004	CA8006	CA8007	CA8008	CA8010	CA8012
Tenderheart Bear	Cheer Bear	Friend Bear	Love-A-Lot Bear	Wish Bear	Good Luck Bear	Baby Tugs Bear

CA8005	CA8009	CA8011	CA8076	CA8077	CA8078	CA8079	CA8080

CA7032	Powerjet XT-7	12	18	30
CA7033	Powerjet XT-7, deluxe set w/CA7061	15	30	45
CA7034	Power On Energizer	10	15	20
CA7035	Phantom Striker	12	18	30
CA7036	Dread Stalker	12	18	20
CA7041	Interlocker	12	18	20
CA7044	Trans-Field Communication Station	12	18	30
CA7045	Trans-Field Base Station	15	25	35
CA7051	Power Base Fortress	12	35	50

Video Tapes CA7061-66

CA7061	Future Force Training (Came w/CA7021)	5	8	10
CA7062	Bio Dread Strike Mission	5	8	10
CA7063	Raid on Valcania	5	8	10
CA7064	Volume 1 "Shattered Past" and "The Abyss"	5	8	10
CA7065	Volume 2	5	8	10
CA7066	Volume 3	5	8	10

CARE BEARS/CARE BEAR COUSINS (Kenner) 1984-85

Care Bears were dveloped by the American Greeting Card Company and were later seen on TV and in a feature-length film. They were franchised for a number of toy products in the mid-'80s.

		CNP	MIP	MMP
CA8001	Tenderheart Bear	2	5	8
CA8002	Bedtime Bear	2	5	8
CA8003	Birthday Bear	2	5	8
CA8004	Cheer Bear	2	5	8
CA8005	Grumpy Bear	2	5	8
CA8006	Friend Bear	2	5	8
CA8007	Love-A-Lot Bear	2	5	8
CA8008	Wish Bear	2	5	8
CA8009	Funshine Bear	2	5	8
CA8010	Good Luck Bear	2	5	8
CA8011	Baby Hugs Bear	2	5	8
CA8012	Baby Tugs Bear	2	5	8
CA8013	Grams Bear	2	5	8
CA8014	Professor Cold Heart	2	5	8
CA8015	Cloudkeeper	2	5	8
CA8031	Love-A-Lot Bear w/Bouquet of Hearts	1	4	7
CA8032	Tenderheart Bear w/Caring Heart Mirror	1	4	7
CA8033	Wish Bear w/Star-A-Scope	1	4	7
CA8034	Friend Bear w/Friendly Sprinkler	1	4	7

| CA8015 | CA8051 | CA8052 | CA8061 |

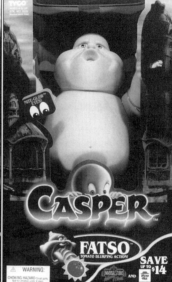

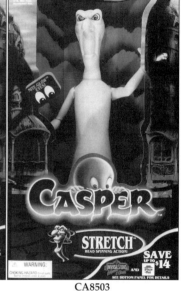

| CA8500 | CA8501 | CA8502 | CA8503 |

CB1001-09

CELESTRA
QUEEN OF THE TRANSFORMING DOLLS

CE0500

CA8035	Funshine Bear w/Sun-Catcher	1	4	7
CA8036	Share Bear w/Share-A-Like Shake	1	4	7
CA8037	Champ Bear w/Good Sport Trophy	1	4	7
CA8038	Bedtime Bear w/Snooze Alarm	1	4	7
CA8039	Baby Hugs Bear w/ Sweet Lickity Lollipop	1	4	7
CA8040	Cheer Bear w/Merry Megaphone	1	4	7
CA8041	Baby Tugs Bear w/Big Diggity Bucket	1	4	7
CA8042	Grams Bear w/Lovin' Basket	1	4	7
CA8051	Rainbow Roller vehicle	4	10	12
CA8052	Cloud Mobile vehicle	4	10	12
CA8061	Care-a-Lot Playset	10	15	20
Care Bear Cousins CA8071-80				
CA8071	Proud Heart Cat w/True Blue Ribbon	1	4	7
CA8072	Loyal Heart Dog w/Waggin' Flag	1	4	7
CA8073	Playful Heart Monkey w/Merry Music Maker	1	4	7
CA8074	Treat Heart Pig w/Sweet Surprise	1	4	7
CA8075	Bright Heart Raccoon w/Clever Candle	1	4	7
CA8076	Gentle Heart Lamb w/Peek-A-Boo Bell	1	4	7
CA8077	Lotsa Heart Elephant w/Mighty Trunk	1	4	7
CA8078	Brave Heart Lion w/Trusty Shield	1	4	7
CA8079	Cozy Heart Penguin w/N'ice Skates	1	4	7
CA8080	Swift Heart Rabbit w/Speedy Skate Board	1	4	7

CASPER (TYCO) 1995

Ghosts don't have much articulation, but four "Mischief Makers" were produced in conjuction with the 1995 film *Casper*. Squeezing the figures activated nifty action features. Two of these were inspired by the line's merchandising tie-in with Pizza Hut: Stinkie burps the smell of pepperoni pizza, and Fatso burps out a tomato. Coupons for Casper toys were also part of a Pepsi 24-pack promotion.

		CNP	MIP	MMP
CA8500	Casper	4	7	12
CA8501	Stinkie	4	7	12
CA8502	Fatso	4	7	12
CA8503	Stretch	4	7	12

CASPER THE FRIENDLY GHOST — See *Dakin and Dakin-Style Figures*

C.B. MCHAUL (Mego) 1977

A not-so-successful offering based on the Citizen's Band radio fad and trucker's lingo.

		CNP	MIP	MMP
CB1001	C.B. McHaul	5	15	30
CB1002	Jim Oakes	5	15	30
CB1003	Kidd Watts	5	15	30
CB1004	Joe Marconi	5	15	30
CB1005	Professor Braine	5	15	30
CB1006	Bad Leroy	5	15	30
CB1007	Sgt. Brown	5	15	30
CB1008	Scowling Jack Jones	5	15	30
CB1009	Speed Johnson	5	15	30
CB1015	Rig (truck)	25	50	150

CELESTRA, QUEEN OF THE TRANSFORMING DOLLS (PLACO) c. 1986

An attempt to combine female heroines, robots, and *Transformers*. A plastic shell and helmet turned each figure into a "robot."

CNP: Complete, no package, with all weapons and accessories; MIP: Mint in package; MMP: Mint item in Mint package. Values in U.S. dollars. See page 11 for details.

| | CE5001 | CE5002 | CE5003 | CE5004 | CE5005 |

| | CE5010 | CE5011 | CE5020 | CE5022 |

| | CE5021 | CE5030 | CE5031 |

| | CE5032 | CE5040 | CE5041 | CE5042 |

		CNP	MIP	MMP
CE0500	Celestra	3	6	10
CB0501	Saturnia	3	6	10
CB0502	Vulcania	3	6	10
CB0503	Zarla	3	6	10

CENTURIONS POWERXTREME (Kenner) 1986

Centurions were 7½" figures. They were modularly designed so that accessories could be rearranged, exchanged or combined with other figures. Assault Weapon Systems were large weapon and vehicle-like attachments for the figures. Figural flashlights, binoculars, and watches were also produced.

		CNP	MIP	MMP
CE5001	Ace McCloud	5	12	25
CE5002	Max Ray	5	12	25
CE5003	Jake Rockwell	5	15	30
CE5004	Dr. Terror	5	15	30
CE5005	Hacker	5	15	30
Doom Drones				
CE5010	Strafer	5	12	15
CE5011	Traumatizer	5	12	20

| | CE5050 | CH0301 | CH0501 |

Assault Weapons Systems CE5020-42

Light Duty				
CE5020	Orbital Interceptor	7	15	20
CE5021	Tidal Blast	7	15	20
CE5022	Wild Weasel	7	15	20
Medium Duty				
CE5030	Hornet	10	18	30
CE5031	Sea Bat	10	18	30
CE5032	Swingshot	10	18	30

Heavy Duty				
CE5040	Skybolt	15	20	35
CE5041	Depth Charger	15	20	35
CE5042	Detonator	15	20	35
CE5050	Power Pack	10	15	25

CHAMPIONSHIP WRESTLING SOUNDS (In Time Products Co., Ltd.) 1991

Two figures and a sound-effects box were packaged together.

CH1001	CH1003	CH1005
CH1006		CH1012
CH1018	CH1021	CH1022
CH1023	CH1024	CH1025 CH1026
CH1031	CH1032	CH1033 CH1041
CH6004	CH6005	CH6006
CH6007	CH6008	CH6009

	CNP	MIP	MMP
CH0301-03 Wrestler sets, ea	3	6	8
CH0311 Wrestling Ring	3	5	6

CHARGERTRON (Buddy L) 1985

A variation on the *Transformers* theme, *Chargertron* launched a figure which could either remain a car or change into a robot.

	CNP	MIP	MMP
CH0501 Antagatron	1	2	4
CH0502 Protagatron	1	2	4
See also: *Robotron*			

CHARLIE'S ANGELS (Hasbro) 1977

These 8½" dolls came on blister packs with a wrap-around logo, or in boxed gift sets. The original logo on the packages showed Farrah Fawcett-Majors as one of the three Angels. Cheryl Ladd replaced Farah's in the logo when the latter left the show.

		CNP	MIP	MMP
CH1001	Jill	10	30	48
CH1002	Sabrina, original logo	10	30	48
CH1003	Sabrina, revised logo	10	30	48
CH1004	Kelly, original logo	10	30	48
CH1005	Kelly, revised logo	10	30	48
CH1006	Kris	10	30	48

		CNP	MIP	MMP
CH1012	Gift Set	-	130	150
CH1018	Flying Skateboard	not determined		
Fashion Costumes CH1021-26				
CH1021	Black Magic	5	10	17
CH1022	Moonlight Flight	5	10	17
CH1023	Gaucho Pizazz	5	10	17
CH1024	Night Caper	5	10	17
CH1025	Russian Roulette	5	10	17
CH1026	Peasantry	5	10	17
Escapades Sets CH1031-33				
CH1031	The Slalom Caper	5	10	17
CH1032	River Race	5	10	17
CH1033	Underwater Intrigue	5	10	17
CH1041	Hideaway House	10	20	30

CNP: Complete, no package, with all weapons and accessories; MIP: Mint in package; MMP: Mint item in Mint package. Values in U.S. dollars. See page 11 for details.

CH6031   CH7001   CH7002   CH7003

CH7021   CH7022   CH7023   CH7024   CH7025

CH7030   CH7040   CH9020

CHIPMUNKS, THE (Ideal) 1984

Action figures and playsets for younger children made a nice addition to the usual Fisher-Price and Playskool fare. A premium figure of Alvin in a Superman-style outfit was available by mail for 3 proof of purchase seals.

		CNP	MIP	MMP
CH6001	Alvin Up for Action	4	7	10
CH6002	Everyday Simon	4	7	10
CH6003	Theodore Ready to Play	4	7	10
CH6004	Fair Brittany	4	7	10
CH6005	Gentle Jeanette	4	7	10
CH6006	Uncle Harry in His Best	4	7	10
CH6007	Sweet Eleanor	4	7	10
CH6008	Alvin in Concert	4	7	10
CH6009	Simon in Concert	4	7	10
CH6010	Theodore in Concert	4	7	10
CH6011	Super Alvin	7	10	15
CH6021	Treat Mobile	10	12	15
CH6022	Chipettes Picnic Buggy	10	12	15
CH6031	Curtain Call Theater	10	12	15

CHiPs (Mego) 1978-81, (LJN) 1983

Proper identification of *CHiPs* figures can be confusing. MCA originally licensed the Mego corporation to produce 8" figures with cloth costumes and a series of 3¾" figures with motorcycles designed for a plastic launcher. Some 3¾" figures were similar to figures from *C.B. McHaul*. When Mego folded in 1982, the molds were obtained by LJN, but no new versions were produced. Figures of Ponch are more common than Jon.

		CNP	MIP	MMP
Mego 8" figures and accessories				
CH7001	Jon	10	25	45
CH7002	Ponch	10	25	45
CH7003	Sarge	10	25	50
CH7010	Motorcycle	10	25	45
Mego 3¾" figures and accessories				
CH7021	Jon	4	10	17
CH7022	Ponch	4	9	15
CH7023	Sarge	5	12	20
CH7024	Wheels Willie	4	10	12
CH7025	Jimmy Squeaks	4	10	12
CH7030	Motorcycle	4	10	20
CH7035	Ponch/Motorcycle set	5	25	45
CH7036	Jon/Motorcycle set	5	25	45
CH7040	Launcher/Mortorcycle Set			not produced

CHUCK NORRIS KARATE KOMMANDOS (Kenner) 1986

Each figure could perform some sort of martial arts action, which was triggered by squeezing the arms or legs. Three different Chuck Norris figures were produced, in addition to five characters from the animated television series. The only accessory was a Corvette with snap-out action features.

		CNP	MIP	MMP
CH9001	Chuck Norris (Battle Gear)	5	10	15
CH9002	Chuck Norris (Kung Fu Training Gi)	5	10	15
CH9003	Chuck Norris (Undercover Agent)	5	10	15
CH9004	Kimo	5	10	15
CH9005	Reed Smith	5	10	14
CH9006	Tabe	5	10	12
CH9007	Super Ninja	5	10	15
CH9008	Ninja Warrior	5	10	15
CH9009	Ninja Master	5	10	15
CH9010	Ninja Serpent	5	10	15
CH9020	Karate Corvette	8	12	17

CINDERELLA — See *Bubble Princess; Musical Princess; Perfume Princess*

CH9001 CH9002 CH9003 CH9004 CH9005

CH9006 CH9007 CH9008 CH9009 CH9010

CL1001 CL1002 CL1003 CL1004 CL1010

CL1015

CL2001 CL2002 CL2003 CL2004

CLASH OF THE TITANS (Mattel) 1980

A less common series, based on the 1980 film by MGM.

		CNP	MIP	MMP
CL1001	Perseus	10	25	40
CL1002	Calibos	10	30	50
CL1003	Thallo	10	25	40
CL1004	Charon	12	32	55
CL1010	Pegasus	15	30	45
CL1015	Kraken	65	95	165
CL1020	Perseus/Pegasus set	25	40	75
CL1031	Bubo the Owl		not produced	
CL1041	Lair Playset		not produced	

CLASSIC MOVIE MONSTERS (Imperial) 1986

These figures were sold on blister cards or individually with tags around their necks.

		CNP	MIP	MMP
CL2001	Dracula	5	9	12
CL2002	Frankenstein	5	9	12
CL2003	Mummy	5	9	12
CL2004	Wolfman	5	9	12

See also: *Lincoln International Monsters; Mad Monster Series, The; Maxx FX; Mini Monsters; Official World Famous Super Monsters; Real Ghostbusters, The; Universal Monsters*

CNP: Complete, no package, with all weapons and accessories; MIP: Mint in package; MMP: Mint item in Mint package. Values in U.S. dollars. See page 11 for details.

CO1001   CO1002   CO1003   CO1004   CO1005   CO1005   CO1006

CO1006   CO1007   CO1008   CO1010   CO1011   CO1012   CO1012

CO1020   CO1021   CO1022

CO1023   CO1024   CO1504

CLASSIC STAR TREK — See *Star Trek*

CLOSE ENCOUNTERS OF THE THIRD KIND (Imperial) 1978

Imperial manufactured a "bendie" figure of the alien from *Close Encounters of the Third Kind.* Although this is technically not an action figure, it was the best method for reproducing the character, and is of interest to some collectors.

	CNP	MIP	MMP
CL5130 Alien bendie	8	22	32

COLLECCION SUPER AMIGOS — See *Super Powers Collection*

COLORFORMS ALIENS — See *Outer Space Men, The*

COMIC ACTION HEROES (Mego) 1975-78

A series of 3¾" action figures, incorporating Marvel and DC heroes. The figures all have bent knees which are non-articulated. Some figure packages include pictures of other characters in the series.

		CNP	MIP	MMP
CO1001	Aquaman	15	65	135
CO1002	Wonder Woman	12	30	50
CO1003	Shazam	12	45	75
CO1004	Superman	12	35	75
CO1005	Batman	12	45	95
CO1006	Robin	12	40	75
CO1007	The Joker	12	45	80
CO1008	The Penguin	12	45	75
CO1009	The Hulk	12	45	85
CO1010	Green Goblin	15	65	135
CO1011	Spider-Man	12	45	90

| CL5130 | CO1601 | CO2201 | CO2421/CO2422 | CO3021 |

| CO3001 | CO3002 | CO3003 | CO3004 | CO3010 |

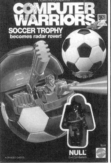

| CO3011 | CO3012 | CO3013 | CO3014 | CO3022 |

CO1012	Captain America	15	65	120
CO1021	Exploding Bridge w/Batmobile		65	150	275
CO1022	The Mangler		75	200	350
CO1023	Collapsing Tower w/Invisible Plane		65	125	225
CO1024	Fortress of Solitude		75	200	275

COMIC HEROINES (Super Queens) (Ideal) 1967
A line similar to Ideal's *Captain Action*, but no connection was promoted. Fully poseable figures were dressed in their super heroine uniforms, but could also wear teenage fashion outfits. Each came in her own comic-art box.

		CNP	MIP	MMP
CO1501	Mera, Queen of Atlantis	600	1250	2500
CO1502	Batgirl	600	1400	4300
CO1503	Wonder Woman	550	1250	2500
CO1504	Supergirl	600	1500	3800

See also: *Comic Action Heroes; DC Comics Super Heroes; Official World's Greatest Super Heroes; Pocket Super Heroes; Super Powers Collection; Wonder Woman*

COMMANDER POWER (Mego) 1975-76
Commander Zack Power came with a motorcycle and "Powerarm." The Powerarm energized the motorcycle for launching.

		CNP	MIP	MMP
CO1601	Commander Power w/ Lightning Cycle	15	30	50

COMMANDO — See *Schwarzenegger Commando*

COMMANDO FORCE (Remco) 1988-89
A revamped version of Remco's *Sgt. Rock* series, sold by Sears. Repainted figures were given new names and weapons.

		CNP	MIP	MMP
CO2201	General Commando	1	2	4
CO2202	Airman Ace	1	2	4
CO2203	Commander Chaos	1	2	4
CO2204	Bombtor	1	2	4
CO2205	Sergeant Stinger	1	2	4
CO2206	Trapper John	1	2	4
CO2207	Ambi-Dextrous	1	2	4
CO2208	Xray Ray	1	2	4
CO2209	Bunker	1	2	4
CO2210	Adamizer	1	2	4
CO2211	Smokescreen	1	2	4
CO2212	Up-Heavel	1	2	4

See also: *Sgt. Rock; U.S. Forces — Defenders of Peace*

COMMANDO RANGER/DEMON RANGER (Concept 2000) c.1987
Another cheap substitute for the popular *G.I. Joe* figures. Figures were sold in 2-packs.

		CNP	MIP	MMP
CO2401	Gunner Bill	1	2	4
CO2402	Trooper Tom	1	2	4
CO2403	Captain John	1	2	4
CO2404	Colonel Jim	1	2	4
CO2405	Sgt. Mike	1	2	4
CO2406	Parachute Pete	1	2	4
CO2407	Major Ed	1	2	4
CO2408	General Len	1	2	4
CO2409	Marine Sam	1	2	4
CO2410	Bazooka Bob	1	2	4
CO2411	Air Force Fred	1	2	4
CO2412	Commando Charlie	1	2	4
CO2421	The Mercenary	1	2	4
CO2422	Mad Dog	1	2	4
CO2423	The Masher	1	2	4
CO2424	The Killer	1	2	4
CO2425	The Terror	1	2	4
CO2426	The Brute	1	2	4

COMPUTER WARRIORS (Mattel) 1989-90
TRON met the *Transformers* in *Computer Warriors*, plastic PC boards and household objects which convert to vehicles and playsets. Each 2" figure came with a gun.

		CNP	MIP	MMP
CO3001	Romm	1	2	4
CO3002	Debugg	1	2	4

CNP: Complete, no package, with all weapons and accessories; MIP: Mint in package; MMP: Mint item in Mint package. Values in U.S. dollars. See page 11 for details.

CO5001	CO5002	CO5005	CO5006	CO5007

CO5201	CO5202	CO5203	CO5204

CO5205	CO5206	CO5207	CO5208

CO3003	Megahert	1	2	4
CO3004	Asynk	1	2	4
CO3010	Minus			
CO3011	Micronn (digital clock)	2	7	10
CO3012	Gridd (Pepsi can)	2	7	10
CO3013	Null (soccer trophy)	2	7	10
CO3014	Dekodar			
CO3021	Book playset	5	12	20
CO3022	Computer w/Chip and Cursor	10	30	40
CO3031	Video tape	1	3	5

CONAN (Remco) 1984

Most of the figures made for the Remco series were of Conan himself. Conan the King and Conan the Warrior were sold individually, while others were planned for playsets.

		CNP	MIP	MMP
CO5001	Conan the King	7	15	35
CO5002	Conan the Warrior	7	15	35
CO5005	Thoth Amon	5	10	20
CO5006	Devourer of Souls	5	10	20
CO5007	Jewel Man	5	10	20

See also: *Official World's Greatest Super Heroes*

CONAN THE ADVENTURER (Hasbro) 1993

This series had a pull-cord mechanism which provided wind-up style action features. The figures had to be larger to accomodate the action features, forcing other shortcuts to be taken. Decoration and articulation suffered as a result. The Greywolf figure was delayed by engineering problems.

		CNP	MIP	MMP
CO5201	Conan the Adventurer	2	7	10
CO5202	Conan the Warrior	2	7	10
CO5203	Zula	2	7	10
CO5204	Wrath-Amon	2	7	10
CO5205	Conan the Explorer	2	7	10
CO5206	Ninja Conan	2	7	10
CO5207	Greywolf	2	7	10

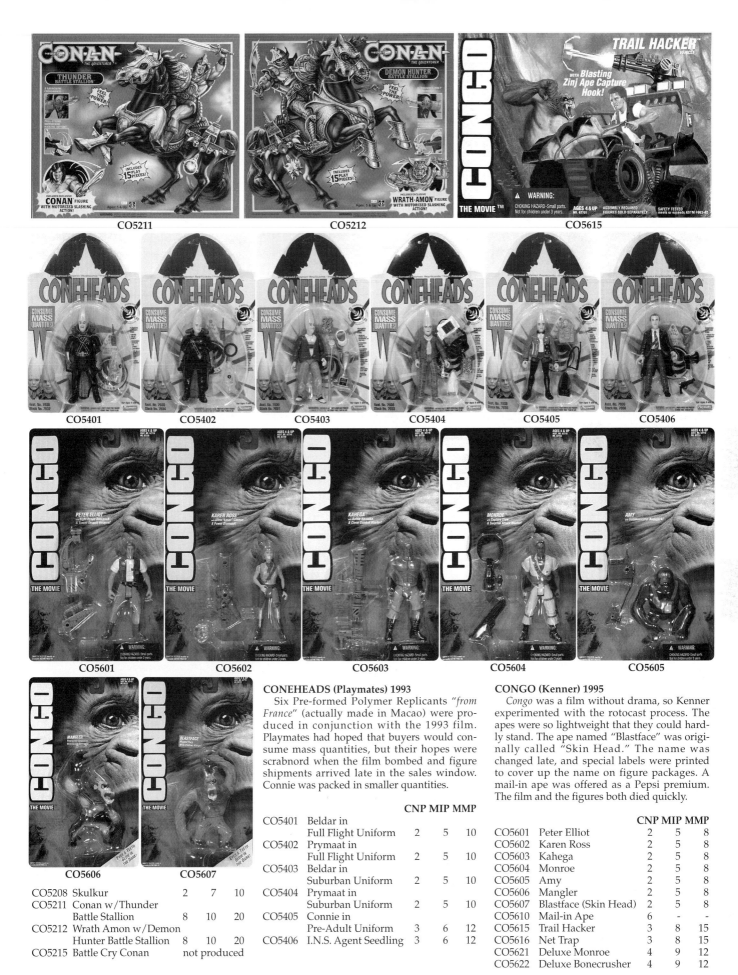

CO5211   CO5212   CO5615

CO5401   CO5402   CO5403   CO5404   CO5405   CO5406

CO5601   CO5602   CO5603   CO5604   CO5605

CO5606   CO5607

CONEHEADS (Playmates) 1993

Six Pre-formed Polymer Replicants *"from France"* (actually made in Macao) were produced in conjunction with the 1993 film. Playmates had hoped that buyers would consume mass quantities, but their hopes were scrabnord when the film bombed and figure shipments arrived late in the sales window. Connie was packed in smaller quantities.

		CNP	MIP	MMP
CO5401	Beldar in			
	Full Flight Uniform	2	5	10
CO5402	Prymaat in			
	Full Flight Uniform	2	5	10
CO5403	Beldar in			
	Suburban Uniform	2	5	10
CO5404	Prymaat in			
	Suburban Uniform	2	5	10
CO5405	Connie in			
	Pre-Adult Uniform	3	6	12
CO5406	I.N.S. Agent Seedling	3	6	12

CONGO (Kenner) 1995

Congo was a film without drama, so Kenner experimented with the rotocast process. The apes were so lightweight that they could hardly stand. The ape named "Blastface" was originally called "Skin Head." The name was changed late, and special labels were printed to cover up the name on figure packages. A mail-in ape was offered as a Pepsi premium. The film and the figures both died quickly.

		CNP	MIP	MMP
CO5601	Peter Elliot	2	5	8
CO5602	Karen Ross	2	5	8
CO5603	Kahega	2	5	8
CO5604	Monroe	2	5	8
CO5605	Amy	2	5	8
CO5606	Mangler	2	5	8
CO5607	Blastface (Skin Head)	2	5	8
CO5610	Mail-in Ape	6	-	-
CO5615	Trail Hacker	3	8	15
CO5616	Net Trap	3	8	15
CO5621	Deluxe Monroe	4	9	12
CO5622	Deluxe Bonecrusher	4	9	12

		CNP	MIP	MMP
CO5208	Skulkur	2	7	10
CO5211	Conan w/Thunder			
	Battle Stallion	8	10	20
CO5212	Wrath Amon w/Demon			
	Hunter Battle Stallion	8	10	20
CO5215	Battle Cry Conan		not produced	

CNP: Complete, no package, with all weapons and accessories; MIP: Mint in package; MMP: Mint item in Mint package. Values in U.S. dollars. See page 11 for details.

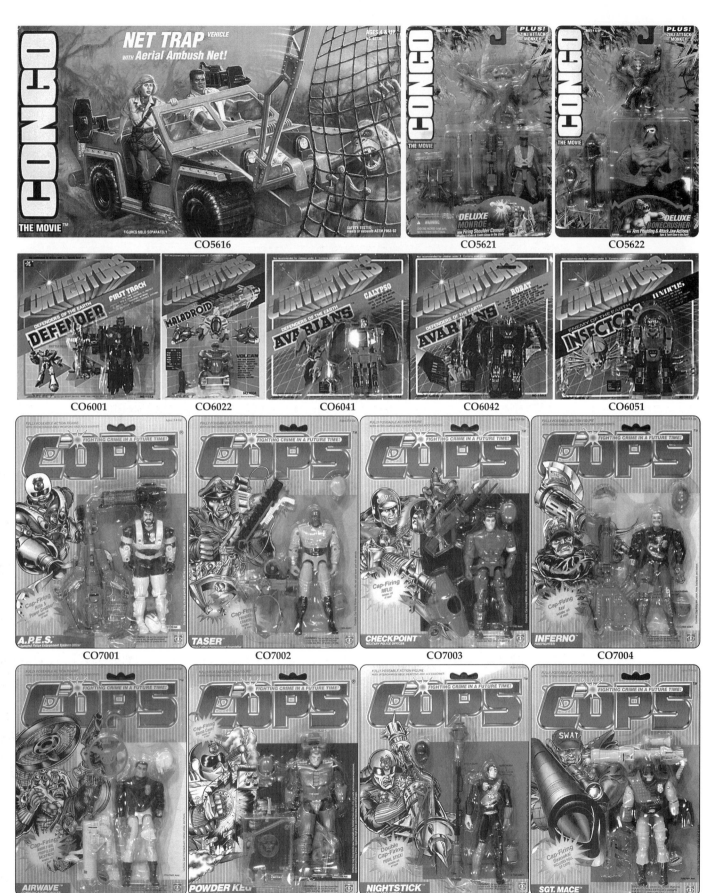

CO5616   CO5621   CO5622

CO6001   CO6022   CO6041   CO6042   CO6051

CO7001   CO7002   CO7003   CO7004

CO7005   CO7006   CO7007   CO7008

CONVERTORS (Select Merchandise) 1984

These were miniature, motorized vehicle-like robots which converted into robot-like vehicles. Another *Transformers* copy cat.

	CNP	MIP	MMP
Defenders			
CO6001 First Track	1	5	8
CO6002 Tanker	1	5	8
Maladroids			
CO6021 Sunyak	1	5	8
CO6022 Volcan	1	5	8

CO6023 Zardak	1	5	8
Avarianss			
CO6041 Calypso	1	5	8
CO6042 Robat	1	5	8
Insectors			
CA6051 Tenticus	1	5	8

| CO7009 | CO7010 | CO7011 | CO7014 |

| CO7021 | CO7022 | CO7023 | CO7024 |

| CO7025 | CO7026 | CO7027 | CO7028 |

COPS ('N CROOKS) (Hasbro) 1988

The Central Organization of Police Specialists (COPS) comprise this Cyberpunk-style series of figures. Each figure came with a cap-firing accessory.

COPS CO7001-14		CNP	MIP	MMP
CO7001	A.P.E.S.	5	10	15
CO7002	Taser	5	10	15
CO7003	Checkpoint	5	10	15
CO7004	Inferno	5	10	15
CO7005	Airwave	5	10	15
CO7006	Powder Keg	5	10	15
CO7007	Nightstick	7	13	18
CO7008	Sgt. Mace	6	12	16
CO7009	Officer Bowzer w/Blitz	6	12	16

CO7010	Bullet-Proof	5	10	15
CO7011	Longarm	6	12	16
CO7012	Barricade	5	10	15
CO7013	Highway	5	10	15
CO7014	Sundown	6	12	20
Crooks CO7021-30				
CO7021	Bullit	5	10	15
CO7022	Koo Koo	5	10	15
CO7023	Nightmare	5	10	15
CO7024	Louie the Plumber	6	14	18
CO7025	Hyena	5	10	15
CO7026	Big Boss	6	12	16
CO7027	Buttons McBoomBoom	6	12	16
CO7028	Berserko	5	10	15
CO7029	Dr. Badvibes	5	10	15
CO7030	Rock Krusher	5	10	15

CO7051	Pursuit Jet	4	8	15
CO7052	Jail Bird Air Speeder	2	5	12
CO7053	Dragster	3	6	15
CO7055	Ironsides Assault Vehicle w/Hardtop	8	12	20
CO7056	Squad Car Highway Interceptor w/Roadblock	8	12	20
CO7057	Roadster w/Turbo Tutone	8	12	20
CO7060	A.T.A.C. w/Heavyweight	8	15	25
CO7070	Lock Up Van	10	18	35
CO7072	Air Raid Cops Helicopter	15	55	75

CORPS!, THE (Lanard Toys) 1986-96

This *G.I. Joe*-style series has been repainted and repackaged in numerous different variations. New variations of the same figures have

DR. BADVIBES
MAD SCIENTIST
CO7029

ROCK KRUSHER
ESCAPED CONVICT
CO7030

PURSUIT JET
CO7051

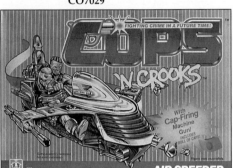

JAIL BIRD AIR SPEEDER
CO7052

DRAGSTER
CO7053

ASSAULT VEHICLE
CO7055

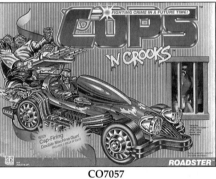

SQUAD CAR HIGHWAY INTERCEPTOR
CO7056

ROADSTER
CO7057

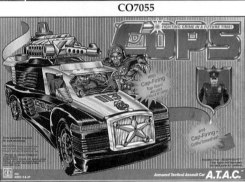

Armored Tactical Assault Car A.T.A.C.
CO7060

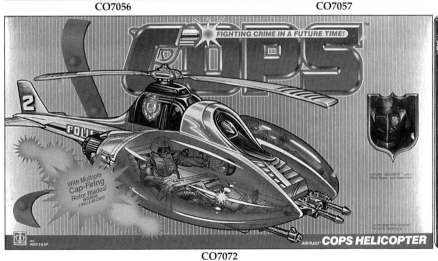

AIR RAID COPS HELICOPTER
CO7072

CO8103   CO8104

CO8111

appeared roughly every 2-4 years since their introduction in 1986. Vehicles were added in 1992, sold on cards with one or nine figures. There was a resurgence of *Corps!* merchandise when Hasbro discontinued 3¾" *G.I. Joes.*

purple 3-packs (c. 1986)	CNP	MIP	MMP
CO8101 Gunner O'Grady/ Whispering Willy/ Hiro Yamata	.50	3	5
CO8102 Large Sarge/John Eagle/Flashfire	.50	3	5

	CNP	MIP	MMP
CO8103 Crowbar/Fox/Bengala	.50	3	5
CO8104 Whipsaw/Jones/Croc	.50	3	5
CO8105 Shark/Tony Tanner/ Dragon Man	.50	3	5
CO8106 Junkyard/Boomerang Billy/Hammer	.50	3	5

CO8115 CO8116 CO8119 CO8120 CO8121

CO8124 CO8128 CO8129 CO8133 CO8134

CO8171 CO8172 CO8173 CO8174 CO8175

CO8185 CO8201 CR2521

yellow cards (1990)											
CO8111	Gunner O'Grady	.50	1	2	CO8118	Fox	.50	1	2	CO8126	Junkyard	.50	1	2
CO8112	Whispering Willy	.50	1	2	CO8119	Bengala	.50	1	2	CO8127	Boomerang Billy	.50	1	2
CO8113	Hiro Yamata	.50	1	2	CO8120	Whipsaw	.50	1	2	CO8128	Hammer	.50	1	2
CO8114	Large Sarge	.50	1	2	CO8121	Jones	.50	1	2	CO8129	Cybor Trooper	.50	1	2
CO8115	John Eagle	.50	1	2	CO8122	Croc	.50	1	2	CO8130	The Gasman	.50	1	2
CO8116	Flashfire	.50	1	2	CO8123	Shark	.50	1	2	CO8131	"Night Laser" Trooper	.50	1	2
CO8117	Crowbar	.50	1	2	CO8124	Tony Tanner	.50	1	2	CO8132	Toxic Waster	.50	1	2
					CO8125	Dragon Man	.50	1	2	CO8133	Artic/Alpine Rescue	.50	1	2

CNP: Complete, no package, with all weapons and accessories; MIP: Mint in package; MMP: Mint item in Mint package. Values in U.S. dollars. See page 11 for details.

CR2501   CR2502   CR2503   CR2504

CR2505   CR2506   CR2511   CR2512

CR2513   CR2514   CR2515   CR2516

CO8134	Chopper	.50	1	2
1992				
CO8141	Two-Packs, ea.	.50	2	4
CO8171	John Eagle w/Armored Wetbike	1	2	4
CO8172	Shark w/Armored Wetbike	1	2	4
CO8173	Whispering Willie w/Chopper Trike	1	2	4
CO8174	Crowbar w/Chopper Trike	1	2	4
CO8175	Chopper w/Pursuit Motorcycle	1	2	4
CO8181	9-pack, type 1	9	18	25
CO8182	9-pack, type 2	9	18	25
CO8183	9-pack, type 3	9	18	25

CO8185	Boxed set (21), type 1	20	30	40
CO8186	Boxed set (21), type 2	20	30	40
CO8191	Tactical Tank	8	16	20
CO8192	Assault boat	8	16	20
1995				
CO8201	Assault vehicle set	8	16	20

See also: *Gung-Ho*

C.O.W. BOYS OF MOO MESA — See *Wild West C.O.W. Boys of Moo Mesa*

CRAIG CUB — See *Official Scout High Adventure*

CRASH DUMMIES — See *Incredible Crash Dummies, The*

CREATURE FROM THE BLACK LAGOON, THE — See *Mini Monsters; Monster Force; Official World Famous Super Monsters; Universal Monsters*

CREEPY CRAWLERS (Toymax) 1994-95

The unique aspect of this line was the ability to make extra accessories using the mold provided with each figure. The *Creepy Crawlers Workshop* oven, a descendant of the "thingmaker," was naturally sold separately, and was never part of the action figure line.

Creepy Crawlers	CNP	MIP	MMP
CR2501 C.C. (Chris Carter)	5	8	12
CR2502 Commantis	5	8	12

| CR9002 | CR9003 | CR9004 | CR9006 | CR9007 |

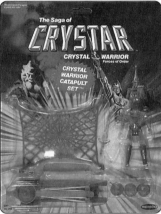
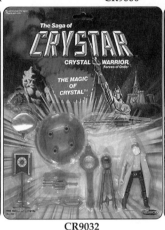

| CR9022 | CR9031 | CR9032 | CR9034 |

CR2503	Hocus Locust	5	8	12
CR2504	Sting Ring	5	8	12
CR2505	T-3 (Tick, Trick, Tick)	5	8	12
CR2506	Volt Jolt	5	8	12
Crime-Grimes				
CR2511	Professor Guggengrime	5	8	12
CR2512	2-Ugly	5	8	12
CR2513	Rumble Bee	5	8	12
CR2514	Shockaroach	5	8	12
CR2515	Spooky Goopy	5	8	12
CR2516	Squirminator	5	8	12
CR2521	Goozooka Vehicle	5	10	15

CRYSTAR (Remco) 1983

This line was sold in conjunction with a Marvel comic book series.

		CNP	**MIP**	**MMP**
CR9001	Crystar	2	5	7
CR9002	Moltar	2	5	7
CR9003	Ogeode	2	5	7
CR9004	Feldspar	2	5	7
CR9005	Warbow	2	5	7
CR9006	Zardeth	2	5	7
CR9007	Magma Man	2	5	7
CR9021	Crystal Dragon w/Dragon Fly	10	15	18
CR9022	Lava Dragon w/Lava DragonWarrior	10	15	18
CR9031	Crystal Warrior Catapult set	10	15	18
CR9032	The Magic of Crystal (includes CR9003)	10	15	18
CR9033	The Spell of the Evil Wizard	10	15	18
CR9034	Crystal Warrior Battle Set	10	15	18
CR9041	Crystal Shatterpult	6	10	12

CR9042	Lava Shatterpult	6	10	12
CR9050	Crystal Castle	10	18	20

CUB SCOUTS — See *Official Scout High Adventure*

CYCLOPS — See *Famous Monsters of Legend; Outer Space Men, The; Power Masters; X-Men*

DAKIN AND DAKIN-STYLE FIGURES (R. Dakin Co.) 1965-77, (I.A. Sutton) 1970-72

R. Dakin and Co. of San Francisco has primarily been a source of fuzzy plush animals and licensed characters. In 1965 they started producing a line of hollow plastic 6" to 9" articulated comic character and advertising figures. The series continued for a little over ten years.

Some figures had cloth costumes or other attachments. They were sold in reclosable bags with plastic handles. Some were also mounted on a variety of plastic bases as award-style greetings called "Goofy Grams."

The special appeal of Dakin figures was the successful capture of each character's personality. The superior sculpting did credit to Dakin, which was one of the few companies to produce Warner Brothers, Disney, and Hanna Barbara characters. As the line changed over the years, selected Disney characters were produced in two sizes. Most advertising figures were one-shot promotions, some only in certain regions, and are therefore rarer.

Dakin's success spawned a number of competitors, most notably I.A. Sutton, who made similar figures and vied for character licenses. The tremendous success of *Star Wars* probably helped to end this popular figure style.

Since Dakin figures do not usually come with separate accessories, only two price categories are used here. Good condition indicates that the figure is complete and reasonably free of wear, though not necessarily in its original package (if any). Mint indicates a perfect specimen with no paint scratches or fading. Mint figures are complete in the original package and/or with all original tags.

See color photos on pages 97-99.

Advertising/Promotional Figures		Good	Mint
DA2001	Big Boy (1974)	125	150
DA2003	Freddy Fast Gas (1976)	65	75
DA2005	Hobo Joe figure w/dog	85	100
DA2007	Li'l Miss Justrite, blonde or brunette (1965)	30	40
DA2011	Miss Liberty Bell (1976)	55	65
DA2013	Quasar Robot	55	65
DA2015	Sambo's mascot, 2 versions	75	100
DA2017	Sambo's Tiger	80	120
DA2019	Smokey Bear (1976)	50	60
DA2021	Woodsy Owl	35	45
Dakin TV Cartoon Theater (boxed, 1976)			
DA2061	Bugs Bunny	20	30
DA2062	Daffy Duck	20	30
DA2063	Wile E. Coyote	10	15
DA2064	Road Runner	12	20
DA2065	Yosemitie Sam	12	20
DA2066	Speedy Gonzales	20	30
DA2067	Tweety Bird	10	15
DA2068	Sylvester	10	15
DA2069	Porky Pig	12	20
DA2070	Elmer Fudd		
DA2071	Dudley Do Right	35	45
DA2072	Rockey the Flying Squirrel	40	55
DA2073	Bullwinkle	45	60

CNP: Complete, no package, with all weapons and accessories; MIP: Mint in package; MMP: Mint item in Mint package. Values in U.S. dollars. See page 11 for details.

| DA2005 | | DA2204 | | DA2241 | | DA2261 |

DA2015

DA7111

DA7112

DA2074	Underdog	50	175
DA2075	Popeye	50	75
DA2076	Olive Oyl	50	75

Disney (1968-72) DA2101-2115

DA2101	Mickey Mouse	15	20
DA2102	Minnie Mouse	15	20
DA2103	Donald Duck, straight legs	20	30
DA2104	Goofy	15	20
DA2105	Pluto	15	20
DA2106	Huey, straight legs	20	30
DA2107	Louie, straight legs	20	30
DA2108	Dewey, straight legs	20	30
DA2111	Pinocchio	15	20
DA2113	Dumbo	15	20
DA2115	Bambi	20	25

Walt Disney Distributing Co.
(manufactured by Dakin, 1972-76) DA2121-30

DA2121	Mickey Mouse	15	20
DA2122	Minnie Mouse	15	20
DA2123	Donald Duck, bent legs	15	20
DA2124	Goofy	15	20
DA2126	Huey, bent legs	8	10
DA2127	Louie, bent legs	8	10
DA2128	Dewey, bent legs	8	10
DA2130	5" Mickey		

Hanna-Barbera (1970-71) DA2141-52

DA2141	Fred Flintstone	20	30
DA2142	Barney Rubble	20	30
DA2143	Dino	50	60
DA2144	Pebbles	20	30
DA2145	Bamm-Bamm	20	30
DA2146	Baby Puss	75	85
DA2147	Hoppy	75	85
DA2148	Yogi Bear	50	60
DA2149	Huckleberry Hound	50	75

DA2150	Snagglepuss	60	125
DA2151	Hokey Wolf	60	125

Popeye DA2201-04 (See also DA2075-76)

DA2201	Popeye (can in L. hand)	60	75
DA2202	Popeye (can in R. hand)	60	75
DA2203	Olive Oyl	35	45
DA2204	Swea' Pea (bean bag body)	20	30
DA2221	Scooby Doo	50	90
DA2222	Scrappy Doo	75	120

Warner Brothers (1968-71, 1976) DA2241-61

DA2241	Bugs Bunny	20	30
DA2242	Bugs Bunny Birthday	20	30
DA2243	Bugs Bunny stars & stripes	20	30
DA2244	Daffy Duck	20	30
DA2245	Porky Pig w/black jacket	20	30
DA2246	Porky Pig w/pink jacket	20	30
DA2247	Sylvester the Cat	20	30
DA2248	Tweety Bird, jointed arms	20	30
DA2249	Tweety Bird, solid arms	20	30
DA2250	Wile E. Coyote	10	15
DA2251	Road Runner	15	20
DA2252	Yosemite Sam	15	20
DA2253	Speedy Gonzales	15	20
DA2254	Elmer Fudd (black jacket)	40	55
DA2255	Elmer Fudd (hunting outfit)	60	75
DA2256	Merlin the Magical Mouse	20	30
DA2257	Second Banana	20	30
DA2258	Cool Cat	35	45
DA2259	Pépé LePew	60	75
DA2260	Foghorn Leghorn	75	85
DA2261	Tasmanian Devil	150	300

Miscellaneous Characters

DA2271	Bozo the Clown (1974)	25	35
DA2273	Deputy Dawg	22	30
DA2275	Mighty Mouse	65	75
DA2277	Stan Laurel	20	35
DA2279	Oliver Hardy	20	35
DA2281	Pink Panther (1971)	15	20

I.A. Sutton
Banana Splits (1970) DA2301-04

DA2301	Fleagle Beagle the Dog	100	150
DA2302	Snorky the Elephant	125	180
DA2303	Drooper the Lion	100	150
DA2304	Bingo the Bear	100	150

DA2310	Casper the Friendly Ghost		
	(I.A. Sutton-1972)	20	40
DA2350	Scooby Doo (1972)	40	80

DARE BROS. (Mego) 1975

The Dare Brothers were two figures that came with a flying glider. The glider was spring-launched, while the figures hung on to the bottom.

		CNP	MIP	MMP
DA5001	Fly Glider set	15	25	40

DARK KNIGHT COLLECTION (Kenner) 1990-91

Kenner was one of several companies which benefited from the merchandise blitz surrounding the 1989 *Batman* film. Since the *Batman* name and logo were already in use on figures being produced by Toy Biz, the Kenner line was named the *Dark Knight Collection.* Even though it was a second line, it was better than other figures available at the time. It also gave Kenner a foot in the door with Warner Brothers, which set the stage for bigger licensing opportunities when *Batman Returns* and other major productions, came along. The *Batman* rights which Kenner eventually acquired as a result ensured the company's position in the action figure market for several years to come. Some of the items listed below were later reproduced as part of Kenner's *Batman Returns* line in 1992.

See color photos on pages 99-100.

		CNP	MIP	MMP
DA7001	Crime Attack Batman	5	10	18
DA7002	Tec-Shield Batman	5	10	20
DA7003	Wall Scaler Batman	5	10	18
DA7004	Sky Escape Joker	5	10	26
DA7005	Bruce Wayne	5	10	16
DA7006	Shadow Wing Batman	5	10	18
DA7007	Iron Winch Batman	5	10	17
DA7110	Batcycle	5	8	15
DA7111	Batcopter	10	20	35
DA7112	Batjet	10	18	38

		CNP	MIP	MMP
DA7113	Batwing	12	22	25
DA7114	Batmobile	10	20	30
DA7115	The Joker Cycle	5	10	18
DA7120	Thunderwhip Batman	10	20	30
DA7121	Powerwing Batman	10	20	30
DA7122	Knock Out Joker	20	50	70
DA7125	Blast Shield Batman	8	20	35
DA7127	Claw Climber Batman	8	18	30
DA7129	Night Glider Batman	8	22	37
DA7141	Strikewing vehicle	3	6	10
DA7142	Bola Bullet	3	6	12

DARKWING DUCK (Playmates) 1991

Based on the Disney cartoon series. Each figure has a unique action feature. Figures of J. Gander Hooter and Chief Agent Gryzlikoff were announced, but were not produced.

See color photos on page 101.

		CNP	MIP	MMP
DA8001	Darkwing Duck	2	5	8
DA8002	Gosalyn	2	5	8
DA8003	Launchpad McQuack	2	5	8
DA8004	Honker Muddlefoot	2	5	8
DA8011	Steelbeak	2	5	8
DA8012	Bushroot	2	5	8
DA8013	Tuskerninni	2	5	8
DA8014	Megavolt	2	5	8
DA8051	Ratcatcher vehicle	3	7	10
DA8052	Thunderquack Jet	8	18	25
DA8061	15" Darkwing Duck	12	20	25

DAVY CROCKETT (Fortune Toy Corp.) 1955, (Mattel) 1993

One of the earliest figures designed for boys was a Davy Crockett doll produced by Fortune Toys in 1955. The figure is a standard doll body with a coonskin cap, leather jerkin, and a plastic rifle. This may be the earliest articulated figure designed with boys in mind.

Mattel later produced a larger figure as part of an ongoing series of 12" Disney Characters.

See color photos on page 101.

		CNP	MIP	MMP
DA8701	Fortune Toys Doll	50	175	250
DA8721	Mattel Figure	8	15	20

See also: *American West Series, The; Legends of the West*

DC COMICS SUPER HEROES (Toy Biz) 1989-90

Each figure in this series has a unique feature. The Penguin originally fired a "safe soft missile," but it wasn't safe or soft enough to bypass federal safety standards. Later figures fired larger missiles or the whole umbrella. Three Batman figures were produced at the same time, but were sold in Batman-specific packaging to take advantage of the 1989 movie (see BA5001-17). The original Flash can be found on two card variations. The first has the regular logo, the second uses the comic book logo. Flash with the Turbo Platform was added to the line in 1991.

See color photos on pages 101-103.

		CNP	MIP	MMP
DC1001	Superman w/Kryptonite ring	10	25	32
DC1002	Lex Luthor	4	12	15
DC1003	Wonder Woman	4	10	12
DC1004	The Penguin, small missile-firing	8	15	28
DC1005	DC1003, large missile-firing	7	12	20
DC1006	DC1003, umbrella-firing	2	9	15
DC1007	The Riddler, w/riddles & clues	5	10	15
DC1008	Mr. Freeze, changes color	5	10	15
DC1010	Robin, karate chop	5	9	12
DC1011	The Flash (reg. card)	5	9	12
DC1012	Green Lantern	9	25	35
DC1013	Aquaman	9	24	30
DC1014	Hawkman	9	23	28
DC1015	Two-Face	9	18	23
DC1021	Flash on Flash card	5	10	14
DC1025	Flash w/Turbo Platform	6	8	12

See also: *Batman; Captain Action; Comic Action Heroes; Comic Heroines; Dark Knight Collection; DC Comics Super Heroes; Die Cast Super Heroes; Official World's Greatest Super Heroes; Pocket Super Heroes; Super Powers Collection; Superman; Wonder Woman*

DEEP SPACE NINE — See *Star Trek*

DEFENDERS, THE (Hasbro) 1976

These figures were issued in 1976 in order to get some use out of leftover *G.I. Joe* accessories and uniforms. Each was a hollow-blown molded figure which moved only at the shoulders, hips, and head. Each blister-carded figure came with a pair of green camouflaged shorts. These items are listed here to help distinguish them from other *G.I. Joe* accessories. Hasbro stock numbers are listed in parenthases where applicable.

See color photos on page 103.

		CNP	MIP	MMP
DE0500	Sniper Patrol	5	15	25
DE0501	Commando Assault	5	15	25
DE0502	Counter Attack	5	15	25
DE0503	Forward Observer	5	15	25
DE0504	Ambush	5	15	25
DE0505	Point Man	5	15	25
DE0510	Command Post (9020)	15	20	30
DE0511	Strong Point (9021)	15	20	40
DE0513	Sea Recovery (9022)	15	20	30
DE0521	Combat Jeep (9030) (similar to GI2603)	30	70	100
DE0522	"Iron Knight" Tank (9031)	60	125	175

See also: *G.I. Joe*

DEFENDERS OF THE EARTH (Galoob) 1986

An unusual combination of King Features Syndicate heroes from the early days of action adventure comprises the *Defenders of the Earth* series. Flash Gordon, The Phantom, and Mandrake the Magician were pitted against Ming the Merciless in anticipation of a TV series. Each figure has a knob on the back which activates a punching action. Gripjaw is a remake of the *Infaceables* Crusher Cruiser from the previous year.

See color photos on pages 103-104.

		CNP	MIP	MMP
DE1001	Flash Gordon	5	15	20
DE1002	The Phantom	5	20	35
DE1003	Mandrake the Magician	5	15	25
DE1004	Ming the Merciless	5	15	25
DE1005	Garax	5	15	20
DE1006	Lothar	5	15	20
DE1011	Claw Copter	8	15	20
DE1012	Phantom Skull Copter	8	15	20
DE1013	Flash Swordship	8	15	20
DE1014	Garax Swordship	8	15	20
DE1021	Mongor Snake vehicle	15	30	35
DE1025	Gripjaw	8	15	20

See also: *Captain Action; Flash Gordon*

DEFINITELY DINOSAURS! (Playskool) 1987-96

A series of jointed plastic dinosaurs, packaged in window or solid boxes. Some window boxes included a caveman figure and a storybook. The cavemen were also sold separately in pairs.

		CNP	MIP	MMP
DE2501	Parasaurolophus	2	8	10
DE2502	Psittacosaurus	2	8	10

CNP: Complete, no package, with all weapons and accessories; MIP: Mint in package; MMP: Mint item in Mint package. Values in U.S. dollars. See page 11 for details.

DE2502: original window box and later solid box. DE2503

DE2504 DE2506 DE2508

DE2509   DE2512   DE2513

DE2515   DE2516   DE2517

DE2521   DE2522   DE2523   DE2524   DE2525

DE5001   DE5002   DE5003   DE5004

DE2503	Anatosaurus w/Zorg	3	10	12
DE2504	Polacanthus	2	8	10
DE2505	Spinosaurus	2	8	10
DE2506	Dimetrodon	2	8	10
DE2507	Ultrasaurus	2	8	10
DE2508	Moschops w/Shindar	3	10	12
DE2509	Tyrannosaurus w/Lexa	5	15	20
DE2510	Struthiomimus w/Grak	3	10	12
DE2511	Ankylosaurus	2	8	10

DE2512	Protoceratops w/Zindar	3	10	12
DE2513	Deinonychus w/Druze	3	10	12
DE2514	Apatosaurus		2	8	10
DE2515	Stegosaurus w/Dron	3	10	12
DE2516	Triceratops		4	12	18
DE2517	Pachycephalosaurus w/Reeve	3	10	12
DE2521	Shonar/Erg	2	5	6
DE2522	Korex/Poldar	2	5	6

DE2523	Nazaar/Zolox	2	5	6
DE2524	Lomex/Shrag	2	5	6
DE2525	Fleb/Trozar	2	5	6

DEMOLITION MAN (Mattel) 1993
    Figures based on the 1993 Stallone movie.
Two different card backs show all eight figures.
Both film and toys were unremarkable.
See page 100 for listings.

DA2001 DA2271 DA2003 DA2007 DA2011 DA2021

DA2061 DA2062 DA2063 DA2064 DA2066 DA2067 DA2068

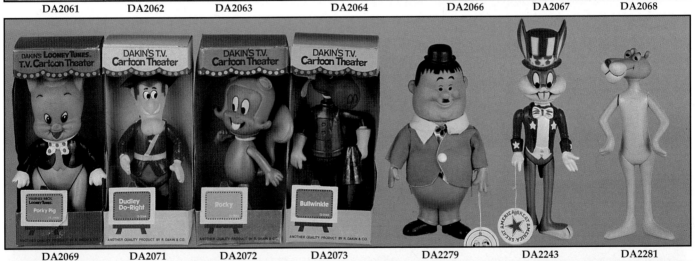

DA2069 DA2071 DA2072 DA2073 DA2279 DA2243 DA2281

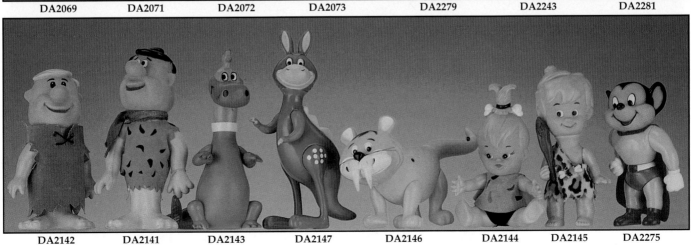

DA2142 DA2141 DA2143 DA2147 DA2146 DA2144 DA2145 DA2275

CNP: Complete, no package, with all weapons and accessories; MIP: Mint in package; MMP: Mint item in Mint package. Values in U.S. dollars. See page 11 for details.

DA2101 DA2102 DA2121 DA2122 DA2103 ◄DA2104 DA2124

DA2105 DA2106 DA2107 DA2126 DA2127 DA2128 DA2113 DA2115 DA2111 DA2130

DA2148 DA2149 DA2150 DA2273 DA2350 DA2301 DA2304 DA2302 DA2303

DA2202 DA2201 DA2203 DA2076 DA2075 DA2019

DA2241	DA2260	DA2258	DA2245	DA2246	DA2259	DA2250	DA2251

DA2247	DA2249	DA2252	DA2254	DA2070	DA2255	DA2253	DA2256	DA2257

DI6101	DI6102	DI6103	DI6105	DI6104	DI6110	DI6106	DI6109	DI6107	DI6120

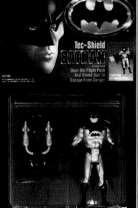

DA7001	DA7002	DA7003	DA7004	DA7005

| DA7006 | DA7007 | DA7120 | DA7121 | DA7122 |

| DA7110 | DA7114 | DA7115 |

| DA7125 | DA7127 | DA7129 |

| DA7113 | DA7141 | DA7142 |

		CNP	MIP	MMP										
DE5001	Battle Baton Spartan	2	4	5	DE5004	Blast Attack Pheonix	2	4	5	DE5008	Battle Hook Friendly	2	4	5
DE5002	Kick-Fighting Spartan	2	4	5	DE5005	Cryo-Claw Tech	2	4	5	DE5011	Bolajet	3	5	15
DE5003	Flame-Throwing Pheonix	2	4	5	DE5006	Bazooka Attack Spartan	2	4	5	DE5012	Fast Blast 442	10	20	30
					DE5007	Combat Cannon Spartan	2	4	5		*See photos on pages 96 and 105.*			

DA8001   DA8002   DA8003   DA8004

DA8011   DA8012   DA8013   DA8014

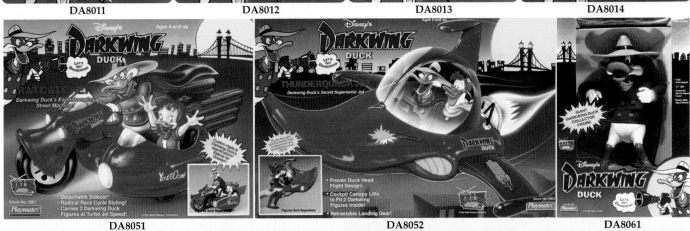

DA8051   DA8052   DA8061

DA8701   DA8721   Penguin missile variations: DC1004, DC1005, and DC1006

DC1001

DC1002

DC1003

DC1004

DC1005

DC1006

DC1007

DC1008

DC1010

DC1011

DC1021

DC1025

DEMON RANGER — See *Commando Ranger*

DEPT. OF DEFENSE (Fishel) 1987

Military figures in dress uniforms.

		CNP	MIP	MMP
DE7001	Marine Seargent	1	3	5
DE7002	Marine Blues	1	3	5
DE7003	Navy Dress Whites	1	3	5
DE7004	Army Dress Greens	1	3	5
DE7005	Air Force Officer w/jacket	1	3	5
DE7006	Air Force Officer w/o jacket	1	3	5

DERRY DARING (Ideal) 1975

The popularity of *Evel Knievel* prompted similar merchandise for girls. *Derry Daring* was the result. Her stunt vehicles were powered by the same gyro-crank mechanism used for the *Evel* toys.

See color photos on page 104.

		CNP	MIP	MMP
DE8001	Western Set	5	15	20
DE8002	Action Reporter	5	15	20
DE8003	Racing Set	5	15	20
DE8004	Mountain Climbing Set	5	15	20
DE8011	Trick Cycle w/figure	7	20	25
DE8012	Wheelie Car w/figure	7	20	25
DE8013	Baja Camper	10	24	28

See also: *Evel Knievel*

DESERT DOGS (Mel Appel) 1991

One of many generic military figure lines inspired by Desert Storm. Figures incorporated sound effects chips.

	CNP	MIP	MMP
DE9001-4 Desert Dogs, ea	1	3	5

DESERT PATROL (Remco) 1991

Another cheap military figure series by Remco, made from the same molds used to create *American Defense, U.S. Forces Defenders of Peace, U.S. Military,* and *Desert Storm.* As usual, the various parts have been assembled in new combinations with a new paint job. "Major Oil Spill" is listed on the back of the card as "Major Reckoning".

DC1012

DC1013

DC1014

DC1015

DE0500-05

DE0510

DE0511

DE0513

DE0521

DE0522

DE1001

DE1002

DE1003

DE1004

DE1005

	CNP	MIP	MMP
DE9011 Sgt. Sand Blaster	1	2	4
DE9012 Major Oil Spill (Major Reckoning)	1	2	4
DE9013 Radar Tech	1	2	4
DE9014 Dead Blow	1	2	4
DE9015 Colonel Striker	1	2	4
DE9016 Black Thunder	1	2	4

DESERT SHIELD (Diversified Specialists Inc.) 1990

Hastily-produced military figures intended to capitalize on the Persian Gulf conflict. They have no names or personality.

	CNP	MIP	MMP
DE9121-32 Desert Shield figures, 12 diff., ea	1	4	5

DESERT STORM (Remco) 1991

Old Remco molds never die, they just get reassembled with new paint jobs. *Desert Storm* featured existing figures painted in desert camo. Each came with a plastic vehicle which was too small for the figure.

	CNP	MIP	MMP
DE9141 Major Metal	2	4	5
DE9142 Captain Combat	2	4	5

CNP: Complete, no package, with all weapons and accessories; MIP: Mint in package; MMP: Mint item in Mint package. Values in U.S. dollars. See page 11 for details.

DE1006

DE1011

DE1012

DE1025

DE1013

DE1014

DE1021

DE8001   DE8002   DE8003   DE8004

DE8002

DE8011

DE8012

DE8013

DI3001

DI3002

DI3003

DI3004

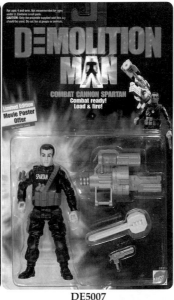

DE5005   DE5006   DE5007   DE5008

DE5011   DE5012

DE7002   DE9001   DE9011   DE9121   DE9142

DICK TRACY (Playmates) 1990

This series appeared shortly before the 1990 *Dick Tracy* film. Each figure was blister-packed with plastic accessories. Cartoons and file card statistics were printed on the back. The figures were produced in massive quantities, only to sit on the shelves when the film failed to meet the expectations of its publicity. The Blank was sold exclusively in Canada. It was initially withheld because the mask (attached to the hat) is removeable, revealing Madonna...and the surprise ending of the film. By the time the figure was cleared, *Dick Tracy* merchandise had died. The figure would never have been released but for a Sears Canada contract which had to be fulfilled up to Christmas '90. Dealers bought up as many as they could find, slowly filtering them into the U.S.

DI1001	Dick Tracy	4	8	12
DI1002	Sam Catchem	5	9	15
DI1003	Al "Big Boy" Caprice	5	9	15
DI1004	The Brow	6	10	18
DI1005	The Tramp	6	10	18
DI1007	Lips Manlis	5	9	15
DI1008	Flattop	6	10	18
DI1009	The Rodent	5	9	15
DI1010	Pruneface	6	10	18
DI1011	Shoulders	5	9	15
DI1012	Influence	5	9	15
DI1013	Mumbles	6	11	19
DI1014	Itchy	6	11	19
DI1015	The Blank	50	150	200
DI1021	Police Squad Car	15	25	50
DI1022	Big Boy's Getaway Car	15	25	50
DI1051	19" Dick Tracy	15	40	60
DI1052	19" Breathless Mahoney	15	40	60

DIE-CAST SUPER HEROES (Mego) 1979

Mego ruled the '70s with Super Heroes, film, and TV-related action figures. It was the company's 25th Anniversary year in 1979. *Micronauts* proved to be a bonanza license in previous years, and Mego was attempting a major expansion into other toy categories. The *Die-Cast Super Heroes* were one of the lean new ideas presented by the decade's dominant action figure producer. It was a bad year to branch out into so many new areas and neglect action figures. *Star Wars* took over the market, and Mego was out of the toy business before it could celebrate its 30th year.

These limited edition die-cast metal super heroes were an oddball product, limited to the number Mego could sell for one-time distribution. The exact number seems to have been

CNP: Complete, no package, with all weapons and accessories; MIP: Mint in package; MMP: Mint item in Mint package. Values in U.S. dollars. See page 11 for details.

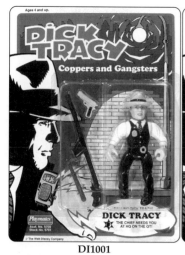
DI1001

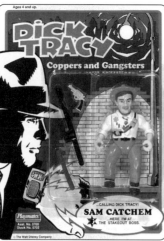
DI1002

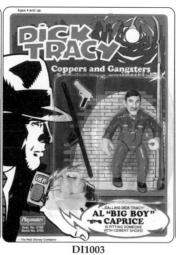
DI1003

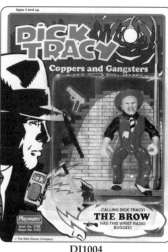
DI1004

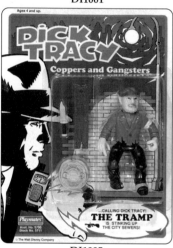
DI1005

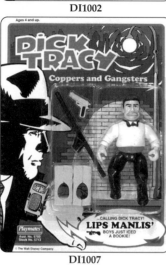
DI1007

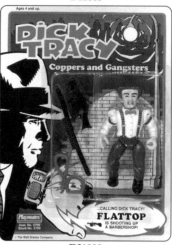
DI1008

DI1009

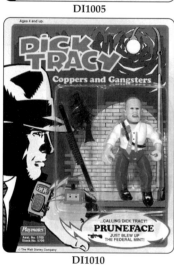
DI1010

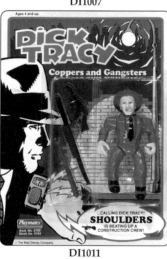
DI1011

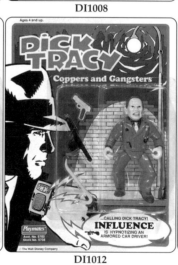
DI1012

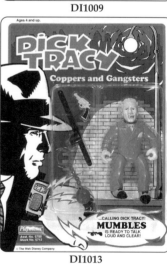
DI1013

DI1021

DI1022

DI1051   DI1052

106

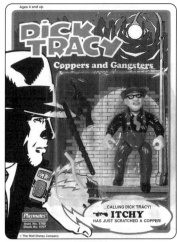

DI1014

DI1015

DI1015 unmasked

DI5002

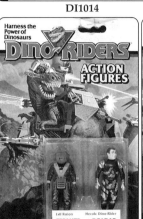

DI5005

DI5006

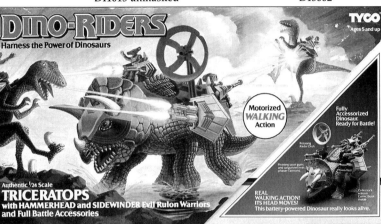

DI5022

DI5051   DI5062   DI5063

DI5087

lost, but the four 5½" figures are fairly difficult to find. For the record, the heads are plastic, and other costume parts are cloth. The articulation and posability are good, and metal is a super medium to show off detail. The packaging is a combination window box and card. Because of the popularity of *Star Wars*, this series was perhaps even more limited than Mego intended.

	CNP	MIP	MMP
DI3001 Spider-Man	20	65	150
DI3002 Batman	25	80	165
DI3003 Hulk	20	50	110
DI3004 Superman	20	55	125

DINO-RIDERS (TYCO) 1987-90

This unusual action figure series combined dinosaurs with science-fiction weaponry. The regular series dinosaurs each came with one or more 2½" figures, and six others were sold indi-

vidually. Most Dino-Riders figures came packaged two per card.

	CNP	MIP	MMP
Dino-Riders Figures, on cards DI5001-08			
DI5001 Questar/Krulos	2	4	8
DI5002 Mind-Zei/Fire	2	4	8
DI5003 Proto/Rattler	2	4	8
DI5004 Orion/Six-Gill	2	4	8
DI5005 Boldar/Termite	2	4	8
DI5006 Nova/Demon	2	4	8
DI5007 Mercury/Fang	2	4	8
DI5008 Quark/Finn	2	4	8
Second Run Figures, on cards DI5011-18			
DI5011 Questar/Krulos	3	5	9
DI5012 Mind-Zei/Sludj	3	5	9
DI5013 Serena/Skwirmv	3	5	9
DI5014 Yungstar/Dedeye	3	5	9
DI5015 Hondo/Drone	3	5	9
DI5016 Graff/Kraw	3	5	9
DI5017 Neutrino/Poxx	3	5	9

		CNP	MIP	MMP
DI5018	Ursus/Snarrl	3	5	9
DI5021	Tyrannosaurus-Rex w/ Krulos/Bitor/Cobrus	10	18	25
DI5022	Triceratops with Hammerhead and Sidewinder	10	18	25
DI5023	Deinonychus w/Antor and Rulon Dinosaur Trap	7	12	15
DI5024	Diplodocus w/Questar, Mind-Zei and Aries	9	16	19
DI5025	Pteranodon w/Rasp & Rulon Dinosaur Trap	7	12	15
DI5026	Monoclonius w/Mako & Rulon Dinosaur Trap	5	10	12
DI5027	Pterodactyl w/Llahd	5	10	12
DI5028	Ankylosaurus w/Sting	5	10	12
DI5029	Torosaurus w/Gunner and Magnus	6	11	14
DI5030	Deinonychus w/Sky	5	10	12

CNP: Complete, no package, with all weapons and accessories; MIP: Mint in package; MMP: Mint item in Mint package. Values in U.S. dollars. See page 11 for details.

DI5501   DI5502   DI5503   DI5504   DI5505   DI5506

DI6061   DI6062   DI6063   DI6064

DI6065   DI6066   DI6067   DI6068

DI6069   DI6070   DI6071   DI6072

DI6081

DI6082

DI6083

DI6084

DI6085

DI6086

DI5031	Quetzalcoatlus			
	w/Youngstar	6	11	14
DI5032	Styracosaurus w/Turret	6	11	14
DI5033	Brontosaurus w/Ikon,			
	Vekto, Serena, Ayce	15	20	30
DI5034	Edmontonia w/Axis	6	11	14
DI5035	Stegosaurus w/Vega			
	and Tark	9	12	15
DI5036	Pachycephalosaurus			
	w/Togg	6	11	14
DI5037	Struthiomimus			
	w/Nimbus	6	11	14
DI5038	Dimetrodon w/Shado	5	10	12
DI5039	Protoceratops w/Kanon	6	11	14
DI5040	Saurolophus w/Lokus	6	11	14
DI5041	Kentrousaurus w/Krok	6	11	14
DI5042	Placerias w/Skate	6	11	14
Dino-Riders Commandos DI5051-56				
DI5051	Astra	2	7	12
DI5052	Bomba	2	7	12
DI5053	Rok	2	7	12
DI5054	Kameelian	2	7	12
DI5055	Faze	2	7	12
DI5056	Glyde	2	7	12
Ice Age figures, on cards DI5061-66				
DI5061	Onk and Buzz	3	8	15
DI5062	Tor and Gorr	3	8	15
DI5063	Urg and Rayy	3	8	15
DI5064	Agga and Gill	3	8	15
DI5065	Wizz and Gutz	3	8	15
DI5066	Ecco and Squish	3	8	15
DI5085	Wooly Mammoth			
	w/Grom	10	18	25
DI5086	Killer Wart Hog			
	w/figure	4	10	15
DI5087	Sabre Tooth Tiger			
	w/Kub	4	10	15
DI5088	Giant Ground Sloth			
	w/figure	4	10	15

See also: *Cadillacs and Dinosaurs*

DINOSAURS (Hasbro) 1991-93

This was one of several Hasbro lines which attempted to produce figures with minimal articulation for younger children. Each figures was articulated only at the waist, and came with two accessories.

		CNP	MIP	MMP
DI5501	Baby Sinclair	1	5	7
DI5502	Charlene Sinclair	1	5	7
DI5503	Robbie Sinclair	1	5	7
DI5504	Earl Sinclair	1	5	7
DI5505	Fran Sinclair	1	5	7
DI5506	B.P. Richfield	1	5	7

DISNEY (R. Dakin Co.) 1968-72, (Remco) 1977, (Mattel/Arco) 1989-90, (Walt Disney Co.) 1990

The Disney characters have been produced as action figures numerous times. The Dakins are the rarest. Figures of Mickey, Minnie, and Donald are usually the easiest to find, with other characters being less common. Clarabelle Cow was the holdout figure for the Mattel series. A series of jointed plastic and vinyl figures were made exclusively for the theme parks by an unknown manufacturer.

See additional color photos on page 99.

		CNP	MIP	MMP
Dakin — See DA2101-2115				
Remco Character Activity Sets DI6021-30				
DI6021	Mickey Mouse			
	w/Tool Box	10	15	25
DI6022	Minnie Mouse w/Swing	10	15	25
DI6023	Donald's Fishing Game	10	15	25
DI6024	Mickey Mouse			
	w/Picnic Lunch	10	15	25
DI6030	Fun Car	10	20	30
Mattel/Arco DI6061-72				
DI6061	Fireman Mickey	3	6	8
DI6062	Cowboy Donald	1	4	5
DI6063	Clarabelle Cow	3	6	8
DI6064	Astronaut Mickey	1	3	4
DI6065	Farmer Donald	3	6	8
DI6066	Scrooge McDuck	3	6	8
DI6067	Pirate Mickey	1	3	4
DI6068	Rock Star Minnie	4	8	12
DI6069	Fireman Donald	1	3	4
DI6070	Fun Time Mickey	1	3	4
DI6071	Carpenter Goofy	2	5	7
DI6072	Pluto	3	6	8
DI6081	Goofy's Dune Buggy	2	5	10
DI6082	Mickey's '57 Chevy	2	5	10
DI6083	Donald's Speed Boat	2	5	10
DI6084	Wild West Goofy	2	5	10
DI6085	Mickey's Safari			
	Adventure	2	5	10
DI6086	Dinosaur Donald	3	7	12
Theme Park Figures DI6101-20				
DI6101	Mickey	8	-	-
DI6102	Minnie	8	-	-
DI6103	Donald	8	-	-
DI6104	Goofy	8	-	-

DI6023   DI6024

DI6105	Pluto	8	-	-
DI6106	Pooh	8	-	-
DI6107	Tigger	8	-	-
DI6109	Tigger, yellow			
DI6110	Pinocchio	8	-	-
DI6120	2½" Mickey (c. 1970)	10	-	-

See also: *Aladdin; Beauty and the Beast: Bedknobs & Broomsticks; Black Hole, The; Dakin and Dakin-Style Figures; Dick Tracy; Dinosaurs; Disney Clubhouse Collection; Gargoyles; Hollywood Mickey; Lion King, The; Little Mermaid, The; Mickey and Friends; Mickey Mouse; Peter Pan; Pirates of the Carribean; Pocahontas; Pooh and Friends; Santa Mickey; Tim Burton's Nightmare Before Christmas; Toy Story; TRON; Walt Disney Characters on Safari; Walt Disney Golden Fantasy; Who Framed Roger Rabbit?; Wuzzles*

DISNEY CLUBHOUSE COLLECTION (Applause) 1987

Clubhouse Collection figures were sold at the Disney theme parks.

		CNP	MIP	MMP
DI6501	Mickey	5	8	15
DI6502	Minnie	5	8	15
DI6503	Donald	5	8	15
DI6504	Daisy	5	8	15
DI6505	Goofy	5	8	15
DI6506	Pluto	5	8	15

DOCTOR DOLITTLE (Mattel) 1967

The Doctor Dolittle figure is a bendie, but with a moveable head. A fuzzy Polynesia the Parrot with feathers was sewn to his right arm.

DO1001	Doctor Dolittle	20	45	65

CNP: Complete, no package, with all weapons and accessories; MIP: Mint in package; MMP: Mint item in Mint package. Values in U.S. dollars. See page 11 for details.

| DI6501 | DI6502 | DI6503 | DI6504 | DI6505 | DI6506 | DO1001 |

| DO2001 | DO2002 | DO2004 | DO2006 |

DO2007

DO3008

DO3005

DO3002

DO3011

DO3031   DO3047

DOCTOR WHO (Denys Fisher Toys) 1976, (Dapol) 1988-95

Doctor Who was the longest-running science fiction television show ever produced. The British Broadcasting Corporation (BBC) first aired it as a children's show in November 1963. The show ran for 26 seasons, until it was put on hold indefinitely in early 1990. Although the show's main character has been played by seven different actors, only two were ever produced as action figures: Tom Baker (the fourth Doctor) and Sylvester McCoy (the seventh).

The original *Dr. Who* series was manufactured by the Mego Corporation and marketed in Britain through Denys Fisher Toys and Palitoy. Mego re-used the Superman body, with a new head and costume to create the Doctor figure. The standard Mego "exchange

chamber" (used in the *Star Trek* and *Wizard of Oz* playsets) was used for the Tardis accessory. K-9 was added late in the line, possibly in conjunction with the character's first appearance on the show in 1977. A number of these British items have made their way overseas.

The Dapol series began in conjunction with the show's 25th anniversary, and was sold in the United States thorough comic stores. Early Davros figures were produced with a left hand, a production error which was replaced with a modified figure. Daleks were molded in every color which appeared in the series.

Dapol's offices and factory were destroyed in a fire on January 30, 1995. Some of the molds for additional *Doctor Who* products were reportedly saved, but production was delayed as a result. Previously announced 3¾" versions

of the Tom Baker Doctor, Silurian, Sea Devil, the Master, plus two 12" figures were among the potential products which had not yet been produced prior to the fire.

Denys Fisher Toys	CNP	MIP	MMP
DO2001 Doctor Who	100	160	200
DO2002 Leela	100	175	225
DO2003 Dalek	100	150	250
DO2004 Giant Robot	125	200	275
DO2005 Cyberman	150	200	300
DO2006 Tardis	175	275	400
DO2007 K-9	150	200	300
Dapol DO3001-3202			
DO3001 The 7th Doctor, brown coat	7	10	15
DO3002 The 7th Doctor, grey coat (came w/DO2080)	10	-	-

| DO3015 | DO3017 | DO3019 | DO3025 |

| DO3100 | DO9001 | DO9002 |

| DO9003 | DO9004 | DO9005 | DO9006 | DO9007 |

DO3005	Mel, blue shirt	7	10	15
DO3006	Mel, pink shirt (came w/DO3100)	10	-	-
DO3008	K-9, grey	5	9	13
DO3009	K-9, green (came w/ DO3100)	10	-	-
DO3011	The 4th Doctor	not determined		
DO3015	Tetrap	7	10	15
DO3017	Cyberman	7	10	15
DO3019	Ice Warrior	7	10	15
DO3025	Ace	7	10	15
DO3030	Davros w/left hand	7	10	15
DO3031	Davros w/o left hand	5	9	13
Daleks DO3040-47				
DO3040	white w/gold spots	15	30	35
DO3041	red w/black spots	15	30	35
DO3042	red w/gold spots	15	30	35

DO3043	red w/silver spots	15	30	35
DO3044	black w/gold spots	15	30	35
DO3045	black w/silver spots	15	30	35
DO3046	grey w/black spots	15	30	35
DO3047	grey w/blue spots	15	30	35
DO3090	Tardis	10	25	30
DO3100	25th Anniversary Commemorative Set	-	120	150
DO3104	Gift Set	-	100	125
DO3110	Dalek Army Set	-	100	125

DOONESBURY — See *Action Figure! — The Life and Times of Doonesbury's Uncle Duke*

DOUBLE DRAGON (TYCO) 1993

This line was based on a popular video game. It was also intended as a movie tie-in, but the film was so bad that it went straight to video after a very short theatrical release. The toys shared a similar fate, showing up on closeout racks shortly after their debut.

		CNP	MIP	MMP
DO9001	Billy Lee	1	4	6
DO9002	Jimmy Lee	1	4	6
DO9003	Vortex	1	4	6
DO9004	Blaster	1	4	6
DO9005	Shadow Master	1	4	6
DO9006	Sickle	1	4	6
DO9007	Trigger Happy	1	4	6
DO9011	Cycle	3	6	9
DO9012	Cruiser	5	10	17
DO9013	Shadow Raven	5	10	17

CNP: Complete, no package, with all weapons and accessories; MIP: Mint in package; MMP: Mint item in Mint package. Values in U.S. dollars. See page 11 for details.

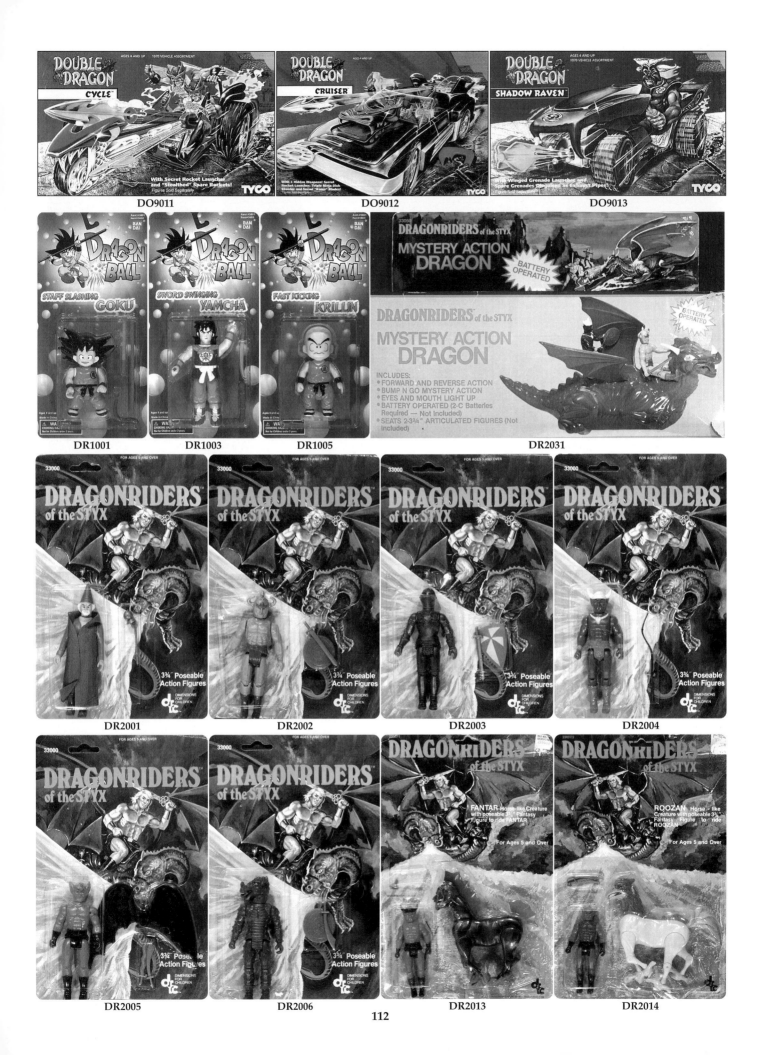

DO9011

DO9012

DO9013

DR1001

DR1003

DR1005

DR2031

DR2001

DR2002

DR2003

DR2004

DR2005

DR2006

DR2013

DR2014

DR2021

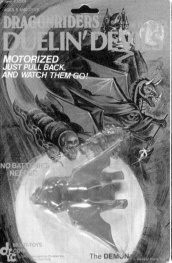

DR2022

DR2023

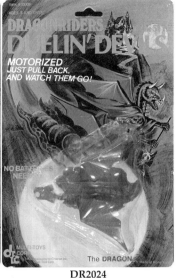

DR2024

DR2010

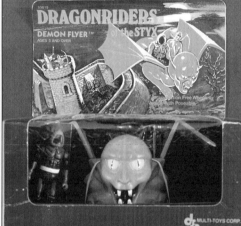

DR2012

DU4002

DU4003

DU4010

DU4011

DU4014

DU4020

DRACULA — See *Classic Movie Monsters; Lincoln International Monsters; Mad Monster Series, The; Maxx FX; Mini Monsters; Monster Force; Official World Famous Super Monsters; Real Ghostbusters, The; Universal Monsters*

DRAGON BALL (Bandai) 1995-96
Figures based on the video game.

	CNP	MIP	MMP
DR1001 Staff Slashing Goku	1	4	6
DR1003 Sword Swinging Yamcha	1	4	6
DR1005 Fast Kicking Krillin	1	4	6

DRAGONRIDERS OF THE STYX (DFC) 1984
A cheaply-made line of 3¾" fantasy figures.

	CNP	MIP	MMP
DR2001 The Wizard	3	5	10
DR2002 Ragnar the Warrior	3	5	10
DR2003 The Black Knight	5	10	12
DR2004 Guliz The Ogre	3	5	10
DR2005 The Demon Warrior	3	5	10

DR2006 Dragon Man	3	5	10
DR2010 Serpent Rider	7	10	18
DR2011 Skull Sled	7	10	18
DR2012 Demon Flyer	7	10	18
DR2013 Fantar	5	10	15
DR2014 Roozan	5	10	15
Duelin' Devils DR2021-24			
DR2021 The Skull	4	7	15
DR2022 The Demon	4	7	15
DR2023 The Spectre	4	7	15
DR2024 The Dragon	4	7	15
DR2031 Mystery Action Dragon	8	18	22

DROIDS — See *Star Wars*

DUKE/RUN JOE RUN (Kenner) 1974-75
Duke and Run Joe Run were German Shepherd dog figures with articulated mouths, legs, tails and heads.

	CNP	MIP	MMP
DU4001 Duke	15	20	40
DU4002 Duke w/Canyon slide	18	25	48

DU5001	DU5005	DU5002	DU5006

DU4003 Run Joe Run	25	30	50
DU4010 Rescue Unit	3	12	16
DU4011 DU4010 w/DU4001	18	32	56
DU4014 Action Firefighter	3	8	12
DU4020 H.Q. playset	8	18	30

DUKES OF HAZZARD (Mego) 1981
Figures based on the TV show were made in two sizes. The Coy and Vance figures were released later when Bo and Luke were temporarily replaced on the show. The cards for the figures still read "Bo" and "Luke," but the faces were Coy and Vance.

CNP: Complete, no package, with all weapons and accessories; MIP: Mint in package; MMP: Mint item in Mint package. Values in U.S. dollars. See page 11 for details.

| DU5001 | DU5002 | DU5003 | DU5004 | DU5005 | DU5006 |

| DU5010 | DU5011 | DU5012 | DU5013 | DU5014 |

| DU5015 | DU5016 | DU5017 | DU5018 | DU5020 |

DU5031

DU5032

DU5033

| DU5012 | DU5020 | DU5012 | DU5013 |

8" figures		CNP	MIP	MMP
DU5001	Bo	10	20	40
DU5002	Luke	10	20	40
DU5003	Daisy	12	40	65
DU5004	Boss Hogg	10	25	50
DU5005	Coy ("Bo" card)	10	25	45
DU5006	Vance ("Luke" card)	10	25	45
3¾" figures and accessories				
DU5010	Bo	5	10	18
DU5011	Luke	5	10	18
DU5012	Daisy, original face	7	10	20
DU5013	Daisy, revised face	8	12	25

DU5014	Boss Hogg	7	14	18
DU5015	Rosco	8	12	28
DU5016	Cooter	8	15	30
DU5017	Uncle Jesse	8	15	30
DU5018	Cletus	8	15	30
DU5019	Coy ("Bo" card)	4	10	15
DU5020	Vance ("Luke" card)	4	10	15
DU5031	General Lee car w/DU5011-12	15	30	65
DU5032	Daisy Jeep w/DU5013	10	25	45
DU5033	Boss Hogg caddy w/DU5014	75	175	250

DUNE (LJN) 1984

Dune figures were inspired by the 1984 film adaptation of Frank Herbert's science-fiction classic. Rock star Sting played the character of Feyd in the film, and this figure is sometimes priced higher. The Sardaukar Warrior is tough to find, but the other five are fairly common.

Eight figures were originally planned — the extras being Lady Jessica and Gurney Halleck — which were produced at the prototype stage. One can only speculate what the value of a Gurney Halleck figure would have been today...the role was played by Patrick Stewart of later *Star Trek* fame. Prototypes were also made for a Harkonnen Thopter vehicle.

Action figures DU8300-05		CNP	MIP	MMP
DU8300	Paul Atreides	10	16	25
DU8301	Stilgar the Fremen	8	12	22
DU8302	Baron Harkonnen	10	18	35
DU8303	Feyd	8	12	25
DU8304	Rabban	12	18	25
DU8305	Sardaukar Warrior	15	25	35
DU8310	Spice Scout	12	20	40
DU8330	Sandworm	15	28	38

| DU8300 | DU8301 | DU8302 | DU8303 | DU8304 |

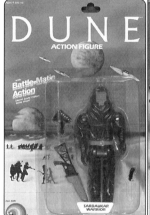

| DU8305 | DU83010 | DU8330 |

| EA2001 | EA2002 | EA2004 | EA2005 | EA2006 |

| EA2021 | EA2022 | EA2023 |

EAGLE FORCE (Mego) 1981

A series of 2½" die-cast metal military figures.

	CNP	MIP	MMP
EA2001 Captain Eagle	2	4	6
EA2002 Stryker	2	4	6
EA2003 Redwing	2	4	6
EA2004 Kayo	2	4	6
EA2005 The Cat	2	4	6
EA2006 Wild Bill	2	3	5
EA2007 Goldie Hawk	2	4	6
EA2008 Nemesis	2	4	6
EA2009 Sgt. Brown	2	4	6
EA2010 General Mamba	2	4	6
EA2011 Baron Von Chill	2	4	6

CNP: Complete, no package, with all weapons and accessories; MIP: Mint in package; MMP: Mint item in Mint package. Values in U.S. dollars. See page 11 for details.

| EA2007 | EA2010 | EA2012 | EA2013 | EA2015 |

| EA2016 | EA2017 | EA2018 | EA2024 |

EA2012	Big Bro'	2	4	6
EA2013	Turk	2	4	6
EA2014	Zapper	2	4	6
EA2015	Shock Trooper	2	4	6
EA2016	Beta Man	2	4	6
EA2017	Savitar	2	4	6
EA2018	Harley	2	4	6
EA2021	"Eliminator" Jeep w/Eagle Mascot	5	12	15
EA2022	"Talon" Tank	5	15	18
EA2023	Communications Adventure Pack w/Zapper	3	6	9
EA2024	V.T.O.L. Jet	8	15	20
EA2041	Eagle Island playset	8	13	26

EARTHWORM JIM (Playmates) 1995-96

Earthworm Jim was a video game-based line in the *TMNT* tradition, incorporating character and play value traits long-proven to attract young buyers…attitude and big guns. When an ultra high-tech super space suit falls to earth, an ordinary worm is transformed into Earthworm Jim (EWJ). Trouble is, every wacko in the galaxy wants the suit. "Snott," a globular sidekick, was thrown in for "gross appeal."

		CNP	MIP	MMP
EA8001	Earthworm Jim	3	5	8
EA8002	EWJ in Special Deep Sea Mission Suit	3	5	8
EA8003	Battle Damage EWJ	3	5	8
EA8004	Peter Puppy	3	5	8
EA8005	Princess What's-Her-Name	3	5	8
EA8006	Psycrow	3	5	8
EA8007	Henchrat	3	5	8
EA8008	Bob & #4	3	5	8
EA8011	Pocket Rocket	5	10	15

EA2041

ELECTROMAN/ZOGG (Ideal) 1977-78

Electroman was a 16" figure equipped with a small lamp and a light sensor. When placed in "radar" mode, the light flashed until it was reflected by an "enemy badge." Zogg the Terrible was a companion figure which Electroman could knock over with a light beam. Zogg also included a gun so that kids could knock him over without Electroman.

		CNP	MIP	MMP
EL2001	Electroman	8	18	25
EL2002	Zogg the Terrible	10	20	30

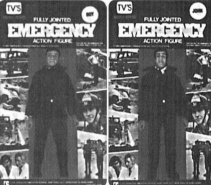

| EM2001 | EM2003 |

ELITE BRIGADE (Cotswold Collectibles) 1995+

These modular figures were designed for fully-articulated display of *G.I. Joe* and other military accessories. Bodies were molded in white and black flesh tones, with a variety of different heads. Two types of hands were available. Figures were shipped in plain boxes with no accessories. Each piece is marked to prevent confusion with original *G.I. Joe* figures.

| EL4001 | Elite Brigade, ea | 35 | - | - |

EMERGENCY (LJN) 1975

A series of 8" costumed figures based on the TV show.

		CNP	MIP	MMP
EM2001	John	10	20	30
EM2003	Roy	10	20	30
EM2005	Accessories Pack	10	18	25
EM2010	Rescue Truck	20	35	65
EM2020	Action Set	15	35	65

EA8001

EA8002

EA8003

EA8004

EA8005

EA8006

EA8007

EA8008

EA8011

EL2001

EL2002

EL4001

EM2010

EM2020

117

ET1012

ET1016

ET1037

ET1045

EV1001   EV1002   EV1003

EV1010

EV1005

EV1021

EV1022

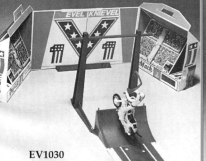
EV1030

EV1041

EV1042

EMPIRE STRIKES BACK, THE — See *Star Wars*

E.T. (LJN) 1982-83

The initial rush for *E.T.* merchandise took the toy industry by surprise. No one had expected the film to be so popular, and manufacturers were unable to keep up with all the requests. Unauthorized figures sprang up to fill the gap. By the time the market recovered, the movie-inspired demand had already died down. Wind-up toys with articulated arms are included in this listing.

Walking Figures		CNP	MIP	MMP
ET1012	Walking figure	4	8	12
ET1016	Figure w/Speak 'n Spell	4	8	12
ET1037	Powered bicycle figure	6	9	16
ET1045	Talking Figure	10	20	25
ET1046	ET1045 w/blue robe	15	25	45

EVEL KNIEVEL (Ideal) 1973-74

Evel Knievel figures were technically "bendies", but were sold as action figures. The figure came in assorted costumes, each with a removeable helmet and "swagger stick," and was sold individually or with certain vehicles. The stunt vehicles were gyro-powered by a crank mechanism similar to a zip cord.

		CNP	MIP	MMP
EV1001	Evel Knievel, white	8	24	32
EV1002	Evel Knievel, red	8	22	30
EV1003	Evel Knievel, blue	9	22	30
EV1005	Stunt Cycle w/figure	12	25	35
EV1010	Scramble Van	9	17	25
EV1021	Stunt and Crash Car w/figure	10	18	26

EV1043   EV1051   EV1052

EV1061   EV1062   EV1063   EV1064   EV1066

EV1065

EV1022	Canyon Sky Cycle w/figure	12	20	28
EV1030	Stunt Stadium	8	17	22
EV1041	Formula 1 Dragster w/figure	12	18	24
EV1042	Trail Bike	6	12	18
EV1043	Chopper	6	12	18
EV1051	Escape From Skull Canyon	12	22	30
EV1052	Road and Trail Adventure Set w/figure and EV1042	10	17	22
EV1061	Racing Set	5	12	18
EV1062	Arctic Explorer Set	5	12	18
EV1063	Rescue Set	5	12	18
EV1064	Explorer Set	5	12	18
EV1065	C.B. Van	8	16	22
EV1066	Stratocycle	6	12	18
EV1070	Bobby Knievel, Teenage Daredevil	12	22	30

See also: *Derry Daring*

EWOKS — See *Star Wars*

EXOSQUAD (Playmates) 1993-96

Exosquad was one of the first animated series produced by Universal Cartoon Studios. The thin storyline features the battle between the Exosquad and the evil, genetically superior Neosapiens.

The line centered around combat E-Frames, a concept which originated with *Robotech*, *Battletech*, and similar stories. The pilot figures were a little smaller, averaging about 3⅛" high. Their exoskeletons, known as "E-Frames," featured multiple shooting weapons, digital sounds, blow-off "battle-damage" parts, and came with sticker sheets to encourage customization. The high-end toy of the first year was to be a Heavy Attack E-Frame with blast-apart smoking action. The prototype was impressive, but bore a close resemblance to one of the heavy 'mechs from the *Battletech* wargame. FASA cried foul, and the toy was killed. Playmates ultimately defeated FASA in a lawsuit over the entire line.

The least-expensive toy in the first series of *Exosquad* products retailed for about $10…a bit high by industry standards. In addition, all of the original toys were boxed. To appeal to lower price points, Playmates added four carded *Jumptroopers* to the line. Each of these figures came with an "Ultralight E-Frame" (i.e. snap-on accessories). Small flip-up window boxes were later replaced with hanging display boxes. All of the smaller E-Frames prior to 1995 are available in both packaging styles. In the same year, *Space Series* and Walking E-Frames which had been proposed in 1994 made their first appearance. A transforming E-Frame and Special Mission E-Frames with wind-up features combined new and old molds. Two carded Neosapien Warriors were also added.

The 1995 line received an additional boost with the introduction of *Robotech*-based toys licensed from Harmony Gold. Unfortunately, most of these toys were cheaply made, and had substantially less play value than the mainstream *Exosquad* product.

1993 Figures/E-Frames		CNP	MIP	MMP
EX7001	Phaeton/Command	6	12	15
EX7002	EX7001 in 1995 box	5	8	10
EX7003	Typhonus/Stealth	7	14	17
EX7004	EX7003 in 1995 box	5	8	10
EX7005	J.T. Marsh/Aerial Attack	6	12	15
EX7006	EX7005 in 1995 box	5	8	10
EX7007	DeLeon/Communications Intelligence	6	12	15
EX7008	EX7007 in 1995 box	5	8	10
EX7011	Shiva/Amphibious Assault	15	22	25
EX7013	Marsala/Rapid Assault	15	22	25
EX7015	Heavy Attack E-Frame	not produced		
1994 Figures/E-Frames				
EX7021	Shawn Napier/ Police Enforcer	6	10	13
EX7022	EX7021 in 1995 box	5	8	10
EX7023	Wolf Bronski/ Ground Assault	6	10	13
EX7024	EX7023 in 1995 box	5	8	10
EX7025	Rita Torres/Field Sgt.	6	10	13
EX7026	EX7025 in 1995 box	5	8	10
EX7027	Nara Burns/ Reconnaissance	6	10	13
EX7028	EX7027 in 1995 box	5	8	10
EX7031	Livanus/Troop Transport	15	22	25
EX7033	Maggie Weston/ Field Repair	15	22	25
Jumptroopers/Ultralight E-Frames				
EX7041	Captain Avery F. Butler/Command	3	5	6
EX7042	Lance Corporal Vince Pellegrino/FireBoss	3	5	6
EX7043	Gunnery Sergeant Ramon Longfeather/ Heavy Gravity	3	5	6
EX7044	Second Lieutenant Colleen O'Reilly/ Rapid Recon	3	5	6
1995 Figures/E-Frames				
EX7051	General Draconis/ Interrogator	5	8	10
EX7053	Jonas Simbacca/ Pirate Captain	5	8	10
EX7055	Peter Tanaka/Samurai	5	8	10
EX7057	Jinx Madison/ Fire Warrior	5	8	10

CNP: Complete, no package, with all weapons and accessories; MIP: Mint in package; MMP: Mint item in Mint package. Values in U.S. dollars. See page 11 for details.

EX7001

EX7003

EX7005

EX7007

EX7002

EX7004

EX7006

EX7008

EX7021

EX7023

EX7025

EX7027

EX7022

EX7024

EX7026

EX7028

EX7011

EX7013

EX7031

EX7033

EX7041   EX7042   EX7043   EX7044

EX7051   EX7053   EX7055   EX7057

EX7065   EX7067   EX7081   EX7083

EX7071   EX7073   EX7075   EX7077

EX7059	Marsala/Sub-Sonic Scout	5	8	10
EX7061	Phaeton/Space Conquest	not produced		
EX7063	J.T. Marsh/Covert Operations	not produced		
EX7065	J.T. Marsh w/Exo-Converting E-Frame	6	10	12
EX7067	Marsala w/Exo-Walking E-Frame	6	15	20
Special Mission E-Frames				
EX7071	Deep Space	6	10	12
EX7073	All-Terrain	6	10	12
EX7075	Deep Submergence	6	10	12
EX7077	Subterranean	6	10	12
Neosapien Warriors				
EX7081	Neo Cat	4	6	7
EX7083	Neo Lord	4	6	7

CNP: Complete, no package, with all weapons and accessories; MIP: Mint in package; MMP: Mint item in Mint package. Values in U.S. dollars. See page 11 for details.

Space E-Frames

EX7091	Kaz Takagi/ExoFighter	7	13	17
EX7093	Thrax/NeoFighter	7	13	17

Robotech 3" (Civil Defense Unit)

EX7101	Excaliber Mk VI	3	5	6
EX7102	Gladiator	3	5	6
EX7103	Raidar X	3	5	6
EX7104	Spartan	3	5	6

Robotech 3" (Tactical Corps Assignment)

EX7105	Excaliber Mk VI	3	5	6
EX7106	Gladiator	3	5	6
EX7107	Raidar X	3	5	6
EX7108	Spartan	3	5	6

Robotech 7" (Attack Mecha)

EX7111	Spartan	4	7	8
EX7112	Gladiator	4	7	8
EX7113	Excaliber Mk VI	4	7	8
EX7114	Raidar X	4	7	8
EX7115	Bioroid Invid Fighter	4	7	8
EX7116	Invid Scout Ship	4	7	8
EX7117	Zentraedi Power Armor (Botoru)	4	7	8
EX7118	Zentraedi Power Armor (Quadrono)	4	7	8

Robotech BattlePods EX7121-23

EX7121	Invid Shock Trooper	6	12	15
EX7122	Tactical BattlePod	6	12	15
EX7123	Officer's BattlePod	6	12	15
EX7125	VeriTech Fighter	9	15	20
EX7026	VeriTech Hover Tank	9	15	20

EX7091

EX7093

EX7125

EX7126

EX7101 EX7102 EX7103 EX7104 EX7105 EX7106 EX7107 EX7108

EX7111 EX7112 EX7113 EX7114 EX7115 EX7116

EX7117 EX7118 EX7121 EX7122 EX7123

FA3001

FA3003

FA3005

FA3007

MR. FANTASTIC™ SUPER STRETCH ARMS!

FA4001

THE THING™ CLOBBERIN' TIME PUNCH!

FA4002

BLACK BOLT™ FLIGHT READY WINGS!

FA4003

MOLE MAN™ TWIRLING COMBAT STAFF!

FA4004

TERRAX™ SPACE SOARING METEOR!

FA4005

SILVER SURFER™ SPACE SURFING!

FA4006

DR. DOOM™ SHOOTING ARM ACTION!

FA4007

DELUXE EDITION HUMAN TORCH™

FA4011

DELUXE EDITION DR. DOOM™

FA4012

DELUXE EDITION SILVER SURFER®

FA4013

FAMOUS MONSTERS OF LEGEND (Tomland) 1977

This series was originally planned as *Famous Monsters of the Movies*, but some rights could not be obtained. The figures are loosely based on characters from *The Voyages of Sinbad*, *The Fly*, H.G. Wells's *The Time Machine*, and *The Abominable Snowman*. American cards bear either the "Tomland" or "Kresge" label, while European versions are labeled "Combex." The same toys were packaged as aliens on *Star Raiders* cards.

		CNP	MIP	MMP
FA3001	Cyclops	25	100	150
FA3003	The Fly	50	160	235
FA3005	Morlock	25	100	150
FA3007	Abominable Snow Man	25	100	150

See also: *Star Raiders*

FANTASTIC FOUR (Toy Biz) 1994-95

Fantastic Four characters have been produced as part of several other lines, but never had a series of their own until 1995. Toy Biz originally included only two members of the famous team in the first assortment — Mister Fantastic and The Thing — but toy retailers demanded all four. Since the molds weren't ready yet, two temporary figures were shipped to fill the gap. Toy Biz repainted the Silver Surfer figure to create the Human Torch, and the *Iron Man* Spider-Woman to create the Invisible Woman. These saw limited release until they were replaced by the new versions. Many ten-inch versions of the same characters were sold in conjunction with this line.

FA4021

FA4022

FA4023

FA4024

FA4025

FA4026

FA4027

FA4028

FA4029

FA4033

FA4034

FA4035

FA4041

	CNP	MIP	MMP			CNP	MIP	MMP			CNP	MIP	MMP
FA4001 Mr. Fantastic	3	5	8	FA4013 10" Silver Surfer	5	10	15	FA4026 Dragon Man	3	4	6
FA4002 The Thing	3	4	6	FA4021 Human Torch				FA4027 Thanos	3	4	6
FA4003 Black Bolt	3	4	6	(repaint of FA4006)	5	10	20	FA4028 Firelord	3	4	6
FA4004 Mole Man w/Moloid	3	4	6	FA4022 Human Torch				FA4029 Blastaar	3	4	6
FA4005 Terrax	3	4	6	(sparking)	3	5	7	FA4033 Mr. Fantastic's			
FA4006 Silver Surfer	3	5	8	FA4023 Invisible Woman				Sky Shuttle	4	8	12
FA4007 Dr. Doom	3	5	7	(repaint of IR7011)	5	15	20	FA4034 The Thing's Sky Cycle	4	8	12
FA4011 10" Human Torch	5	10	15	FA4024 Invisible Woman (clear)	3	4	6	FA4035 Fantasticar	10	22	30
FA4012 10" Dr. Doom	5	10	15	FA4025 Gorgon	3	4	6	FA4041 Galactus	5	10	15

THE THING II — UNDERCOVER DISGUISE!

FA4044

ANNIHILUS — COSMIC CONTROL ROD TRANSFORMING MUTANT!

FA4045

NAMOR THE SUB-MARINER — POWER PUNCH WITH UNDERSEA TRIDENT AND SHIELD!

FA4046

SUPER SKRULL — SUPER EXTENDING POWER PUNCH ACTION!

FA4047

TRITON — SWIMMING ACTION WITH ATTACK SHARK & SEA TRUMPET!

FA4048

ATTUMA — SWORD SLASHING ACTION!

FA4049

DELUXE EDITION — JOHNNY STORM — 10" TALL • FULLY POSEABLE • ACCESSORY INCLUDED

FA4051

DELUXE EDITION — THE THING — 10" TALL • FULLY POSEABLE • ACCESSORY INCLUDED

FA4052

METAL MANIA — THING vs. BLASTAAR

FA4056

METAL MANIA — HUMAN TORCH vs. DRAGON MAN

FA4057

METAL MANIA — MR. FANTASTIC vs. DR. DOOM

FA4058

METAL MANIA — SILVER SURFER vs. TERRAX

FA4059

FA4044	The Thing II	3	4	6
FA4045	Annihilus	3	4	6
FA4046	Namor, the Sub-Mariner	3	4	6
FA4047	Super Skrull	3	4	6
FA4048	Triton	3	4	6
FA4049	Attuma	3	5	7

FA4051	10" Johnny Storm	5	10	15
FA4052	10" The Thing	5	10	15
Metal Mania die-cast figures FA4056-59				
FA4056	Thing/Blastaar	2	4	6
FA4057	Human Torch/ Dragon Man	2	4	6

FA4058	Mr. Fantastic/ Dr. Doom	2	4	6
FA4059	Silver Surfer/Terrax	2	4	6
FA4061	Thing II	3	8	12
FA4063	Johnny Storm	3	8	12
FA4065	Medusa	3	8	12

FA4069   FA4063   FA4061   FA4067   FA4065

FA4501   FA4502   FA4503   FA4504

FA4067	Psycho Man	3	8	12
FA4069	Wizard	3	8	12

See also: *Fantastic Four/Iron Man Collectors Edition; Marvel Team-up; Marvel Super Heroes; Official World Famous Super Heroes; Projectors*

FANTASTIC FOUR/IRON MAN COLLECTORS EDITION (Toy Biz) 1995

This set of four two-packs was produced exclusively for Wal-Mart. Each package included a bonus "collector pin." Individual figures were identical to those sold in their respective figure lines.

		CNP	MIP	MMP
FA4501	Mr. Fantastic/Iron Man Hydro Armor	5	12	25
FA4502	Dr. Doom/Iron Man	5	12	25
FA4503	Silver Surfer/Mandarin	5	11	20
FA4504	Thing/War Machine	5	11	20

See also: *Fantastic Four; Iron Man*

FANTASY WORLD (Arron's) 1986

A He-Man knock-off.

		CNP	MIP	MMP
FA5001	Fantastar	2	4	6
FA5002	Hellord	2	4	6
FA5003	Herocon	2	4	6
FA5004	Ironmask	2	4	6
FA5005	Trikin	2	4	6
FA5006	Dragonman	2	4	6
FA5007	Nizard	2	4	6
FA5008	Piro	2	4	6

FERNGULLY (Toys 'N Things) 1992

A single figure of Crysta was produced.

		CNP	MIP	MMP
FE7051	Crysta	1	3	6

FIGHTING TALK! (Toy Island) 1991

These military figures were Toy Island's first 3½" figures, no doubt inspired by the *G.I. Joe* line.

FA5001   FE7051   FI1501   FI2000

Digital sounds from the larger *Voice Squad* figures were re-used in the talking backpacks, but with slightly different electronics that make the figures sound like they have inhaled helium. All of the figures have the same legs, and three different torsos have been given six different paint jobs. Three sets of assorted accessories were also included, with two different color schemes.

Tiger Team FI1501-05		CNP	MIP	MMP
FI1501	Commando Ops. Chief	2	5	7
FI1503	Special Recon Cmdr.	2	5	7
FI1505	Tactical Supply Officer	2	5	7
Eagle Team FI1511-15				
FI1511	Combat Engineer	2	5	7
FI1513	Special Forces Leader	2	5	7
FI1515	Special Ops. Cmdr.	2	5	7

FIGHTING YANK (Mego) 1974

Fighting Yank was a short-lived 8" action figure and costume series designed to capitalize on the popularity of Hasbro's *G.I. Joe* line. Outfits were packaged in boxes or on blister packages.

		CNP	MIP	MMP
FI2000	Fighting Yank figure	5	15	20
Outfits FI2001-10				
FI2001	Frog Man	1	5	7
FI2002	MP Outfit	1	5	7
FI2003	Flight Outfit	1	5	7
FI2004	Air Force	1	5	7
FI2005	Marine Dress	1	5	7
FI2006	Special Forces	1	5	7
FI2007	Navy Dress	1	5	7
FI2008	West Point Cadet	1	5	7
FI2009	Snowbound	1	5	7
FI2010	Ski Patrol	1	5	7

FILMATION'S GHOSTBUSTERS (Schaper) 1986

The *Ghost Busters* was originally a live-action Saturday morning TV program for kids, starring character actors Forrest Tucker and Larry Storch, plus Bob Burns in the gorilla suit. The characters were named Spencer, Tracy, and Kong. Younger readers may not recognize the humor. Spencer Tracy was a famous leading man of many films; King Kong was the most

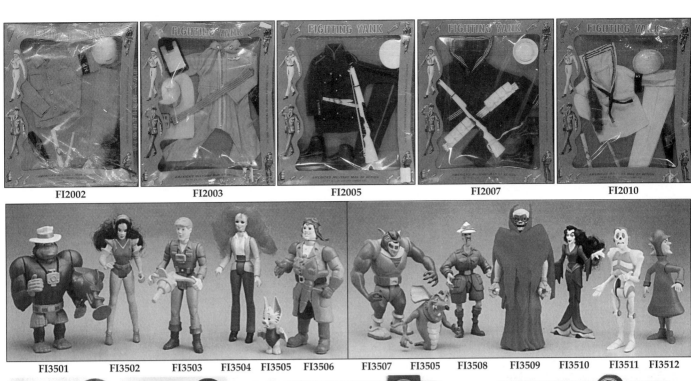

FI2002   FI2003   FI2005   FI2007   FI2010

FI3501   FI3502   FI3503   FI3504   FI3505   FI3506   FI3507   FI3505   FI3508   FI3509   FI3510   FI3511   FI3512

FI3510   FI3521   FI3522   FI3525

famous movie ape. The twist was Kong in The Ghost Busters was played by Tucker…the gorilla was called Tracy. The program was produced by Filmation and aired for two complete seasons starting September 6, 1975 on the CBS network. Fifteen episodes were produced in a breakneck nine-week taping schedule, and ran on a rotating basis…Saturday mornings in '75 and Sundays in '76.

Even though the show continued to grow in popularity, no new episodes were created. Not much thought was given to the property until news began to circulate regarding a script Dan Aykroyd was writing for Columbia Pictures, which was based in part on the 1940 Bob Hope film *Ghostbreakers*. The name *Ghostbreakers* had to be changed to *Ghostbusters* because of a legal conflict. Executives at Filmation noted the familiar ring and decided to convert the old live-action idea into an animated series called The *Ghost Busters*. Columbia objected and filed a lawsuit to prevent Filmation from using the name. There was a counter-suit, and the court ruled in Filmation's favor. In return for a handsome payoff, Filmation used their name in front of the title for the Saturday morning TV series, and gave clearance for the film's title to remain as planned. For licensing however, Columbia was required to differentiate their product from Filmation's. The resulting title "The Real *Ghostbusters*" was used as identification on authorized products, including a second animated series.

The *Filmation's Ghostbusters* characters were the "children" of those in the live-action series to prevent any royalty problems. The figures were produced by Schaper in 1986 — one would guess none of the major toy companies wanted to risk offending Columbia Pictures. Tracy the Ape was the only original character carried over (no royalties required on an ape suit). The figures were extremely well done and a small comic was initially included with each figure. The Ghost Buggy was the standout accessory. It was an incredible transforming car which could become several different surface and "flying" vehicles.

		CNP	MIP	MMP
FI3501	Tracy	5	8	12
FI3502	Futura	5	8	12
FI3503	Jake	5	8	12
FI3504	Jessica	5	8	12
FI3505	Belfry and Brat-A-Rat	6	9	15
FI3506	Eddie	5	8	12
FI3507	Fangster	5	8	12
FI3508	Haunter	5	8	12
FI3509	Prime Evil	5	8	12
FI3510	Mysteria	8	10	15
FI3511	Scared Stiff	5	8	12
FI3512	Fib Face	5	8	12
FI3521	Time Hopper vehicle	2	5	8
FI3522	Scare Scooter vehicle	3	7	9
FI3524	Bone Troller vehicle	2	5	8
FI3525	Ghost Buggy vehicle	6	12	15
FI3531	Ghost Command set	8	16	30

See also: *Real Ghostbusters, The*

FISHER-PRICE ADVENTURE PEOPLE (Fisher-Price) c. 1976-83

The *Fisher-Price Adventure People* were land, sea, air, and space-related settings, designed to stimulate the imaginations of kids age 4-9. Often unnoticed in later years, this line had a powerful impact on the action figure industry. It was one of the first line to use 3¾" figures, probably because of its emphasis on vehicles and accessories. As a side note, *Fisher-Price Adventure People* were the basis for the original *Star Wars* prototypes. Figures and accessories are listed alphabetically.

Action Figures		CNP	MIP	MMP
FI6001	Alpha Pilot	1	3	6
FI6003	Astro Knight	1	3	6
FI6005	Brainoid	1	3	6
FI6007	Clawtron	1	3	6
FI6009	Dune Buster	1	3	6
FI6011	Frogman	1	3	6
FI6013	Highway Trooper	1	3	6
FI6015	Opticon	1	3	6
FI6017	Rescue Pilot	1	3	6
FI6019	Space Commander	1	3	6
FI6021	Super Sonic Pilot	1	3	6
FI6023	X-Ray Man	1	3	6
FI6025	X-Ray Woman	1	3	6
FI6031	3-figure closeout packs	3	9	22
Figure and Accessory Sets				
FI6051	Aero-Marine Search Team	6	12	25
FI6053	Alpha Probe	6	12	25
FI6055	Alpha Recon	6	12	25
FI6057	Cycle Racing Team	6	12	25

CNP: Complete, no package, with all weapons and accessories; MIP: Mint in package; MMP: Mint item in Mint package. Values in U.S. dollars. See page 11 for details.

FI6025

FI6031

FI6055

FI6065

FI6067

FI6073

FL5610

FL5600

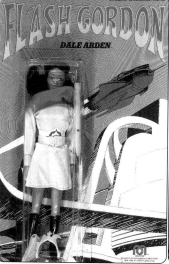

FL5601

FL5602

FL5603

FI6059	Daredevil Sport Van	6	12	25
FI6061	Deep Sea Diver	6	12	25
FI6063	Dune Buster	6	12	25
FI6065	Firestar I	6	12	25
FI6067	Land Speed Racer	6	12	25
FI6069	Northwoods Trailblazer	6	12	25
FI6071	Scuba Divers	6	12	25
FI6073	Sea Shark	6	12	25
FI6075	Weeelie Dragster	6	12	25
FI6077	White Water Kayak	6	12	25

See also: *Flipper*

FLASH, THE — See *DC Comics Super Heroes; Super Powers Collection*

FLASH GORDON (Mego) 1976, (Mattel) 1979

A 9" series of *Flash Gordon* figures was produced in 1976. Smaller figures were made by Mattel in 1979, not associated with the film released the following year. Mego and Mattel figures were based on the original animated TV series.

Playmates developed a new line for an all-new animated series scheduled to air in 1996.

Mego (1976)		**CNP**	**MIP**	**MMP**
FL5600	Flash	45	95	150
FL5601	Dale	40	65	95
FL5602	Dr. Zarkov	42	75	135
FL5603	Ming	40	70	100
FL5610	Playset	40	75	125
Mattel (1979)				
FL5755	Flash Gordon	10	35	50
FL5756	Dr. Zarkov	8	25	40
FL5757	Thun the Lion Man	8	20	35
FL5758	Ming the Merciless	8	15	25
FL5759	Beastman	10	55	80
FL5760	Lizard Woman	8	15	25
FL5761	Vultan	40	135	200
FL5762	Captain Arak	35	95	180
FL5771	Boxed set of 4 (FL5755, FL5757, FL5760, FL5762; Sears exclusive)	-	70	115
FL5785	Inflatable Rocket Ship	18	35	65
FL5786	Ming's Shuttle	15	30	65

See also: *Captain Action; Defenders of the Earth*

FLEX•A•TRON (S & T Sales Inc.) 1987

A *Thundercats* knock-off.

FL5903   FL5916

		CNP	**MIP**	**MMP**
FL5901	Flexor	2	5	7
FL5902	Zorn	2	5	7
FL5903	Varyk	2	5	7
FL5904	Herr Bone	2	5	7
FL5905	Vipen	2	5	7
FL5906	Devilor	2	5	7
FL5911	Flexor w/Ran	3	8	10
FL5912	Zorn w/Raj	3	8	10
FL5913	Varyk w/Devilcat	3	8	10

FL5755 FL5756 FL5757 FL5758

FL5759 FL5760 FL5761 FL5762

FL5771

FL5785

FL6001

FL5914	Herr Bone w/Devilcat	3	8	10
FL5915	Vipen w/Devilcat	3	8	10
FL5916	Devilor w/Devilcat	3	8	10

FLINTSTONE KIDS, THE (Coleco) 1987

This series was based on a short-lived cartoon, a spin-off of the *Flintstones* TV show.

		CNP	MIP	MMP
FL6001	Freddy Flintstone	3	6	10
FL6002	Barney Rubble	3	6	10
FL6003	Wilma Slaghoople	3	6	10
FL6004	Betty Jean Bricker	3	8	12
FL6005	Fang	3	6	10
FL6006	Dino	3	6	10
FL6007	Dreamchip Gemstone	8	15	20

FL6008	Nate Slate	8	15	35
FL6009	Philo Quartz	8	20	35
FL6010	Cavey, Jr.	10	20	35
FL6011	Micki	8	15	20
FL6012	Rocky Ratrock w/Stalagmutt	8	15	20
FL6013	Mailman (from FL6031)	8	-	-
FL6014	Girl (from FL6032)	8	-	-
FL6021	Dreamchip Limo	4	8	15
FL6022	Bedrock Firefighter	4	8	15
FL6023	Bedrock Airlines	4	8	15
FL6031	Town of Bedrock	8	15	20

FL6032	Bedrock Elementary School	8	15	20

FLINTSTONES, THE (Mattel) 1993-94

Figures based on the live-action film. Figures looked like the human actors rather than the famous cartoon characters.

		CNP	MIP	MMP
FL6551	Hard Hat Fred	1	3	6
FL6552	Big Shot Fred	1	3	6
FL6553	Lawn Mowin' Barney	1	3	6
FL6554	Fillin' Station Barney	1	3	6

CNP: Complete, no package, with all weapons and accessories; MIP: Mint in package; MMP: Mint item in Mint package. Values in U.S. dollars. See page 11 for details.

FL6002

FL6003

FL6004

FL6006

FL6008

FL6009

FL6010

FL6012

FL6021

FL6022

FL6023

FL6031

FL6032

FL6555	Wilma & Pebbles	3	8	10	FL6564	Dyno-Drilling Barney	4	6	10
FL6556	Betty & Bamm-Bamm	3	8	10	FL6571	Flintmobile	5	10	15
FL6557	Licking Dino	3	8	10	FL6572	Le Saber Tooth 5000	5	10	15
FL6558	Evil Cliff Vandercave	2	5	8	FL6581	Yabba-Dabba-Doo Fred	7	10	15
FL6561	Big Bite Fred	4	6	10	**See also:** *Dakin and Dakin-Style Figures*				
FL6562	Bowl-o-rama Fred	4	6	10					
FL6563	Crash Test Barney	4	6	10					

FLINTSTONES IN ACTION, THE (Irwin) 1985

The best *Flintstones* action figure series was produced by Irwin, a Canadian toy company. Many figures were sold through U.S. comic store distribution channels, but very few retail stores carried them. The vehicles and playsets were very difficult to find in the U.S.

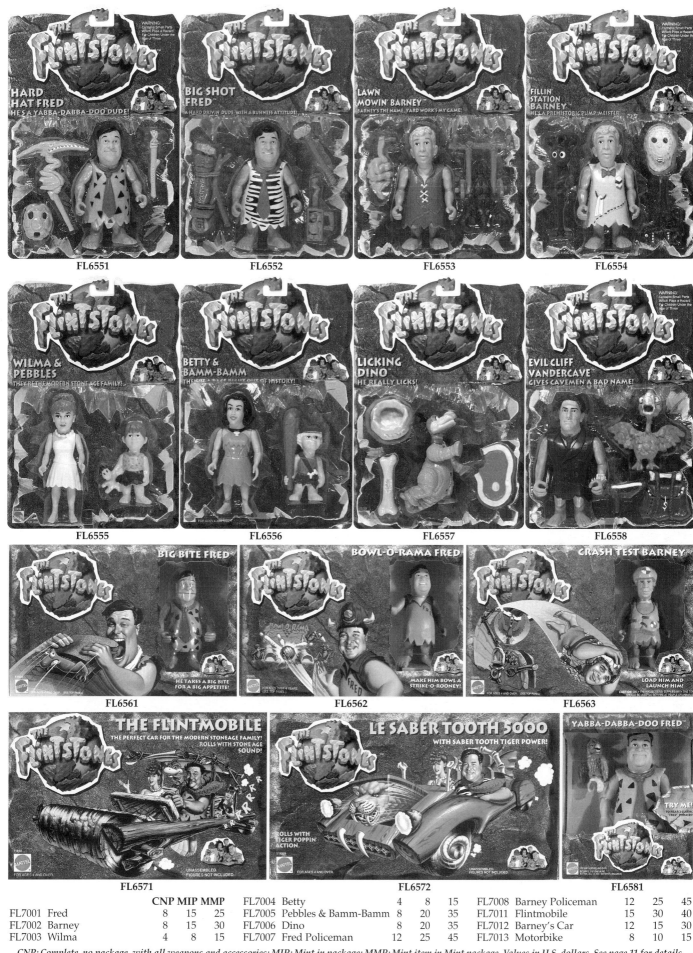

| FL6551 | FL6552 | FL6553 | FL6554 |

HARD HAT FRED — HE'S A YABBA-DABBA-DOO DUDE!
BIG SHOT FRED — A HARD DRIVIN' DUDE WITH A BUSINESS ATTITUDE!
LAWN MOWIN' BARNEY — BARNEY'S THE NAME, YARD WORK'S MY GAME!
FILLIN' STATION BARNEY — HE'S A PREHISTORIC PUMP-MEISTER!

| FL6555 | FL6556 | FL6557 | FL6558 |

WILMA & PEBBLES — THEY'RE THE MODERN STONE AGE FAMILY!...
BETTY & BAMM-BAMM — THE GREATEST PAIR OUT OF HISTORY!
LICKING DINO — HE REALLY LICKS!
EVIL CLIFF VANDERCAVE — GIVES CAVEMEN A BAD NAME!

BIG BITE FRED — HE TAKES A BIG BITE FOR A BIG APPETITE!
BOWL-O-RAMA FRED — MAKE HIM BOWL A STRIKE-O-ROONEY!
CRASH TEST BARNEY — LOAD HIM AND LAUNCH HIM!

| FL6561 | FL6562 | FL6563 |

THE FLINTMOBILE — THE PERFECT CAR FOR THE MODERN STONEAGE FAMILY! ROLLS WITH STONE AGE SOUND!
LE SABER TOOTH 5000 — WITH SABER TOOTH TIGER POWER!
YABBA-DABBA-DOO FRED

| FL6571 | FL6572 | FL6581 |

		CNP	MIP	MMP									
FL7001	Fred	8	15	25	FL7004	Betty	4	8	15	FL7008	Barney Policeman	12	25	45
FL7002	Barney	8	15	30	FL7005	Pebbles & Bamm-Bamm	8	20	35	FL7011	Flintmobile	15	30	40
FL7003	Wilma	4	8	15	FL7006	Dino	8	20	35	FL7012	Barney's Car	12	15	30
					FL7007	Fred Policeman	12	25	45	FL7013	Motorbike	8	10	15

CNP: Complete, no package, with all weapons and accessories; MIP: Mint in package; MMP: Mint item in Mint package. Values in U.S. dollars. See page 11 for details.

FL7001

FL7002

FL7003

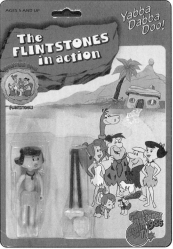

FL7004

FL7005

FL7006

FL7011

FL7012

FL7013

FL8001

		CNP	MIP	MMP
FL7014	Police Car	25	40	65
FL7015	Fred and Motorbike	15	50	75
FL7016	Barney w/car & ladder	15	50	75
FL7017	Deluxe set w/Betty, Wilma, Table & utensils	15	50	100
FL7018	Pebbles, Bamm-Bamm, and Dino	15	50	100
FL7019	Boxed Set w/FL7007, FL7008, and FL7014	55	75	135
FL7020	Flintmobile w/Fred, Wilma, Pebbles, and Bamm-Bamm	50	75	135
FL7021	Deluxe set w/Fred, Barney, Dino, Betty, Wilma, Table & utensils	55	75	140
FL7030	The Flintstones' House	not confirmed		

FLIPPER (Fisher-Price) 1976

The *Flipper* playset included a boat, two action figures, a diving platform, and scuba tanks. The rubber Flipper was hollow so that it could shoot water out of its "spout." This set was probably a licensing tie-in with the *Fisher-Price Adventure People*.

		CNP	MIP	MMP
FL8001	Flipper Sea Explorer	18	35	50

FLY, THE — See *Famous Monsters of Legend*

FOOD FIGHTERS (Mattel) 1988-89

Grab something leftover from the refrigerator, add arms, legs and commando weapons, and you've got a *Food Fighter*. Each came with a plastic weapon and backpack. Figures were painted with "catsup" or "mustard" variations.

		CNP	MIP	MMP
FO5001	Burgerdier General	1	2	3
FO5002	Major Munch	1	2	3
FO5003	Sergeant Scoop	1	2	3
FO5004	Private Pizza, light or dark cheese	1	2	3
FO5005	Lieutenant Legg	1	2	3
FO5006	Short Stack	1	2	3
FO5007	Mean Weener	1	2	3
FO5008	Chip-The-Ripper	1	2	3
FO5009	Fat Frenchy	1	2	3
FO5010	Taco Terror	1	2	3
FO5021	Combat Carton	4	10	14
FO5022	Fry Chopper	2	5	8
FO5023	BBQ Bomber	2	5	8

FORT APACHE FIGHTERS — See *Best of the West*

FOX'S PETER PAN AND THE PIRATES (THQ (HK) Ltd.) 1991

Based on the Fox cartoon series, this line was one of the first to target both boys and girls, combining action figures with "miniature dolls." Peter Pan, Captain Hook, and other male figures came with weapons, pop-off hats, and falling pants. Female figures had rooted hair and combs for girls. Peter Pan and Tinker Bell had hidden "flight hooks." The Mermaid figure came with a red or blue tail, and had red hair — different from the blonde one shown on the package back.

		CNP	MIP	MMP
FO9001	Peter Pan	1	3	4
FO9002	Captain Hook	1	3	4
FO9003	Robert Mullins	1	3	4
FO9004	Alf Mason	1	3	4
FO9005	Smee	1	3	4
FO9006	Wendy	1	3	4
FO9007	Tinker Bell	1	3	4
FO9008	The Mermaid, red tail	5	15	18
FO9009	The Mermaid, blue tail	1	3	4

FRANKENSTEIN — See *Classic Movie Monsters; Lincoln International Monsters; Mad Monster Series, The; Maxx FX; Mini Monsters; Monster Force; Official World Famous Super Monsters; Real Ghostbusters, The; Universal Monsters*

FREDDY FAST GAS — See *Dakin and Dakin-Style Figures*

FO5001 FO5002 FO5003 FO5004 FO5005

FO5006 FO5007 FO5008 FO5009 FO5010

FO5021 FO5022 FO5023

FO9001 FO9002 FO9003 FO9004

GALAXIE GIRL (Woolworth) c. 1986
A Golden Girl/Princess of Power "me too" series manufactured for Woolworth.

GALAXY ADVENTURE GIRL (Soma) 1985
Another *Golden Girl* knock-off.

		CNP	MIP	MMP
GA0501	Mace & bird shield	2	5	7
GA0502	Spear & leaf shield	2	5	7

		CNP	MIP	MMP
GA0503	Sword & leaf shield	2	5	7
GA0504	Spear & round shield	2	5	7
GA0505	Sword & lion shield	2	5	7
GA0506	Sword & round shield	2	5	7
GA0507	Mace & lion shield	2	5	7
GA0508	Sword & bird shield	2	5	7

		CNP	MIP	MMP
GA1001	Ventura	2	5	7
GA1002	Noblest	2	5	7
GA1003	Supra	2	5	7

CNP: Complete, no package, with all weapons and accessories; MIP: Mint in package; MMP: Mint item in Mint package. Values in U.S. dollars. See page 11 for details.

FO9005

FO9006

FO9007

FO9009

GA0501

GA1002

GA2001

GA4501

GA4981

GA5008

GA5011

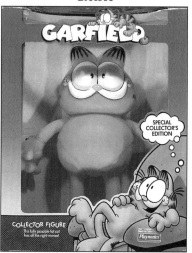

GA6501

GA1004	Werra	2	5	7
GA1005	Yfele	2	5	7
GA1006	Virago	2	5	7
GA1011	Balius (horse)	3	7	10
GA1012	Xaufus (horse)	3	7	10

GALAXY FIGHTER (Jak Pak) 1984

A series of six die-cast metal figures. The only variation among the figures were their heads, weapons, and paint jobs.

		CNP	MIP	MMP
GA2001	Thunder Prince	1	2	3
GA2002	Demon Man	1	2	3
GA2003	Power Lord	1	2	3
GA2004	Evil Karzu	1	2	3

GA2005	Zodiac	1	2	3
GA2006	Lava Monster	1	2	3

See also: *Galaxy Warriors*

GALAXY FIGHTERS (Madison Ltd.) 1987

		CNP	MIP	MMP
GA3001	Magon	1	2	3
GA3002	Sun Hawk	1	2	3
GA3003	Mace Ape	1	2	3
GA3004	Centurn	1	2	3
GA3005	Baltard	1	2	3
GA3006	Iguana	1	2	3
GA3007	Anubi	1	2	3
GA3008	Kobra	1	2	3
GA3009	Pegasurus	1	2	3

GALAXY RIDER (Silver Industrial) c. 1985

A series of three motorcycle vehicles, each with a semi-poseable figure. The figure is the same for all three.

		CNP	MIP	MMP
GA4501	Eagleman	1	2	3
GA4502	Lion Rider	1	2	3
GA4503	Crazyhorser	1	2	3

GALAXY WARRIORS (Woolworth) 1987

Galaxy Warriors is a trademark owned by Woolworth. Two lines are known to have been produced under this name. The first is a series of die-cast metal figures similar to the *Galaxy Fighter* series, with slight changes and new colors.

| | GA6701 | | GA6703 | | GA6705 | | GA6707 | | GA6709 |

| | GA6711 | | GA6713 | | GA6715 | | GA6723 | | GA6725 |

| | GA6727 | | GA6729 | | GA6731 | | GA6733 | | GA6735 |

	CNP	MIP	MMP
First Series GA4981-86			
GA4981-86 Die-cast metal			
Galaxy Warriors, ea	2	4	6
Second Series GA5001-11			
GA5001 Ygg	2	4	6
GA5002 Dragoon	2	4	6
GA5003 Dino Man	2	4	6
GA5004 Huk	2	4	6
GA5005 Baltard	2	4	6
GA5006 Magnon	2	4	6
GA5007 Thor	2	4	6
GA5008 Tiger Man	2	4	6
GA5009 Anubi	2	4	6
GA5010 Shark	2	4	6
GA5011 Triton	2	4	6

GARFIELD (Playmates) 1991

This 12" collector figure of Universal Features' famous fat cat featured "posable paws." A similar figure of Odie was proposed, but not produced.

	CNP	MIP	MMP
GA6501 Garfield, 12"	15	45	65
GA6511 Odie, 12"		not produced	

GARGOYLES (Kenner) 1995-96

Characters from the popular Disney animated series inspired some of the better Kenner toys from this period.

	CNP	MIP	MMP
1st Series Figures (8-back cards) GA6701-15			
GA6701 Quick Strike Goliath	2	5	8
GA6703 Stone Armor Goliath	2	5	8
GA6705 Broadway	2	5	8
GA6707 Lexington	2	5	8
GA6709 Brooklyn	2	5	8
GA6711 Xanatos	2	5	8
GA6713 Demona	2	5	8
GA6715 Steel Clan Robot	2	5	8
GA6721 Rippin' Rider Cycle	5	8	12
2nd Series Figures (13-back cards) GA6723-35			
GA6723 Hudson	2	5	8
GA6725 Claw Climber Goliath	2	5	8
GA6727 Bronx	2	5	8
GA6729 Battle Goliath	2	5	8
GA6731 Strike Hammer			
MacBeth	2	5	8
GA6733 Power Wing Goliath	3	6	12
GA6735 Mighty Roar Goliath	3	6	12

CNP: Complete, no package, with all weapons and accessories; MIP: Mint in package; MMP: Mint item in Mint package. Values in U.S. dollars. See page 11 for details.

GA6741

GA6745

GA6746

GA6751

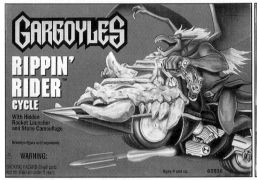

GA6721

GA6739

GE5001

GE5011

GE5021

GE5033

GE5034

GE5035

GE5036

GE5037

GE5038

		CNP	MIP	MMP
GA6739	Night Striker vehicle	3	6	9
GA6741	Elisa Miza	2	5	8
Series 2				
GA6745	Stone Camo Broadway	2	5	8
GA6746	Stone Camo Lexington	2	5	8
GA6751	Castle Playset	10	20	30

GEN. PATCH (Galoob) 1983

Figures included a mini-comic and plastic weapons scented with the "smell of battle." Imagine the smell of battle! Burning flesh, perhaps ... or smoke inhalation ... or the whiff of a freshly fired gun. "Smell don't sell" was the kids' verdict. Paratrooper figures included a working parachute and stick-on patch.

		CNP	MIP	MMP
GE5001	Gen. Patch w/Ammo	3	4	8
GE5002	Gen. Patch w/Detonator	3	4	8
GE5003	Flamethrower	3	4	8
GE5004	Bazooka Man	3	4	8
GE5005	Mortar Man	3	4	8
GE5006	Machine Gunner	3	4	8
Paratroopers GE5011-14				
GE5011	Gen. Patch	3	6	9
GE5012	Gen. Patch	3	6	9
GE5013	Evil Enemy	3	6	9
GE5014	Evil Enemy	3	6	9
"Evil Enemy" troops GE5021-26				
GE5021	Bazooka Man	3	5	8
GE5022	Mortar	3	5	8

		CNP	MIP	MMP
GE5023	Flamer	3	5	8
GE5024	Machine Gunner	3	5	8
GE5031	Battery Operated Mobile Tank w/figure	3	6	8
GE5032	Laser Cannon w/figure	3	6	8
GE5033	Flying platform	2	5	6
GE5034	Patrol Boat w/figure	3	6	8
GE5035	Interceptor w/figure	3	6	8

GENERAL OF THE ARMY (Marx) c. 1965

A single figure of Dwight Eisenhower is known to exist under this name. Other generals may have been produced.

		CNP	MIP	MMP
GE6001	Dwight D. Eisenhower	100	500	600

GE6001

GH5001

GH5003

GH5005

GH5007

GH6501

GH6511

GH6513

GH6515

GH6517

GH6519

GH6521

GENERATIONS — See *Star Trek*

GHOST BATTALLION/BONE BRIGADE (Jasman Inc.) 1995

This series of military skeleton figures was probably created in response to *Skeleton Warriors*. Figures were sold in two-pack bubble cards labelled *Ghost Battallion* or *Bone Brigade*. Army and Space figures were produced.

GH5001	Sgt. Robert Clay/			
	Major Alex Tripp	2	4	6
GH5003	Lt. Buster Hill/			
	Cpl. Charles Rod	2	4	6
GH5005	Captain Johnathan			
	Comet/Chief Petty			
	Officer Matthew Fry	2	4	6
GH5007	Lt. J. G. Peter Cook/			
	Ensign William S. Aster	2	4	6

GHOST RIDER (Fleetwood Toy Co.) 1976, (Toy Biz) 1995-96

The Fleetwood Toys figure and cycle set was a one-shot toy sold on a blister card. The figure came with two different heads.

Collector demand for *Ghost Rider* figures was strong in the early '90s, but it wasn't until Halloween of 1995 that product finally began to appear. Glow-in-the-dark features called

GH6531

GH6532

GH6533

GH6541

GH6542

GH6543

"flame glow details" were extensively used.

The Zarathos figure was originally intended for the first series. Retailer demand for smaller case assortments caused it to be delayed until the second group of figures.

The line featured two different kinds of motorcycles. Bubble-carded *Flamin' Stunt Cycles* were zip cord-powered toys with non-removable figures attached. Though not technically action figures, they were designed to interact with other figure toys in the line, and are thus of some interest to action figure collectors. *Spirits of Vengeance* cycles and riders were boxed sets which included articulated figures and cycles with spring-launcing features.

		CNP	MIP	MMP
Fleetwood Toy Co.				
GH6501	Ghost Rider	40	200	300
Toy Biz Assortment I				
GH6511	Ghost Rider	3	5	6
GH6513	Ghost Rider II	3	5	6
GH6515	Blaze	3	5	6
GH6517	Vengeance	3	5	6
GH6519	Blackout	3	5	6
GH6521	Skinner	3	5	6
GH6531	10" Ghost Rider	5	10	12
GH6532	10" Blaze	5	10	12
GH6533	10" Vengeance	5	10	12
Flamin' Stunt Cycles				
GH6541	Ghost Rider	5	10	12
GH6542	Blaze	5	10	12
GH6543	Vengeance	5	10	12
Spirits of Vengeance Cycles & Riders				
GH6551	Ghost Rider	5	10	15
GH6552	Blaze	5	10	15
GH6553	Vengeance	5	10	15
Toy Biz Assortment II				
GH6561	Original Ghost Rider	3	5	6
GH6563	Exploding Ghost Rider	3	5	6
GH6565	Armor Blaze	3	5	6
GH6567	Outcast	3	5	6
GH6569	Zarathos	3	5	6

GHOSTBUSTERS — See *Filmation's Ghostbusters; Real Ghostbusters, The*

GH6551   GH6552   GH6553

GH6569   GH6563   GH6567   GH6561   GH6565

GI0501

G.I. COMBAT (Chitech Industries) 1983

A *G.I. Joe* knock-off.

		CNP	MIP	MMP
GI0501	U.S. Marauder	3	6	10
GI0502	U.S. Fighter Pilot	3	6	10
GI0503	Russian Officer	3	6	10
GI0504	Japanese Officer	3	6	10
GI0505	Chinese Guerilla Fighter	3	6	10
GI0506	British Commando	3	6	10
GI0507	Anzac Bush Fighter	3	6	10
GI0508	U.S. Fighting Seabee	3	6	10
GI0509	British Paratrooper	3	6	10
GI0510	French Infantryman	3	6	10
GI0511	German U-Boat Commander	3	6	10
GI0512	U.S. Paratrooper	3	6	10

G.I. JOE (Hasbro) 1964–78

G.I. Joe, Hasbro's American fighting man, was a toy with a mission. The brainstorm of toy inventors at Hasbro, the idea was to create a posable fighting man (the sales force was told never to call the *G.I. Joe* figure a doll) and carve a niche into the boy's toy market which would last for years to come.

Hasbro had been working on the concept of *G.I. Joe* for more than a year, and it was originally thought they would start out small, releasing only one figure — the Action Soldier — and release the remaining 3 services if it sold well. But it was successfully argued that if Hasbro didn't release figures for all 4 services, some other toy company would and capture that segment of the market. So by 1964, Hasbro was ready for *G.I. Joe* to make its debut at the February Toy Fair. The buyers were cautious, but enough orders came in to begin *G.I. Joe's* tour of duty, which for the large 12" figures lasted until 1976.

Once *G.I. Joe* hit the toy store shelves, it became apparent something big had hit boys toys. The 1964 production run of *G.I. Joe* was a complete sellout. The rest is history. Hasbro was overwhelmed by the success of their new figure line. All 4 services were represented with the Action Soldier, Action Marine, Action Sailor and Action Pilot. Most of the first year accessories and uniforms were made for the Action Soldier and Marine figures because they sold better than the Action Pilot and Action Sailor.

The very first boxes for the *G.I. Joe* figures were marked with ™ at the lower right corner of the large *G.I. Joe* logo. Below the *G.I. Joe* logo is the name of what the item is, such as "Action Soldier." This name would also have ™ placed to the right and just below the words. The second issue of the boxes has a registered symbol ® below the *G.I. Joe* logo rather than the ™, but below the words Action Soldier, it still has the trademark symbol. The third version of the boxes has the registered symbol both below the *G.I. Joe* logo and below the name of the figure. This is true for all 4 services; so in essence, there are 3 different boxes for each of the 4 services using the first year box design. The first year accessory boxes and small cards also followed this marking sequence.

Each *G.I. Joe* figure in the box came with his appropriate uniform and accessories, including a pair of boots. The very first issue boots for *G.I. Joe* have smooth bottoms as opposed to the ridged bottoms of the later issue, and most importantly, the boots were made of rubber. They came in both brown and black. If found today, these boots are usually hard as a rock and nearly impossible to actually put on a fig-

CNP: Complete, no package, with all weapons and accessories; MIP: Mint in package; MMP: Mint item in Mint package. Values in U.S. dollars. See page 11 for details.

ure, but a few pairs have survived in good condition. They are something to behold because of their beautiful detailing. In this line, the first issue G.I. Joe feet were smaller and less detailed than the feet which would later be used. Later-issue figures have highly detailed feet with distinct toes, even showing toenails and joints. The first issue did not have this detailing, but only the smaller first issue feet would fit into the first issue rubber boots.

There were different field manuals for each of the 4 services: Action Soldier, Action Marine, Action Sailor or Action Pilot. Since the box for the G.I. Joe figures was narrow, the manual packaged with the figure was actually smaller than the manual which came packaged with the accessory cards. Manuals for the figure boxes measured 3½" x 4". The accessory cards came with manuals measuring 4" x 4".

Each service manual was color coded: Action Soldier manuals were beige; Action Marine, olive green; Action Sailor, dark blue; Action Pilot, light blue. These colors held true for both sizes of manuals. Each manual contained basic information about G.I. Joe, like how to pose the figure, put on or take off the boots, dress the figure, or where to place paper sticker insignia.

Leftover or overrun pieces from various adventures were issued in bags with a standard header card printed with "Official Backyard Patrol." The accessories in the package varied and a listing of each bag's contents was rubber stamped on the header card along with an adventure identification; i.e., River Adventure. The value of these packages depends on the contents in them.

Many collectors use Hasbro stock numbers to reference 12" G.I. Joe figures and accessories. Unfortunately, these numbers do not uniquely identify G.I. Joe items, as they do not appear on all products, and are sometimes re-used. When applicable, these numbers are listed in parentheses.

See color photos on pages 145-167.

	CNP	MIP	MMP
G.I. Joe Action Soldier & Accessories GI2001-92			
GI2001 G.I. Joe Action Soldier (7500)	100	150	300
GI2002 Field Jacket Set (7501)	40	100	130
GI2003 Combat Field Pack (7502) w/cloth first aid pouch	75	100	200
GI2004 GI2003 w/green plastic first aid pouch (1965 and later)	55	80	150
GI2005 Combat Fatigue Shirt (7503)	8	40	68
GI2006 Combat Fatigue Pants (7504)	8	40	68
GI2007 Combat Field Jacket (7505)	20	75	115
GI2008 Combat Field Pack (7506)	35	80	90
GI2009 Combat Helmet (7507)	20	35	50
GI2010 Combat Sandbags (7508)	18	30	40
GI2011 Combat Mess Kit (7509)	20	35	55
GI2012 Combat Rifle Set (7510)	30	60	75
GI2013 Combat Camouflage Netting (7511)	15	20	40
GI2014 Bivouac Sleeping Bag Set (7512)	45	110	130
GI2015 Bivouac Pup Tent Set (7513)	50	160	180
GI2016 Bivouac Machine Gun (7514)	20	40	70
GI2017 Bivouac Sleeping Bag (7515),	20	40	60
GI2018 Sabotage Set (7516)	150	750	1000
GI2019 GI2018, 1968 photo box	150	600	800
GI2020 Bivouac Tent Set (7516) (1964-65 version)	150	250	350
GI2021 Command Post Poncho Set (7517)	50	100	150
GI2022 Command Post Small Arms (7518)	40	75	125
GI2023 GI2022, w/green plastic first aid pouch (1965+)	15	35	60
GI2024 Command Post Poncho (7519), green	30	50	70
GI2025 Command Post Field Radio & Telephone (7520)	20	35	50
GI2026 Military Police Set (7521) w/olive green Ike jacket & pants	200	700	1000
GI2027 GI2026, w/brown Ike M.P. jacket & pants	125	400	600
GI2028 Jungle (7522)	30	100	160
GI2029 Military Police Duffel Bag (7523)	25	40	55
GI2030 Military Police Ike Jacket (7524), green	65	145	175
GI2031 GI2030 w/brown jacket	20	40	50
GI2032 Military Police Ike Pants (7525), green	60	135	160
GI2033 GI2032 w/brown pants	15	40	55
GI2034 Military Police Helmet & Small Arms (7526)	40	65	80
GI2035 Ski Patrol (7527) w/water decal helmet emblem	50	75	90
GI2036 GI2035 w/sticker helmet emblem	40	65	80
GI2037 Rocket Firing Bazooka (7528)	40	65	110
GI2038 Snow Trooper (7529)	30	60	80
GI2039 Mountain Troops (7530)	45	125	150
GI2040 Ski Patrol (7531)	155	650	850
GI2041 Special Forces (7532)	135	650	800
GI2042 Green Beret (small card-7533)	50	100	150
GI2043 Green Beret set (7536)	275	1000	1500
GI2043b Green Beret in Action Soldier box	200	300	400
GI2044 GI2043 w/o scarf (revised box art)	85	750	1000
GI2045 West Point Cadet (7537)	225	500	800
GI2046 GI2045, 1968 photo box	225	800	1100
GI2047 Heavy Weapons Set (7538), 1967 window box	100	750	1000
GI2048 GI2047, 1968 photo box	100	700	900
GI2049 Military Police Set (7539), tan jacket, 1967 window box	700	1450	2000
GI2050 GI2049 in 1968 photo box, tan or green jacket	650	1350	1900
GI2051 Combat Field Pack Set (7540), 1968 photo box	65	650	960
GI2052 Army Bivouac Series (7549.83), 1968 w/Action Soldier, GI2002 & GI2003	150	650	960
GI2053 Mountain Troops (7557.83), w/talking Action Soldier and accessories GI2035, GI2039, GI2040 (1968)	200	800	1000
GI2055 Green Beret talking Adventure set	200	1100	1600
GI2060 Combat Engineer (7571)	75	200	275
GI2061 Combat Construction (7572)	80	210	300
GI2062 Combat Demolition (7573)	30	125	225
GI2090 Talking Action Soldier (7590)	150	300	375
GI2092 Action Soldier Negro (7900)	500	900	1400
G.I. Joe Action Sailor & Accessories GI2101-90			
GI2101 G.I. Joe Action Sailor (7600)	75	250	350
GI2102 Sea Rescue Set (7601)	75	175	250
GI2103 Navy Frogman Underwater Demolition Set (7602) in 1967 window box	135	350	500
GI2104 GI2103, 1968 photo box	150	375	425
GI2105 Navy Frogman Scuba Top (7603)	20	50	60
GI2106 Navy Frogman Scuba Bottom (7604)	20	40	60
GI2107 Frogman Accessories (7605)	20	40	60
GI2108 Navy Frogman Scuba Tanks (7606)	20	35	50
GI2109 Navy Attack Set (7607)	50	120	185
GI2110 Navy Attack Work Shirt (7608)	20	45	80
GI2111 Navy Attack Dungaree Pants (7609)	20	60	75
GI2112 Navy Attack Helmet Set (7610)	30	50	70
GI2113 Navy Attack Life Preserver (7611), orange	20	40	60
GI2114 GI2113, gold	30	60	75
GI2115 Shore Patrol Set (7612) jumper zips all the way to cuff of shirt	120	350	450
GI2116 GI2115, except jumper only zips to armpit	120	350	450
GI2117 GI2115 w/snap closure on arm band, white S.P. helmet & field radio	600	1500	1750
GI2118 Shore Patrol Jumper (7613) w/zipper to sleeve cuff	40	70	100

GI2005   GI2044   GI2045

GI2117

GI2130

GI2218

GI2305   **GI2307**

		CNP	MIP	MMP
GI2119	GI2118 w/zipper to armpit	25	65	80
GI2120	Shore Patrol Dress Pants (7614)	25	55	75
GI2121	Sea Bag (7615)	15	50	60
GI2122	Shore Patrol Helmet (7616)	25	75	90
GI2123	Machine Gun (7618)	25	60	75
GI2124	Dress Parade (7619)	35	90	180
GI2125	Deep Sea Diver (7620)	150	850	1200
GI2126	GI2125, 1968 photo box	150	750	1000
GI2127	Landing Signal Officer (7621)	125	450	600
GI2128	Sea Rescue (7622)	75	250	300
GI2129	Deep Freeze Set (7623) w/white combat boots, window box	175	900	1100
GI2130	GI2129 w/arctic ice boots	160	750	850
GI2131	GI2130 in photo box	160	450	750
GI2132	Annapolis Cadet (7624), window box	250	750	900
GI2133	GI2132, 1968 photo box	250	700	850
GI2134	Breeches Buoy set (7625) in 1967 window box	175	700	900
GI2135	GI2134, 1968 photo box	175	750	850
GI2136	LSO (7626)	40	70	90
GI2137	Life Ring (7627)	30	55	70
GI2138	Navy Basics (7628)	30	65	80
GI2139	Navy Scuba Series (7643.83) w/Action Sailor & accessories from GI2103 & GI2128	200	800	1100
GI2190	Talking G.I. Joe Action Sailor (7690)	160	500	750

G.I. Joe Action Marine & Accessories GI2201-91

		CNP	MIP	MMP
GI2201	G.I. Joe Action Marine (7700)	80	260	335
GI2202	Communications Post & Poncho Set (7701) w/green comouflage field phone	150	300	400
GI2203	GI2202 w/brown field phone	75	175	225
GI2204	Communications Post Poncho (7702)	55	115	160
GI2205	Communications Post Field Set (7703) w/green field phone	100	150	200
GI2206	GI2205 w/brown field phone	50	75	90
GI2207	Communications Flag Set (7704)	125	200	250
GI2208	Combat Paratrooper Parachute Pack Set (7705) w/cloth first aid pouch	40	95	160
GI2209	GI2208 w/plastic first aid pouch (1965+)	40	100	125
GI2210	Paratrooper Small Arms (7706) w/cloth first aid pouch	50	100	150
GI2211	GI2210 w/plastic first aid pouch (1965+)	25	55	75
GI2212	Paratrooper Helmet (7707)	25	40	55
GI2213	Paratrooper Tent Camouflage (7708)	20	38	50
GI2214	Paratrooper Parachute (7709)	60	135	165
GI2215	Dress Parade Set (7710), window box	75	200	250
GI2216	GI2215 w/dress shoes	75	250	300
GI2217	GI2216, 1968 photo box	75	325	425
GI2218	Beachhead Assault Tent Set (7711) w/cloth first aid pouch	50	150	210
GI2219	GI2218 w/plastic first aid pouch (1965+)	40	100	150
GI2220	Beachhead Assault Field Pack Set (7712)	40	150	175
GI2220b	Beachhead Assault Field Pack Set (7713)	45	165	190
GI2221	Beachhead Assault Fatigue Shirt (7714)	10	65	110
GI2222	Beachhead Assault Fatigue Pants (7715)	10	65	110
GI2223	Beachhead Assault Mess Kit Set (7716)	5	35	45
GI2224	Beachhead Assault Rifle Set (7717)	25	45	55
GI2225	Beachhead Assault Flame Thrower (7718)	30	45	65
GI2226	Marine Medic Set (7719)	90	300	400
GI2227	Medic (7720)	30	80	100
GI2228	First Aid (7721)	40	80	110
GI2229	G.I. Basics (7722)	30	70	75
GI2230	Bunk Bed (7723)	75	200	300
GI2231	Mortar Set (7725)	60	90	150
GI2232	M-60 (7726)	65	150	200
GI2233	Weapons Rack (7727)	95	175	250
GI2234	Demolition Set (7730)	70	225	350
GI2235	GI2234, 1968 photo box	60	550	750
GI2236	Tank Commander (7731), window box	150	1300	1700
GI2237	GI2236, 1968 photo box	150	750	1000
GI2238	Jungle Fighter (7732), window box	225	1750	2000
GI2239	GI2238, 1968 photo box	225	1500	1750
GI2240	Super Value Adventure Pack Marine Medic Series (7733.83), w/basic Marine in uniform & accessories from GI2226 & GI2228	225	800	1350
GI2290	Talking G.I. Joe Action Marine (7790)	60	700	875

G.I. Joe Action Pilot & Accessories GI2301-90

		CNP	MIP	MMP
GI2301	G.I. Joe Action Pilot (7800)	125	300	400
GI2302	Survival Equipment Set (7801)	100	550	700
GI2303	Survival Life Raft (7802)	60	150	225
GI2304	Dress Uniform (7803)	225	1000	1500
GI2305	Dress Jacket (7804)	40	150	200
GI2306	Dress Pants (7805)	30	140	175
GI2307	Dress Shirt & Service (7806)	35	140	175
GI2308	Scramble Set (7807)	75	300	400
GI2309	Scramble Flight Suit (7808)	30	100	125
GI2310	Scramble Air Vest and Accessories (7809)	30	80	100
GI2311	Scramble Crash Helmet (7810)	35	80	125
GI2312	Scramble Parachute Pack (7811)	25	55	80
GI2313	Communications (7812)	30	65	95
GI2314	Air Police (7813)	110	180	210
GI2315	Pilot Basics (7814)	35	75	110
GI2316	Air Security (7815)	200	400	500
GI2317	Mae West Life Vest (7816)	75	125	150

CNP: Complete, no package, with all weapons and accessories; MIP: Mint in package; MMP: Mint item in Mint package. Values in U.S. dollars. See page 11 for details.

GI2318	Crash Crew (7820),			
	window box	75	250	375
GI2319	GI2318, 1968 photo box	100	300	400
GI2320	Air Cadet (7822),			
	window box	200	600	800
GI2321	GI2320, 1968 photo box	200	550	750
GI2322	Fighter Pilot w/Working			
	Parachute (7823)	400	2000	2500
GI2324	GI2322, 1968 photo box	400	1450	1900
GI2325	Astronaut Suit (7824)	80	800	1000
GI2326	GI2325, 1968 photo box	80	800	900
GI2327	Air Sea Rescue (7825)	150	650	750
GI2328	GI2327, 1968 photo box	150	600	800
GI2390	Talking G.I. Joe Action			
	Pilot (7890)	200	650	850

Action Soldiers of the World & Accessories GI2501-30

The following series of figures was introduced by Hasbro in 1966, and featured soldiers of 6 different nationalities — German, Japanese, Russian, French, British and Australian — all with corresponding uniforms and equipment. These new figures also had a new head with a thinner, more European-looking scarless face. The Japanese soldier had a unique head with distinctive slanted eyes. With the exception of the Japanese soldier, who always had black hair, the foreign soldiers were painted with one of the four standard *G.I. Joe* hair colors. All but the Japanese figure have been found mint in the box with the standard scar *G.I. Joe* head as well as the no-scar foreign head. This was probably done to fulfill early orders before the foreign heads were produced. Non-scar figures are preferred by most collectors.

There are 2 different body types for the Japanese soldier. The standard figure is flesh colored like all the other G.I. Joe figures, but with the ethnic Japanese face. The second, and less common, figure still has a Japanese face in flesh color, but the body has a yellowish tint. Since this second body type is only rarely seen, it is speculated that this was a test run of a different body color and quickly abandoned by Hasbro.

Figures and accessories were packaged together in large display boxes, but were also sold seperately. Foreign Soldiers without accessories came packaged in narrow boxes, each with a paper illustrated tab which fits into a slot on the front of the box about a third of the way up from the bottom. When the shrinkwrap is taken off the box, this tab is frequently missing. It is an important part of the value of the box. Accessories for Foreign Soldiers were available on cards.

A Canadian Commando was produced by Hasbro of Canada. It came in the same box as the British Commando, but with the designation "British and Canadian Commando, copyright 1966, Canada Montreal Ltd. Litho in Canada" printed on the box.

Foreign Soldiers with accessories GI2501-06
GI2501	German Storm Trooper			
	(8100)	400	1200	1700
GI2502	Japanese Imperial			
	Soldier (8101)	500	1400	1900
GI2503	Russian Infantryman			
	(8102)	350	1100	1600
GI2504	French Resistance			
	Fighter (8103)	280	1200	1500
GI2505	British Commando			
	(8104)	300	1150	1600
GI2506	Australian Jungle			
	Fighter (8105)	255	1050	1550

GI2602

Foreign Soldiers without accessories GI2511-16
GI2511	German Storm Trooper			
	(8200)	215	675	900
GI2512	Japanese Imperial			
	Soldier (8201)	275	775	1000
GI2513	Russian Infantryman			
	(8202)	235	675	900
GI2514	French Resistance			
	Fighter (8203)	220	575	800
GI2515	British Commando			
	(8204)	225	675	850
GI2516	Australian Jungle			
	Fighter (8205)	220	575	800

Carded accessories GI2521-26
GI2521	German Equipment			
	Pack (8300)	185	275	300
GI2522	Japanese Equipment			
	Pack (8301)	200	350	400
GI2523	Russian Equipment			
	Pack (8302)	105	225	275
GI2524	French Equipment			
	Pack Equip. (8303)	50	150	225
GI2525	British Equipment			
	Pack (8304)	135	200	300
GI2526	Australian Equipment			
	Pack (8305)	55	225	300
GI2530	Foreign Soldier Series			
	w/Talking G.I. Joe			
	(8111.83), 1968 with			
	Russian, German &			
	Japanese uniforms and			
	accessory cards	—	1500	2500
GI2535	Canadian Mountie Gift			
	Set (no Hasbro #)	300	1500	2000

G.I. Joe Action Nurse
GI2590	Action Nurse Figure			
	(8060) w/white medic			
	bag	1200	1850	3000
GI2591	GI2590 w/green			
	medic bag	500	1100	1300

Heavy Equipment & Other Vehicles
GI2601	Five Star Jeep (7000)			
	(1965-67)	100	300	400
GI2602	GI2601 w/o engine			
	sound and shooting			
	rifle (1968-75)	75	225	325

GI2603

GI2603	Combat Jeep Vehicle &			
	Trailer (7000)	40	100	150
GI2610	G.I. Joe Desert Patrol			
	Attack Jeep (8030) w/			
	desert fighter figure	500	800	1000
GI2611	GI2610 w/o figure	400	650	900
GI2612	G.I. Joe Crash Crew			
	Fire Truck Set (8040)			
	w/figure	700	1400	1800
GI2613	GI2612 w/o figure	500	1000	1400
GI2614	G.I. Joe Astronaut Suit			
	& Space Capsule Set			
	(8020)	150	225	300
GI2620	Sea Sled & Frogman			
	Set (8050) w/frogman	100	275	375
GI2621	GI2620, except figure			
	"wears" navy blue			
	swimming trunks	100	275	375
GI2622	Official Sea Sled &			
	Frogman (5957): GI2620			
	w/sea cave & buoy			
	marker (Sears)	125	325	425
GI2623	GI2622 w/o frogman			
	(5962) (Sears)			

See also: *Defenders*

Irwin Vehicles (licensed by Hasbro) GI2631-37
GI2631	Staff Car (5652)	400	700	900
GI2632	Motorcycle & Sidecar			
	(5651)	150	225	325
GI2633	Armored Car	100	150	225
GI2634	Jet Aeroplane (5396)	200	550	750
GI2635	Personnel Carrier &			
	Mine Sweeper (5694)	250	700	900
GI2636	Jet Helicopter (5395)	175	350	500
GI2637	Amphibious Duck			
	(5693)	350	600	750
GI2640	Action Joe State Trooper			
	w/Action Motorcycle			
	(5300)	300	750	1000

GI2631

GI2641	Action Joe Race Car Driver w/Action Race Car (5305)	300	700	900
GI2650	Machine Gun Emplacement Set (5931) (Sears)	150	375	500
GI2651	Forward Observer Set (5969) (Sears)	160	375	500
GI2652	Green Beret Machine Gun Outpost Set (5978) (Sears)	175	700	900
GI2654	Space Capsule & Space Outfit Set (5979) (Sears)	200	385	550

Miscellaneous Accessories

GI2660	G.I. Joe Foot Locker (8000) w/paper wrapper	30	55	70
GI2661	Foot Locker Gift Set (8000.83) (1968) w/snowshoes, ice pick, etc.	70	155	225
GI2662	Foot Locker Gift Set (8001.83) (1968) w/ski troop equipment, etc.	70	155	225
GI2663	Foot Locker Gift Set (8002.83) (1968) w/Jungle Fighter equipment, etc.	70	155	225
GI2667	Four in One sets w/description card, ea.	-	300	400

The G.I. Joe Adventurers

GI2700	G.I. Joe Adventurer (7905), figure, 1969	225	300	500
GI2701	GI2700, Negro figure w/sticker on box	500	1000	1250
GI2702	Sears issue of GI2701 w/French Resistance Fighter outfit	450	950	1200
GI2703	G.I. Joe Aquanaut (7910)	400	1250	1750
GI2704	Talking Astronaut (7915) w/white cloth headpiece	150	400	600
GI2705	GI2704 w/white plastic cap	140	350	550
GI2711	The Adventure of the Danger of the Depths (7920)	75	200	250
GI2712	The Adventure of the Mysterious Explosion (7921)	75	175	225
GI2713	The Adventure of the Secret Mission to Spy Island (7922)	75	175	225
GI2714	The Adventure of the Perilous Rescue (7923)	100	250	350
GI2720	Adventure Locker (7940), wooden	75	125	175
GI2721	GI2720, green vinyl	100	150	225
GI2722	Aqua Locker (7941)	100	150	200
GI2723	Astro Locker (7942)	100	150	200
GI2730	The Eight Ropes of Danger Adventure (7950)	75	200	250
GI2731	The Fantastic Freefall Adventure (7951)	85	200	250
GI2732	The Hidden Missile Discovery Adventure (7952)	65	150	200
GI2733	The Mouth of Doom Adventure (7953)	65	150	200
GI2740	The Adventure of the Shark's Surprise (7980)	75	200	250
GI2740b	GI2740 w/o figure (7980.16) (Sears)			
GI2741	G.I. Joe Spacewalk Mystery Adventure (7981)	75	150	225

GI3021

GI3023

GI2742	The Fight for Survival Adventure (7982) w/tall white ice boots	125	200	300
GI2743	GI2742 w/white jack boots (from foreign soldier mold)	150	225	350
GI2744	GI2742 w/o figure (7982.16) (Sears)			

The Adventure Team GI3001-63

GI3001	G.I. Joe Land Adventurer (7270)	60	100	140
GI3002	G.I. Joe Adventurer (7271), black body	90	170	250
GI3003	G.I. Joe Man of Action (7272)	60	90	125
GI3006	G.I. Joe Eagle Eye Commander (7276)	50	125	150
GI3007	G.I. Joe Eagle Eye Man of Action (7277)	40	100	125
GI3008	G.I. Joe Eagle Eye Commando (7278) black body	90	140	200
GI3011	Land Adventurer w/Kung Fu Grip (7280)	60	120	160
GI3012	Land Adventurer, Carded (1-7280)	50	110	140
GI3013	Sea Adventurer (7281)	60	125	150
GI3014	Sea Adventurer, carded	60	110	140
GI3015	Air Adventurer (7282)	50	125	150
GI3016	Air Adventurer (7282), carded	50	110	140
GI3017	Black Adventurer (7283)	100	150	225
GI3018	Black Adventurer (7283), carded	100	140	210
GI3019	Man Of Action (7284)	50	100	150
GI3020	Talking Adventure Team Commander (7290)	90	150	200
GI3021	Life-Like Talking Commander (7290)	50	140	175
GI3022	Talking Black Adventure Team Commander (7291)	250	375	500
GI3023	GI3022 w/blue molded shorts	100	175	250
GI3024	Talking Man of Action (7292)	90	155	225
GI3025	G.I. Joe Talking Man of Action (7292) w/kung fu grip	75	100	150
GI3030	Talking Adventure Team Commander (7400)	80	155	225
GI3031	Land Adventurer (7401)	60	125	160
GI3032	Sea Adventurer (7402)	70	160	210

GI3033	Air Adventurer (7403) w/pistol & holster	65	135	190
GI3034	GI3033, w/rifle	50	130	175
GI3035	Negro Adventurer (7404)	110	170	240
GI3040	Talking Astronaut (7405) w/lace-up boots	120	200	300
GI3041	GI3040 w/space boots	120	175	275
GI3042	Black Talking Adventure Team Commander (7406)			
GI3046	Man of Action (7500)	75	160	240
GI3047	Talking Man of Action (7590)	90	155	240
GI3050	Mike Power, Atomic Man (8025)	20	40	65
GI3051	GI3050, boxed (salesman's sample)		undetermined	
GI3060	Bulletman (8026),	55	125	175
GI3061	Intruder Commander (8050)	25	50	75
GI3062	Intruder Warrior (8051)	25	50	75
GI3070	G.I. Joe Foot Locker (8000)	25	50	90

G.I. Joe Adventures

GI3100	Secret Mission to Spy Island (7411) w/TNT & detonator	30	60	80
GI3101	GI3100 w/o TNT & detonator	20	40	60
GI3102	Danger of the Depths (7412)	60	75	85
GI3103	Revenge of the Spy Shark (7413)	60	90	130
GI3104	Black Widow Rendezvous (7414) w/Sten gun (silver stock & black shoulder strap)	50	80	130
GI3105	GI3104 w/black gun	25	45	55
GI3106	Hidden Missile Discovery (7415)	35	75	100
GI3107	Peril of the Raging Inferno (7416)	50	85	135
GI3108	Search for the Stolen Idol (7418)	62	115	140
GI3109	Attack at Vulture Falls (7420) w/black & yellow vulture & orange storage box	50	85	135
GI3110	GI3109 w/black vulture & tan storage box	20	40	55
GI3111	Jaws of Death (7421) w/orange scuba suit, white mouthpiece on scuba tanks	60	130	160

CNP: Complete, no package, with all weapons and accessories; MIP: Mint in package; MMP: Mint item in Mint package. Values in U.S. dollars. See page 11 for details.

GI3112 GI3111 w/gray scuba suit, yellow mouthpiece on scuba tanks. | 35 | 60 | 75
GI3113 Eight Ropes of Danger (7422) | 100 | 140 | 200
GI3114 Fantastic Freefall (7423) | 100 | 170 | 235
GI3115 Flying Space Adventure (7425) | 95 | 200 | 300
GI3116 Fight for Survival (7431) | 100 | 125 | 165
GI3117 White Tiger Hunt (7436) w/pith helmet & rubber campfire | 100 | 140 | 200
GI3118 GI3117 w/bush hat & rubber campfire | 55 | 75 | 100
GI3119 GI3118, w/plastic fire | 50 | 70 | 90
GI3120 Capture of the Pygmy Gorilla (7437) | 50 | 85 | 135
GI3121 Devil of the Deep (7439) | 50 | 77 | 115
GI3122 Sky Dive to Danger (7440) | 70 | 100 | 135
GI3123 The Secret of the Mummy's Tomb (7441) | 60 | 100 | 175
GI3124 The Shark's Surprise (7442) | 110 | 175 | 275
GI3125 G.I. Joe Spacewalk Mystery (7445) | 110 | 175 | 275
GI3126 The Secret of the Mummy's Tomb (7445) 1976 issue of GI3123 | 40 | 65 | 80
GI3127 The Fate of the Trouble Shooter (7450) | 75 | 90 | 100

Other Adventure Team Vehicles

GI3140 Adventure Team Vehicle (7005) | 40 | 70 | 90
GI3141 Space-A-Matic Astro-Space Vehicle (7010) | not produced
GI3142 Combat Jeep Vehicle & Trailer | 40 | 100 | 150

Small-Packaged Adventure Team Equipment

GI3150 Underwater Demolition (7310) | 20 | 40 | 50
GI3151 Laser Rescue (7311) | 15 | 35 | 45
GI3152 Sonic Rock Blast (7312) | 15 | 35 | 45
GI3153 Chest Winch (7313) | 10 | 25 | 35
GI3154 Solar Communicator (7314) | 10 | 25 | 35
GI3155 Rocket Pack (7315) | 10 | 25 | 35
GI3156 Missile Recovery (7340) | 10 | 25 | 35
GI3157 Radiation Detection (7341) | 10 | 25 | 35
GI3158 High Voltage Escape (7342) | 20 | 35 | 45
GI3159 Hurricane Spotter (7343) w/belt | 25 | 45 | 60
GI3160 GI3159 w/o belt | 20 | 40 | 55
GI3161 Volcano Jumper (7344) | 20 | 40 | 55
GI3162 Aerial Recon (7345) w/belt | 20 | 40 | 55
GI3163 GI3162 w/o belt | 20 | 35 | 50
GI3164 Rescue Raft (7350) | 10 | 25 | 40
GI3165 Fire Fighter (7351) | 10 | 25 | 40
GI3166 Life Line Catapult (7352) | 12 | 25 | 42
GI3167 Sail Car (7353) | 15 | 30 | 45
GI3168 Windboat (7353), same as GI3167 | 15 | 30 | 45
GI3169 Underwater Explorer (7354) | 25 | 37 | 50
GI3170 Escape Car (7360) | 17 | 28 | 48
GI3171 Flying Rescue (7361) | 17 | 30 | 45
GI3172 Signal Flasher (7362) | 17 | 30 | 45
GI3173 Turbo Copter (7363) | 25 | 35 | 50
GI3174 Drag Bike (7364) | 25 | 40 | 55

Large Window-Boxed AT Accessories

GI3180 Demolition (7370) | 35 | 65 | 80
GI3181 Dangerous Removal (7370) | 30 | 60 | 75
GI3182 Smoke Jumper (7371) | 30 | 75 | 90
GI3183 Karate (7372) | 40 | 80 | 120
GI3184 Jungle Survival (7373) | 30 | 70 | 85

GI3185 Emergency Rescue (7374) | 40 | 75 | 90
GI3186 Secret Agent (7375) | 40 | 75 | 90
GI3187 Helicopter (7380) (from GI3108) | 50 | 75 | 100
GI3188 Sea Wolf (7460) | 65 | 80 | 140
GI3189 Skyhawk (7470) | 50 | 75 | 105
GI3190 Super Adventure Set (7480) | 200 | 300 | 400
GI3191 Capture Copter (7480) | 50 | 75 | 100
GI3192 GI3191 w/Intruder Figure (7481) | 65 | 80 | 125
GI3193 Adventure Team Headquarters (7490) | 50 | 75 | 100
GI3194 Sandstorm Survival (7493) | 85 | 125 | 210
GI3196 Big Trapper w/Intruder figure (7494) | 40 | 75 | 120
GI3197 Training Center/Slide for Survival (7495) | 60 | 90 | 160
GI3198 Big Trapper (7498) GI3196 w/o figures | 25 | 75 | 90
GI3199 Mobile Support Vehicle/Search for the Radioactive Satellite (7499) | 60 | 80 | 120

Small Window-Boxed AT Accessories

GI3200 Hidden Treasure | 10 | 25 | 40
GI3201 Fight For Survival (7301) w/bush hat or machete | 15 | 30 | 45
GI3202 Copter Rescue w/camera or binoculars | 10 | 25 | 40
GI3203 Secret Rendezvous | 10 | 25 | 40
GI3204 Dangerous Mission | 10 | 25 | 40
GI3205 Desert Survival | 10 | 20 | 35
GI3206 Winter Rescue | 10 | 20 | 35
GI3207 Desert Explorer | 20 | 30 | 50
GI3208 Jungle Ordeal | 20 | 30 | 50
GI3209 Undercover Agent | 20 | 30 | 50
GI3210 Secret Mission | 10 | 20 | 35

Small Carded Adventure Team Accessories

GI3220 Mobile Escape Slide | 10 | 20 | 30
GI3221 Escape Slide (same as GI3220) (7319-1) | 10 | 20 | 35
GI3222 Magnetic Flaw Detector (7319-2) | 10 | 20 | 35
GI3223 Sample Analyzer | 10 | 20 | 35
GI3224 Thermal Terrain Scanner (7319-3) | 10 | 20 | 35
GI3225 Seismograph (7319) | 10 | 20 | 35
GI3226 Equipment Tester | 10 | 20 | 35

Later Boxed Accessories

GI3227 Secret Courier | 15 | 28 | 40
GI3228 Thrust into Danger | 15 | 28 | 40
GI3229 Long Range Recon | 15 | 28 | 40
GI3230 Green Danger | 15 | 28 | 40
GI3231 Buried Bounty | 15 | 28 | 40
GI3232 Diver's Distress | 15 | 28 | 40
GI3233 Raging River Dam Up | 20 | 30 | 45
GI3234 Jettison to Safety | 20 | 30 | 45
GI3235 Mine Shaft Breakout | 20 | 30 | 45
GI3236 Danger Ray Detection | 20 | 30 | 45
GI3237 Night Surveillance | 20 | 30 | 45
GI3238 Shocking Escape | 20 | 30 | 40
GI3239 Infiltration | 15 | 20 | 30
GI3240 Photo Recon (8201) | 15 | 20 | 30
GI3241 Dangerous Climb (8202) | 20 | 30 | 45
GI3242 Magnum Power | 28 | 40 | 60

Carded re-packs of GI3200-10

GI3250 Hidden Treasure | 30 | 40 | 60
GI3251 Fight For Survival | 30 | 40 | 60
GI3252 Copter Rescue | 30 | 40 | 60
GI3253 Secret Rendezvous | 30 | 40 | 60
GI3254 Dangerous Mission | 30 | 40 | 60
GI3255 Desert Survival | 30 | 40 | 60
GI3256 Winter Rescue | 30 | 40 | 60
GI3257 Desert Explorer | 30 | 40 | 60
GI3258 Jungle Ordeal | 30 | 40 | 60
GI3259 Undercover Agent | 30 | 40 | 60
GI3260 Secret Mission | 30 | 40 | 60

Adventure Team Sears Exclusives

GI3270 Recovery of the Lost Mummy (59092) | 60 | 110 | 150
GI3271 Search for the Abominable Snowman (7430.16) | 50 | 100 | 150
GI3272 Mystery of the Boiling Lagoon (7431.16) | 60 | 125 | 175
GI3273 Training Center (7495.16-1), Sears version of GI3197, no escape slide or black bar on tower top, vulture substituted for snake | 45 | 120 | 140
GI3274 Avenger Pursuit Craft (7497.16) | 40 | 90 | 125
GI3275 Super Adventure Set (7441.16) | 125 | 160 | 200
GI3276 Trouble at Vulture Pass (7432.16) | 65 | 125 | 140
GI3277 Trapped in the Coils of Doom (59301) | 65 | 125 | 140

Adventure Team J.C. Penney's Exclusive

GI3279 Desert Patrol Adventure (7000.18) | 100 | 165 | 225

Mike Power Atomic Man Accessories

GI3280 Secret Mission (8030) | 30 | 45 | 60
GI3281 Dive to Danger (8031) | 25 | 40 | 55
GI3282 Challenge of Savage River (8032) | 25 | 40 | 55
GI3283 Command Para Drop (8033) | 35 | 45 | 65
GI3284 Secret Mountain Outpost (8040) | 50 | 75 | 105
GI3285 GI3284, "Bionivac-4" changed to "Maxitron 80," accessories added | 25 | 45 | 60
GI3286 Race for Recovery (8028) | 25 | 45 | 70
GI3287 Fangs of the Cobra | 25 | 45 | 70
GI3288 Special Assignment | 25 | 45 | 70

Super Joe Adventure Team (8" figures)

GI3300 Super Joe Commander (7501) | 5 | 20 | 30
GI3301 Super Joe Commander (7502) | 10 | 30 | 50
GI3302 Super Joe (7503) | 5 | 20 | 35
GI3303 Super Joe (7504), black figure | 10 | 30 | 50
GI3304 The Shield (7505) | 10 | 20 | 30
GI3305 Luminos (7506) | 10 | 20 | 30
GI3306 Darkon (7508) | 20 | 40 | 55
GI3307 Gor (7510) | 15 | 35 | 50
GI3310 Laser Communicator (7550) | 5 | 15 | 25
GI3320 Rocket Command Center (7570) | 25 | 40 | 60
GI3321 Rocket Command Center Super Adventure (7571), GI3320 w/GI3307 | 40 | 60 | 75
GI3330 Terron (7580) | 30 | 65 | 80
GI3335 Super Joe Equipment Case (8000) | 45 | 70 | 90
GI3340 Aqua Laser | 5 | 15 | 25
GI3341 Treacherous Dive w/ yellow bellows pump | 5 | 15 | 25
GI3342 GI3341 w/black pump | 5 | 15 | 25
GI3343 Fusion Bazooka | 5 | 15 | 25
GI3344 Invisible Danger | 5 | 15 | 25
GI3345 Edge of Adventure (7511) | 5 | 15 | 25
GI3346 Emergency Rescue (7514) | 5 | 15 | 25
GI3347 Paths of Danger | 20 | 40 | 70
GI3348 Magna Tools (7531) | 15 | 25 | 40
GI3349 Helipak (7530) | 15 | 25 | 40
GI3350 Sonic Scanner (7532) | 15 | 25 | 40

Super Joe Sears Exclusives

GI3400 Adventure Pursuit Craft (7497.16) (orange version of GI3254) | 35 | 50 | 75
GI3401 Super Joe Strategic Command Center (8001.16) | 40 | 60 | 80

See also: *Defenders; Elite Brigade*

GI200   GI2002   GI2003   GI2004

GI2006   GI2007   GI2008   GI2009   GI2010   GI2011   GI2012

GI2013   GI2015   GI2016   GI2017   GI2022   GI2023   GI2024

GI2014   GI2018   GI2019   GI2020

GI2021   GI2027   GI2039   GI2040

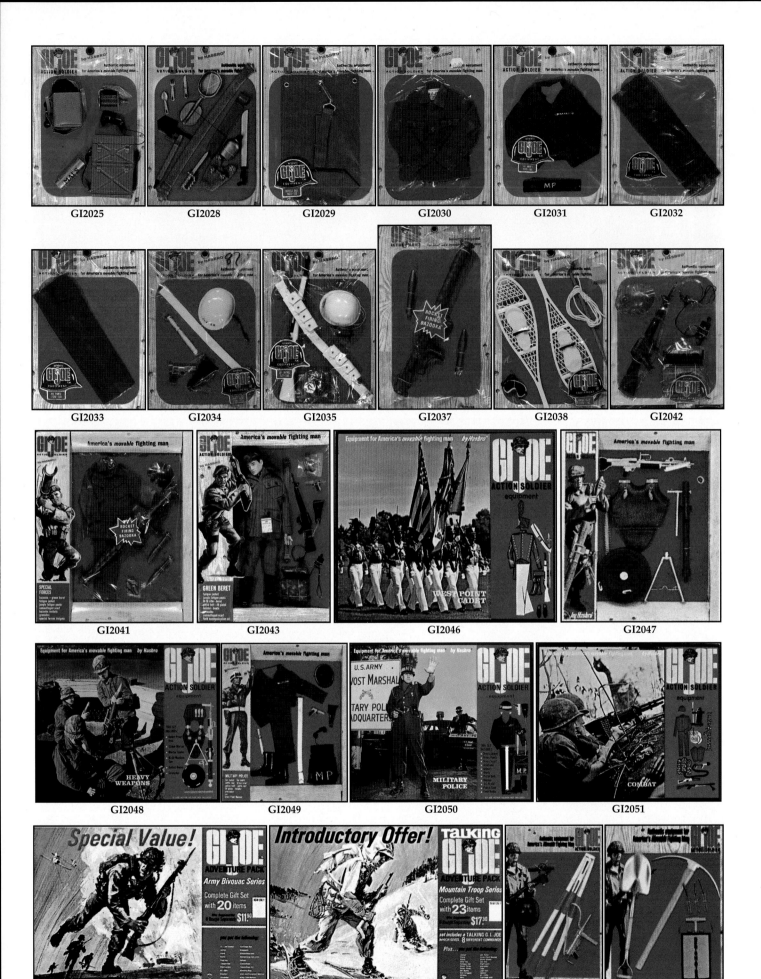

GI2025

GI2028

GI2029

GI2030

GI2031

GI2032

GI2033

GI2034

GI2035

GI2037

GI2038

GI2042

GI2041

GI2043

GI2046

GI2047

GI2048

GI2049

GI2050

GI2051

GI2052

GI2053

GI2060

GI2062

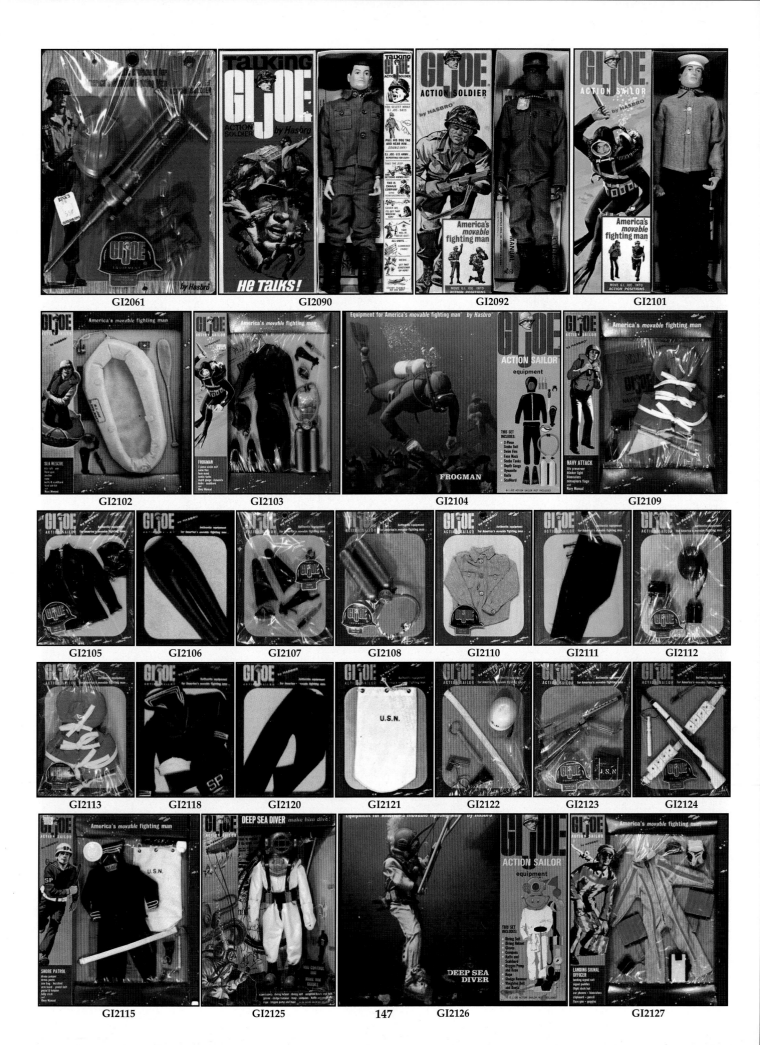

GI2061

GI2090

GI2092

GI2101

GI2102

GI2103

GI2104

GI2109

GI2105

GI2106

GI2107

GI2108

GI2110

GI2111

GI2112

GI2113

GI2118

GI2120

GI2121

GI2122

GI2123

GI2124

GI2115

GI2125

147

GI2126

GI2127

GI2128

GI2129

GI2131

GI2132

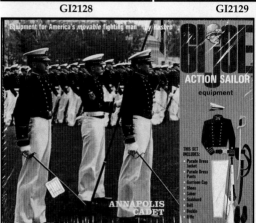
GI2133

GI2134

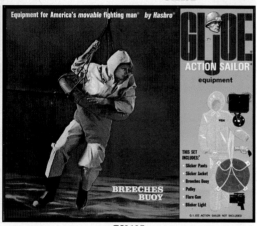
GI2135

GI2136

GI2137

GI2138

GI2139

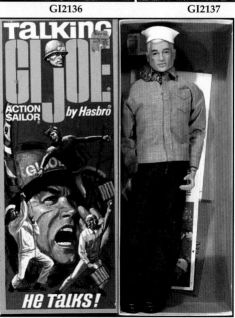
GI2190

GI2201

GI2202

GI2204 GI2205 GI2212 GI2213 GI2214 GI2220b GI2221

GI2207 GI2208 GI2210 GI2215 GI2217

GI2219 GI2220 GI2226 GI2230

GI2222 GI2223 GI2224 GI2225 GI2227 GI2228 GI2229

GI2231 GI2232 GI2233 GI2235

CNP: Complete, no package, with all weapons and accessories; MIP: Mint in package; MMP: Mint item in Mint package. Values in U.S. dollars. See page 11 for details.

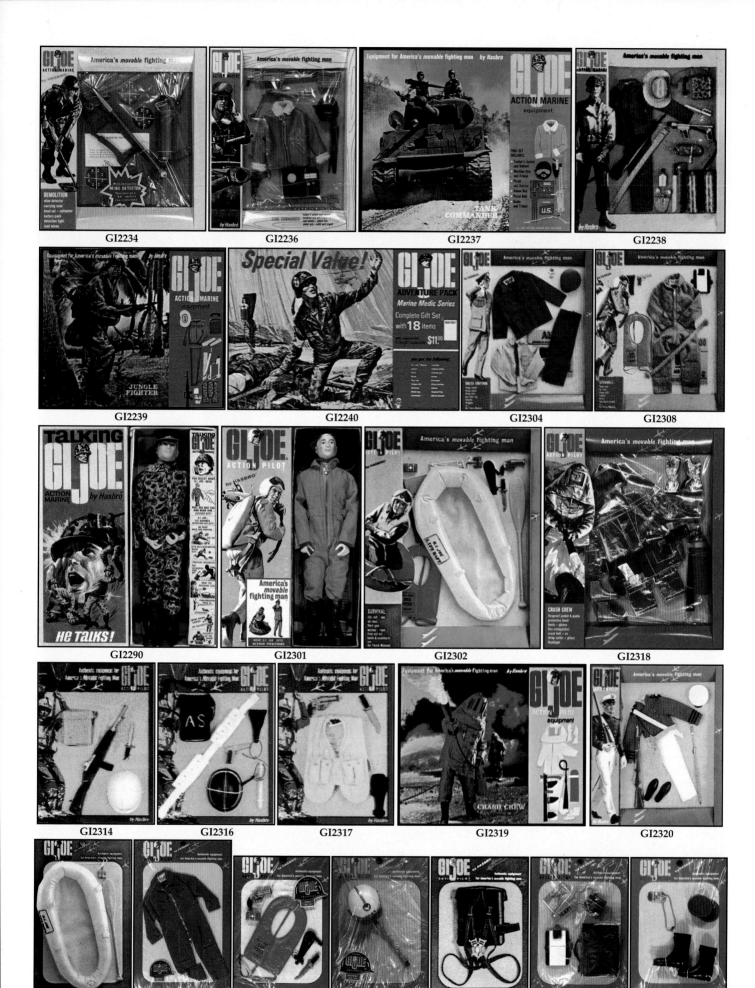

GI2234

GI2236

GI2237

GI2238

GI2239

GI2240

GI2304

GI2308

GI2290

GI2301

GI2302

GI2318

GI2314

GI2316

GI2317

GI2319

GI2320

GI2303

GI2309

GI2310

GI2311

GI2312

GI2313

GI2315

150

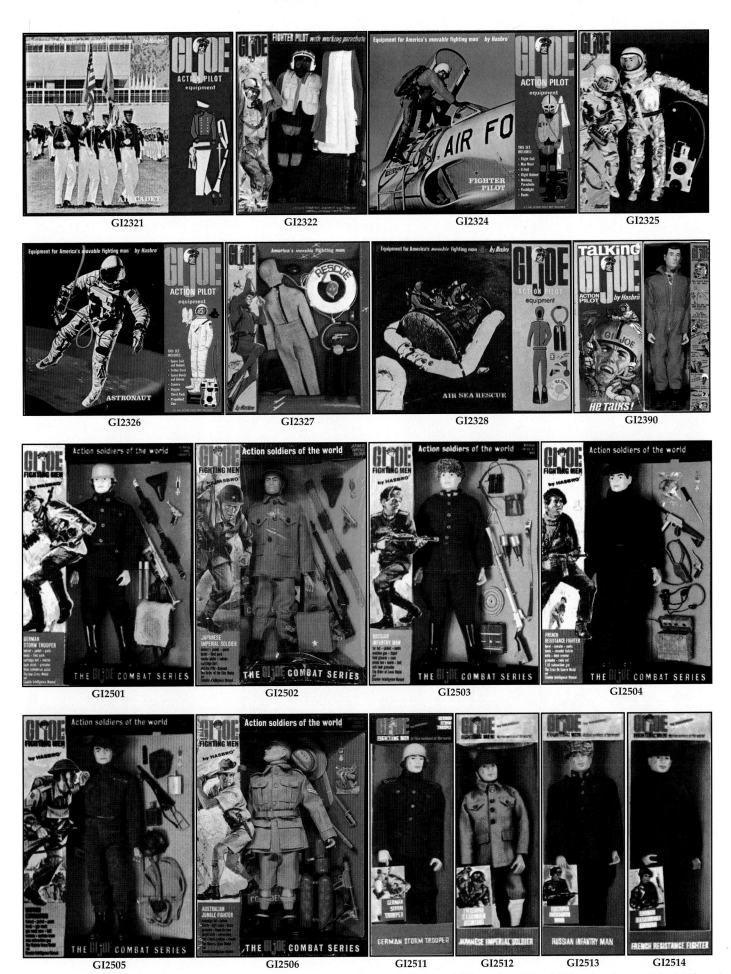

GI2321   GI2322   GI2324   GI2325

GI2326   GI2327   GI2328   GI2390

GI2501   GI2502   GI2503   GI2504

GI2505   GI2506   GI2511   GI2512   GI2513   GI2514

CNP: Complete, no package, with all weapons and accessories; MIP: Mint in package; MMP: Mint item in Mint package. Values in U.S. dollars. See page 11 for details.

GI2515   GI2516

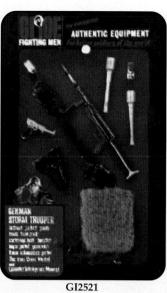

GI2521

GI2522

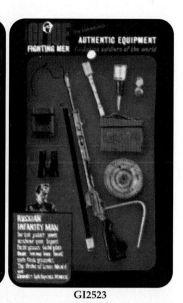

GI2523

GI2524

GI2525

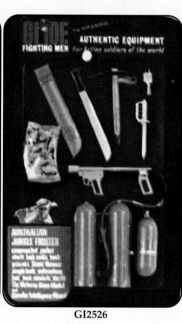

GI2526

GI2535

GI2530

GI2601

GI2590

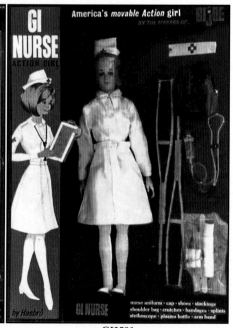

GI2591

152

GI2610

GI2613

GI2620

GI2614

GI2622

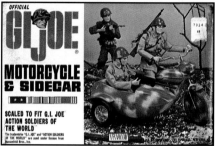

GI2632

GI2634

GI2635

GI2636

GI2637

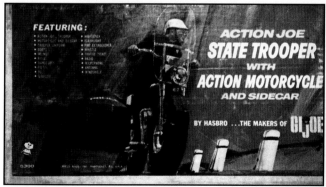

GI2640

GI2641

GI2660

GI2661

GI2662

GI2663

GI2650

GI2651

GI2652

GI2654

GI2667

GI2700

GI2701

GI2702

GI2703

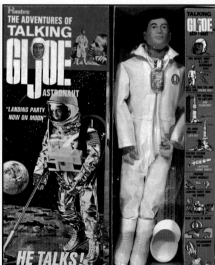

GI2705

GI2741

GI2720

GI2722

GI2723

GI2711

GI2712

GI2713

GI2714

GI2730

GI2731

GI2732

GI2733

GI2740

GI2742

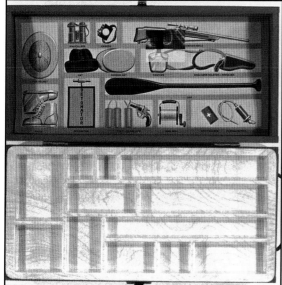
GI2720 interior

GI3001

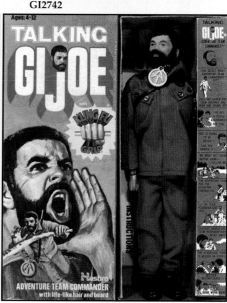
GI3020

GI3002

GI3003

GI3006

GI3007

GI3012

GI3013

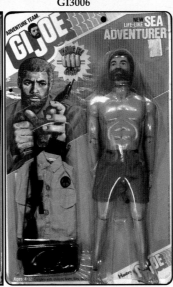

GI3014

GI3015

GI3017

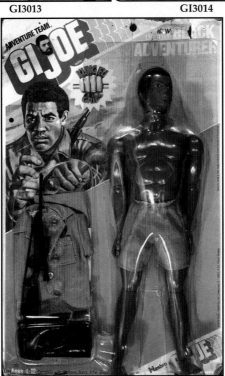

156   GI3018

GI3019

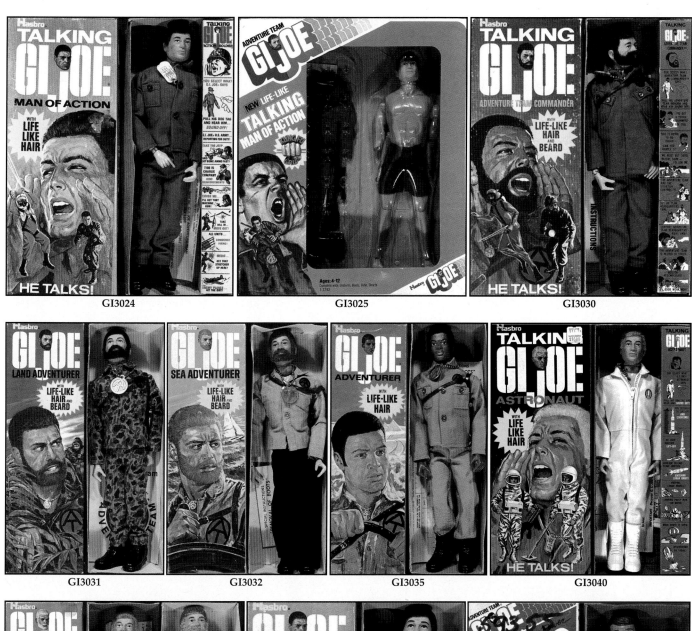

GI3024   GI3025   GI3030

GI3031   GI3032   GI3035   GI3040

GI3033   GI3034

GI3033 lid detail   GI3034 lid detail   GI3046   GI3051

CNP: Complete, no package, with all weapons and accessories; MIP: Mint in package; MMP: Mint item in Mint package. Values in U.S. dollars. See page 11 for details.

GI3050

GI3060

GI3061

GI3062

GI3100

GI3101

GI3102

GI3103

Gun from GI3104

GI3105

GI3106

GI3107

GI3108

GI3109

GI3110

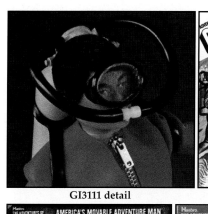

GI3111 detail

GI3112

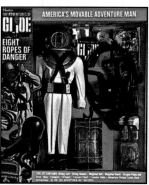

GI3113

GI3114

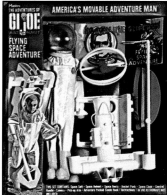

GI3115

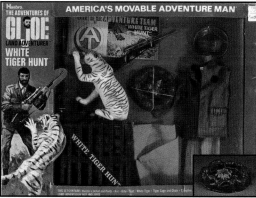

GI3118

GI3119

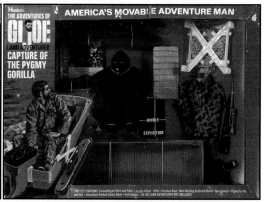

GI3120

GI3121

GI3122

GI3123

GI3127

GI3142

GI3150

GI3151

GI3152

GI3153

GI3154

GI3155

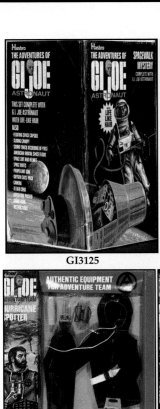

GI3125

GI3156

GI3157

GI3158

GI3159

GI3161

GI3163

GI3164

GI3165

GI3166

GI3167

GI3168

GI3170

GI3171

GI3172

GI3169

GI3173

160   GI3174

GI3189

GI3180

GI3181

GI3182

GI3183

GI3184

GI3185

GI3186

GI3190

GI3187

GI3188

GI3193

GI3197

GI3191

GI3194

GI3200

GI3201

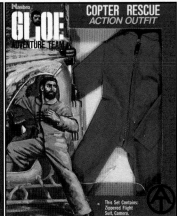

GI3202

GI3203

GI3204

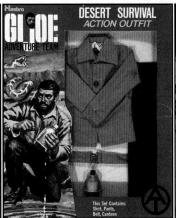

GI3205

GI3206

GI3207

GI3208

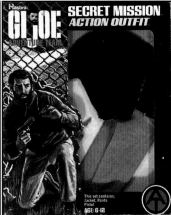

GI3210

GI3240

GI3241

GI3196

GI3199

GI3220 GI3222 GI3223 GI3224 GI3225 GI3226

GI3227 GI3228 GI3229 GI3230 GI3231 GI3232 GI3233

GI3234 GI3235 GI3236 GI3237 GI3238

GI3239 GI3250 GI3251 GI3252 GI3253

CNP: Complete, no package, with all weapons and accessories; MIP: Mint in package; MMP: Mint item in Mint package. Values in U.S. dollars. See page 11 for details.

GI3254

GI3255

GI3258

GI3259

GI3270

GI3272

GI3273

GI3274

GI3277

GI3271

GI3279

GI3287

GI3288

GI3284

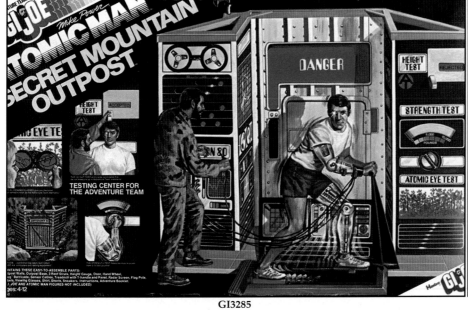

GI3285

GI3286

CNP: Complete, no package, with all weapons and accessories; MIP: Mint in package; MMP: Mint item in Mint package. Values in U.S. dollars. See page 11 for details.

GI3300

GI3302

GI3303

GI3305

GI3307

GI3304

GI3321

GI3330

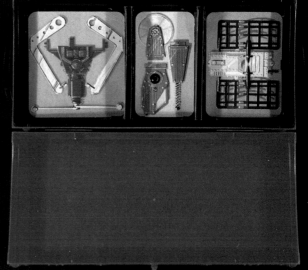

GI3335